An Environmental History of Latin America

This book, in a series of short historical episodes, narrates the mutually vital and reciprocally mortal relationship between tropical nature and human culture in Latin America. Covering a period that begins with ancient Amerindian civilizations and concludes in today's pulsating cities, the work offers an original synthesis of the current scholarship on Latin America's environmental history and argues that tropical nature has played a central role in shaping the region's historical development. Human attitudes and appetites, from Aztec cannibalism to more contemporary forms of conspicuous consumption, figure prominently in the story. However, characters such as hookworms, whales, hurricanes, bananas, dirt, butterflies, and guano make more than cameo appearances. Recent scholarship has overturned many of our egocentric assumptions about humanity's preeminent role in history. Seeing Latin America's environmental past from the perspective of many centuries illustrates that former American civilizations were more powerful than previously thought, and that current civilizations are potentially as vulnerable.

Shawn William Miller is the author of *Fruitless Trees: Portuguese Conservation and Brazil's Colonial Timber* (2000) and has published on Latin America's environmental history in the *Hispanic American Historical Review*, *Forest & Conservation History*, and *Colonial Latin American Historical Review*.

New Approaches to the Americas

Edited by Stuart Schwartz, *Yale University*

Also published in the series:

If there is an earthly paradise anywhere on earth, I judge it is not far from these regions.

Amerigo Vespucci

AN ENVIRONMENTAL HISTORY OF LATIN AMERICA

Shawn William Miller

Brigham Young University

CAMBRIDGE
UNIVERSITY PRESS

CAMBRIDGE UNIVERSITY PRESS
Cambridge, New York, Melbourne, Madrid, Cape Town, Singapore, São Paulo, Delhi

Cambridge University Press
32 Avenue of the Americas, New York, NY 10013-2473, USA

www.cambridge.org
Information on this title: www.cambridge.org/9780521848534

First published 2007

A catalog record for this publication is available from the British Library.

Library of Congress Cataloguing-in-Publication Data

Miller, Shawn William, 1964-
An Environmental history of Latin America / Shawn William Miller.
p.   cm.
Includes bibliographical references and index.
ISBN-13: 978-0-521-61298-2 (pbk.)
ISBN-10: 0-521-61298-5 (pbk.)
ISBN-13: 978-0-521-84853-4 (hardback)
ISBN-10: 0-521-84853-9 (hardback)
1. Human ecology – Latin America – History.   2. Nature – Effect of human beings on –
Latin America – History.   3. Rain forest ecology – Latin America – History.   4. Rain forest
conservation – Latin America – History.   5. Forest management – Latin America – History.
6. Environmental degradation – Latin America – History.   7. Latin America –
Environmental conditions – History.   I. Title.

ISBN   978-0-521-84853-4 hardback
ISBN   978-0-521-61298-2 paperback

Contents

List of Illustrations

Cover Illustration: Laborers begin to clear away three centuries of forest growth from the ruins of Tulum, Mexico. Frederick Catherwood, *Views of Ancient Monuments in Central America, Chiapas, and Yucatan* (London: F. Catherwood, 1844), plate XXIII, detail.

Maps

Figures

ACKNOWLEDGMENTS

Despite the youthful nature of environmental history both in and of Latin America, there is a small but growing body of exciting work on which I have depended heavily. New historical studies are appearing each year on an ever-expanding range of topics. Moreover, Latin America's environmental past has interested more than just historians, and I have consulted excellent studies by geographers, anthropologists, natural scientists, and others. I have kept footnotes and other scholarly apparatus to a minimum, but those authors whose names appear in this book's "Suggested Further Readings" have made direct contributions to this survey's contents as well as to my own thinking. Some of the research and conclusions are my own, for which I take sole responsibility. As the field is new, consistently bear in mind that we have only just begun to seek answers to questions about the historical experience in tropical nature, and we have certainly not yet asked the most important questions. Many of my most forceful assertions may in fact be open questions, and the best measure of this book's success will be if readers take an interest in the questions rather than accept what I present as uncontested ground.

By name, I thank Herbert Klein, Stuart Schwartz, Kendall Brown, and Jeffrey Shumway for their personal encouragements and professional contributions to this book. Above all, I thank my family, especially Kelly, to whom this too is dedicated.

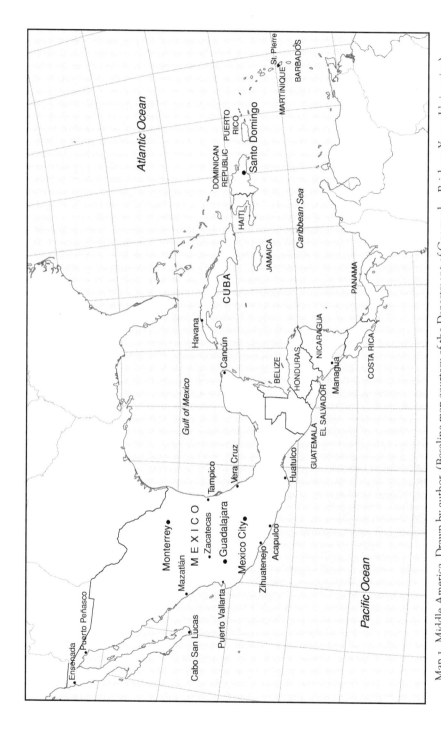

Map 1. Middle America. Drawn by author. (Baseline map courtesy of the Department of Geography, Brigham Young University.)

Map 2. South America. Drawn by author. (Baseline map courtesy of the Department of Geography, Brigham Young University.)

Props and Scenery

Without contradiction, this land is the best of all for the life of man: the air is exceptionally healthful, and the soil extremely fertile; all that is before you is delightful and pleasing to the human eye to a great degree.[1]

In 1519, Hernán Cortés advanced on Aztec Mexico to accomplish the foremost event of America's conquest. Launching from Cuba, his armies sailed the coral reefs of Cozumel, marched through rainforests in Vera Cruz, skirted smoking volcanoes in the Sierra Madre, and crossed the reflective lakes of the Valley of Mexico, some of the earth's most stunning and diverse geography. Remarkably, the conquistadors had very little to say about the nature they encountered along their paths to empire. Nature was unacknowledged, taken for granted. The conquest's chroniclers – Cortés, Francisco López de Gómara, Bernal Díaz del Castillo – emphasized, rather, the subjugation of an exotic American culture, an antagonist whose story and defeat were worthy of the telling. American nature, it was assumed, had already been conquered by Amerindian cultures. America's human empires might resist for a time, but nature would supinely yield her possessions immediately upon the transfer of imperial title to her new rulers.

Cortés and his men shared a limited although all too common view of history, one in which men of professed superior culture, technology, and religion succeed one another in an unbroken chain as rulers of

[1] Pero de Magalhães de Gandavo, *Tratado da terra do Brasil & história da Província Santa Cruz a que vulgarmente chamamos Brasil*, 1576, 12th ed. (Recife, Brazil: Editora Massangana, 1995), 53–4, my translation.

civilization. To them, the past was exclusively a human pageant, the triumphal march of conquering men, as if nature had no role in the course and shape of time's passage. It was a view that blinded Cortés as he later marched south to extend his conquests into Central America's dark forests. Entering the former lands of the Maya, a landscape riddled with the ruins of a once vigorous civilization, Cortés, and many to follow, could not see the past for the trees, even as they tripped over it. The obscuring jungle, which was only 600 years old, had forced its roots into the Maya cities' prostrate cadavers, dismembering monoliths and dislocating forensic material that might have betrayed the causes of Maya collapse. To the Spanish passersby, the great former Maya cities were little more than thickly vegetated hillocks, urban burial mounds with no notable headstones. Cortés went on conquering, but he failed to observe that conquistadors had come this way before. Whatever the cause of the Maya collapse, after an impressive half millennium of cities, art, writing, trade, and roads, nature had ultimately prevailed, covering up civilization's triumphs and its mistakes.

We still think of our history much as did the conquistadors, a series of cultural events that came to pass entirely independent of nature. The stage for the human drama, we suppose, is stocked with culture's props but is barren of nature's scenery. Until recently, there have been few beasts, creeks, food crops, dirt clods, or raindrops in our histories. Yet nature is more than mere backdrop to the human drama, more than the resource that sustains it. Nature's troupe – vegetable, animal, and mineral – forms part of the production's cast, actors whose agency rivals that of the human players. History without nature is not only self-serving: it is inaccurate, shortsighted, and potentially perilous to the human story line. For the drama to be complete, we must cast both nature and culture in the roles of protagonist, for each have dealt the other health and sickness, aid and harm, and life and death. Yet neither nature nor culture has been able to determine the other's destiny entirely. Quite the contrary. Both culture and nature interpret characters that are too wily, cunning, and unpredictable to be altogether bullied by the other. However, the very same tenacious qualities in each have resulted in nature and culture shaping each other profoundly, in ways mundane and catastrophic. All of our histories need not be environmental, but in some of our histories, nature and culture deserve equal billing.

This is a history of humans and nature in the Neotropics, the bioregion of tropical and subtropical America that ranges from Mexico and the Caribbean well down into South America's southern cone. In time,

I will attempt to span roughly six centuries, from strategies to eat in Aztec Tenochtitlán, to the struggle to breathe in today's Mexico City. And in subject I will range as broadly, from yesterday's tropical agriculture to today's ecotourist zoo. My primary focus, however, will be on humans striving to make themselves a tropical home. In a landscape that many, since Columbus, have described as nigh unto the original Eden, what shape did human habitats take, and what relationships did they form with the nature on which they were ensconced? Home is the term we will use to describe the human habitat, the place where culture and nature meet and contest each other's desired accommodations. Home, whether speaking of an individual shelter or an entire civilization, is among our most powerful cultural symbols, an ideal that embraces security, comfort, beauty, belonging, place, and memory. Environmental history has something to say about each of those homely qualities, but our chief concern will consider whether the project of tropical civilization has been sustainable. To what extent have human habitats in Latin America succeeded and failed to provide for themselves, their children, and their children's children? Did Indian homes function in long-term harmonious balance with nature; did colonial homes, cities, and farms built by European settlers and African workers substantially degrade America's landscapes; did Latin America's independent nations export nature's wealth faster than it could renew itself, forcing them to make drastic leaps from one unsustainable enterprise to the next; and, ultimately, are Latin Americans' current homes, most of them dense urban agglomerations, on a warped trajectory toward cultural collapse? The latest answers to some of these questions may surprise you.

Do not confuse sustainable development, an issue outside our interest, with sustainability. This environmental history, unlike most history, will be less interested in civilization's material progress or social equality than in its permanence and longevity. And, although it may seem at first impression hard-hearted, it is also more interested in the survival of human civilization than in the biological and material successes of individual humans. As a species, humans have been as tenacious as bacteria, more like rodents than dinosaurs, surviving cultural and natural disasters of all sorts. Although high Maya civilization now lays tragically silent beneath tangled forests, the Maya as a vital people are still very much with us. Nature, so far, has posed no substantial threat to human biological survival. However, Neotropical America's history is replete with examples of civilization's repeated collapse. To the Maya case you can add dozens of other cultures of whose demise we are aware, and probably many more of which we are not. Civilization, the human species' highest expression of home, has proven most vulnerable, and its loss, which entails the loss of security, comfort, beauty, belonging, place, and even history itself, is the greatest of all human tragedies, short of our biological extinction.

To address the question of sustainability, I will emphasize four recurring themes: population, technology, attitudes toward nature, and attitudes toward consumption. Among other variables, these factors have substantially shaped civilization's environmental sustainability. All else being equal, large populations are less sustainable than small ones. All else, however, is seldom equal; small voracious populations that consume without restraint will be less sustainable than large ones of more modest material demands. Hence consumption, another instance where culture and nature make intimate contact, will figure prominently in our journey across landscapes and time. Humans, like all species, must consume nature to survive, but only the human species has demonstrated the capacity to consume exponentially more than its basic biological needs. Technology as a theme is ambivalently double-edged: some human instruments, such as the Inca woodstove and the electric streetcar, have permitted cultures to satisfy their needs for heat and transportation, for example, with fewer resources and less pollution; others, such as the chainsaw and the private automobile, have heartened cultures to use resources wastefully and have entailed substantial collateral damage.

Cultural attitudes toward nature set the tone of the human relationship with the environment and can potentially be a most significant factor in a culture's sustainability. Ideas often matter. In practice, however, attitudes toward nature have yet to prove themselves historically significant. History has shown that regardless of a culture's religious or scientific views of nature, we of the human race have joined hands in reshaping and devastating the earth, its diversity and vitality. Indians, many of whom had sharply less inimical attitudes toward nature than Europeans, still deforested, hunted beasts to extinction, and carved the face of the landscape to meet their material and cosmological needs. In some ways more striking, twenty-first-century westerners live in the most enlightened era ever as regards positive, even amicable, attitudes toward nature. Due to the popular environmental movement, not yet a half a century old but one of the most profound revolutions in recent human thought, nature is valued, loved, reverenced, and cherished possibly as in no other time. But the developed nations, which have the strongest claim to environmentalism's revolution, consume, pollute, and kill the nature we profess to admire and respect at rates entirely unprecedented. As Wallace Stegner reminded us, nature appreciation and natural destruction are utterly compatible. Ideologies are important, and hence will not be ignored, but as in nearly every party and creed, anachronisms survive and hypocrites abound.

One of the tasks of history is to expand human memory beyond a single generation. Few humans have lived as long as a century, and none of us can say exactly what a landscape looked like even at the time of our birth. In fact, many Latin Americans, like North Americans, have begun to transform their landscapes so quickly, and they have themselves become so mobile, flitting from one location to the next in search of better lives, few can guess what the landscape they currently call home looked like even 20 years ago. We are hardly aware of the visible impact we have had on the earth, and we remain largely ignorant of what may have been lost with time's passing. The work of environmental history is to recover, in a sense, what has been lost, and to make it dear to our historical consciousness. Only by putting nature in our official past can we potentially grasp its substantially altered place in our present and future.

J. R. McNeill has concisely defined environmental history as the history of humans and "the rest of nature." As much as we may protest, humans are nature too. Humans will remain at center stage in our drama lest environmental history shade into natural history; however, the stories of nonhuman life and of the inanimate resources on which life depends will be given place in our plots. In addition to Indians, colonists, slaves, industrialists, peasants, urbanites, and tourists, our cast will include soils, smallpox, sugar, mercury, egrets, butterflies, guano, whales, hurricanes, and reefs. To the story's benefit, the rest of nature in Latin America is overwhelming in its diversity. Despite the racial and ethnic diversity of hominids in the region, humans constitute just one species. By contrast, there are more than 30,000 species of vascular plants, three times as many as Africa or Asia despite Latin America being significantly smaller than either of those tropical continents. Of orchids alone there are some 8,000 species. The region holds more than 3,000 species of birds, and the Amazon and its tributaries carry in excess of 2,000 kinds of fish. Little Peru sustains 3,532 species of butterfly, more than any other nation. And single trees are known to support 50 varieties of ant. Of course, all these tallies are current. What was lost before we cared to count will never be known, but we do know that of those who remain, many are threatened, about 650 species in Brazil alone.

Due to our rather limited ability to comprehend the immensities of cosmological time and space, we have thus far failed to grasp fully just how rare life is. The universe is mostly vacuum and lifeless elements. As far as we know, life on this terrestrial bestiary of breeding, breathing creatures may be unique in all space and in all time. We share much with the rest of nature, but the characteristic that should connect our mutual fortunes most persuasively is our astonishing rarity. That we generally value things by their scarcity, then, makes an odd contradiction in the face of our often thoughtless actions toward living things, human and nonhuman. More of us would treasure life, even its most bizarre and frightening forms, if we truly understood how cosmologically vulnerable it is.

While sustainability will serve as our foremost rule for cultural judgment throughout the book, sustainability is largely a human-centered aspiration. It promises nothing to the rest of nature's health and survival, just to that of humans. Sustainability so focuses on building successful, long-lived human societies that it neglects those elements of nature that make no apparent contribution to human welfare and, in fact, mercilessly attacks natural objects and creatures that threaten it. We have seen progress. We have rescued a few favored species, such as whales, that hardly entered human consciousness even 50 years ago, and we have cleaned up some bodies of water and a few pockets of urban air that troubled our growing sensibilities. However, the fact that by our own estimation we fall well short of achieving sustainability in most fields of human endeavor hardly bodes well for the rest of life on the planet.

Sustainability remains a commendable cultural goal, but even if achieved it will be insufficient to reverse nature's miserable fortunes. Safeguarding nature will require a yet more revolutionary change in human attitudes that must grant nonhuman life, even inanimate landscapes, fuller consideration as regards their own rights to sustainable existence. And it will require relinquishing our obsession with perpetual material growth. Such a change would not deny humans their right to kill and eat, something all living things must carry out to survive; nor will it require that we reintroduce smallpox into the wild as we have done with wolves. We will, rather, have to reorient our cultural goals toward living satisfied and happy in nature's company rather than single-mindedly progressing by its demise, for the danger is the sneaking probability that many of us seem all too willing to embrace: that humans can sustain themselves over the long-term not only without smallpox and wolves, but also without forests and birds, corals and fishes, and fields and grasses. As human technologies and arts advance, we may just be able to create a sustainable existence for ourselves without nature, or with substantially less of it than we currently have. Like the space travelers of science fiction who sever themselves from earth's life-sustaining services, we may come to be able to biologically sustain ourselves on synthesized food, purified oxygen, filtered urine, and an artificially controlled climate – indefinitely. And we may satisfy our spiritual need for nonhuman nature through art, broadcasting birdsong to wireless earphones and projecting the images of stately forests and meandering wildlife into every corner of our increasingly virtual existence. Such bleak, dystopic futures are frequently depicted in film and books, and they are universally hellish, sustainable or not. In our long struggle with nature, true victory cannot envisage *Homo sapiens* as the last one standing. Even if our clever civilizations will hereafter not require the biodiversity that much of the rest of nature provides, the next evolution in environmental thought must be the realization that we desperately want it anyway.

CHAPTER ONE

An Old World Before It Was "New"

Oh God, my father, my mother, Holy Huitz-Hok, Lord of the hills and valleys, Lord of the forest, be patient. I am doing as always has been done . . . but perhaps you will suffer it. I am about to damage you, I am about to work you so that I may live. . . . With all my soul I am going to work you.[1]

Christopher Columbus refused to accept that he had discovered a new world, two entire continents of which his own world had been ignorant. He doggedly held that he had discovered a new route to the backside of the known world, the coveted Orient, even the original human home, the garden planted by God eastward in Eden – just as he intended. In his first report penned to Ferdinand and Isabella, Columbus described his island discoveries as immense gardens of useful trees perpetually in foliage, flower, and fruit, flowing with honey and bounded by fertile fields. Significantly, neither Columbus nor his seafaring successors saw their discoveries as empty wilderness. To Columbus, the Edenic landscapes he described were no more pristine than the Europe from which he had sailed. Eden was, after all, a garden, not a wilderness. The paradise he described, whether in origin divine or manmade, was a cultivated artifact, and as Columbus pronounced repeatedly, it was full of "innumerable people." If America was in fact news to Europe, as Columbus' successors figured out, Europeans also clearly understood that it was by no means new. The so-called "New World," once removed from the

---

[1] Maya prayer, quoted in J. Eric S. Thompson, *Maya Archaeologist* (Norman: University of Oklahoma Press, 1975), 139–40.

perspective of Columbus' astonishing landfall, is seen more accurately as just another old world.

Pre-Columbian America, however, we have long idealized as one big leafy preserve inhabited by an inconsequential smattering of Indians, all of whom we have ecologically sainted. This Pristine Myth, which depicts precontact America as an unspoiled, lightly peopled wilderness in environmental harmony and ecological balance, is an image that manages to remain standing even though recent scholarship has cut off its legs. Some have held to the myth because an empty land justifies America's conquest and colonization. But we cannot blame the Iberians, the Spanish and Portuguese conquerors, for creating the myth. Such men had no qualms and made no excuses for subjugating two densely peopled continents. Conquest justified itself, and the more people conquered, converted, and taxed, the better.

The Iberians struck few deserted shores; nearly every place they landed was inhabited by plentiful peoples who greeted them with gifts or arrows. From Columbus in the Caribbean to Magellan in Tierra del Fuego, all described the Americas as "densely peopled," and "full." Bartolomé de Las Casas observed in 1542 that the Caribbean islands were "as populous and filled with native-born peoples, the Indians, as any peopled land upon the earth."[2] Gaspar de Carvajal, chaplain on the first European descent of the Amazon, found even its banks heavily settled, noting "cities that glistened white" with tens of thousands of people. One city, he reported, ran unbroken for nearly 30 kilometers along the river's bank. The inventor of the title "New World," Amerigo Vespucci, who also became America's namesake, encountered so many people on his multiple voyages to South America that he proclaimed it was more densely peopled than Europe, Asia, or Africa. Such claims were only amplified when the Iberians encountered highly developed empires in the highlands of Mexico and Peru. Las Casas described Mexico's mainland as "all filled as though the land were a beehive of people," as if "God did set down upon these lands the entire multitude, or greatest part, of the entire human lineage."[3] Until recently, these observations were believed the boastful exaggerations of men bent on embellishing their conquests (or in Las Casas' case, amplifying the tragedy). Since at least

---

[2] Bartolomé de Las Casas, *An Account, Much Abbreviated, of the Destruction of the Indies*, ed. Franklin W. Knight (Indianapolis, IN: Hackett Publishing, 2003), 4–5.

[3] Ibid.

the late eighteenth century, men as eminent as Adam Smith questioned the veracity of unschooled soldiers and irrational priests who in the sixteenth century dared suggest that Indian America was anything more than a primitive polity of meager, scattered tribes. However, mounting new evidence is corroborating the conquerors' crude accounting.

Estimates of the precontact American population remain crude, and we will never know Indian numbers with certainty, but changing assumptions have increased them considerably. Scholars in the 1930s estimated the New World's 1492 population at 8–15 million, their figures influenced by racist assumptions about the Indians' incapacity for civilization and the tropics' incapacity for intensive agriculture. Historical demographers and archeologists have turned those assumptions on their heads, and particularly since the 500th anniversary of Columbus' voyage, scholars have argued persuasively that American cultures created societies supporting some of the world's densest populations. Today, we believe that the American population in 1492 ranged from 40 to 70 million (some estimates go as high as 115 million), and the large majority lived in what is today Latin America. Mexico and Central America combined may have held some 24 million; South America about the same number. The Caribbean islands alone held 3–7 million. By contrast, North America (without Mexico) held a mere 2–3 million. Unfortunately, the story has been too often told from a North American perspective and with a rather late beginning. In fact, the Pristine Myth itself originated in later centuries among European settlers whose evidence for an empty wilderness was not an un-peopled landscape, as they assumed, but a depopulated one. As best we can tell, before the conquest, there were no frontiers. Civilizations and tribes jostled one another everywhere. The empty American frontier was created, not discovered, by the conquest.

Likewise, what would become Latin America was dotted with significant urban centers. The Aztec cities of Tenochtitlán and Texcoco, in the Valley of Mexico, each had more than 200,000 inhabitants, larger than contemporary Paris, London, or Lisbon. Zempoala, to the east of Mexico, had 100,000. Inca Cuzco held 50,000 within its constricted city limits, and that many again within a day's walk. In Spain and Portugal, there were no cities comparable in size to those of America, and during the three succeeding centuries of the colonial era, the Iberians built no enduring colonial city that could match them for size. In 1492, the Valley of Mexico had 1 million inhabitants, to use the more conservative estimate. Although the valley would embrace

Mexico City, America's largest city in 1600, 1800, and 2000, the entire valley would not house a million people again until the twentieth century. In the gulf lowlands of Vera Cruz, the precontact population of half a million was not surpassed until the 1990s. And as large as indigenous populations were in 1492, it is probable that they had been yet larger in the Classic Period before A.D. 1000. America had been heavily peopled thousands of years before the Iberians arrived. It is now believed that civilization took shape in the Andes before it did in China or India, contemporary with Egypt just before 3000 B.C. Much of the evidence of these early cultures and their numbers, of course, has been overlain by time and dust. Civilized peoples tend toward tidiness, constantly sweeping clean their homes, streets, and temples. When civilization and brooms disappear, the dust accumulates, and many American ruins, like those of the Old World, came to be buried meters below the earth's current surface. In America, until rather recently, few thought there was any reason to dig.

SHAPING FERTILE LANDSCAPES

What impact did millions of people through thousands of years have on the Neotropical landscape? If the land was not pristine, to what extent was it humanized, refashioned to meet the needs of the human species? New World agriculture is an instructive window through which to examine these questions. Culture transformed American nature in myriads of ways, but strategies for securing food were among the most powerful shapers of the landscape. As examples, we will examine agricultures that were contemporary to America's European discovery, the farming techniques of the Aztecs, Incas, and Brazil's lowland Tupi, not of those cultures buried under time's accumulated dust. But keep in mind that the indigenous peoples contacted by Europeans were only the latest in what was a long chain of cultures. The terms Aztec, Inca, and Tupi are in essence new names for ancient cultural processes. While each added something to agricultural technique and technology, for the most part successors copied those they conquered, and some of the practices and impacts we will describe were as old as American agriculture.

Unlike North America, where settled agriculture was the exception, in tropical America it was the rule, and much of the region was intensively farmed. Agriculture had developed in America independently in both Mesoamerica and Peru, uninfluenced by old-world precedent, and by 1492, farming was the primary food source in Mexico, Central America, the Caribbean, the Andes, the coastal Pacific, and portions of the Amazon basin. And farming was at least an ancillary source of food nearly everywhere outside cold Patagonia. Hence, the impact of farming in tropical America is, in fact, more similar to that of old-world systems than the North American experience. And in some places, its visible environmental impact was arguably greater than any example from European agriculture.

Of course, for much of America's prehistoric past, hunting and gathering were the primary strategies to secure food, and while less consequential than settled agriculture, even the wandering nomads had notable impacts. They have been blamed for the disappearance of the New World's mega-fauna, including the giant sloth, giant beaver, horses, mastodons, and a handful of other peculiar creatures. In colder North America, climate change remains a primary explanation for the disappearance of these large mammals, but at least some few survived, such as deer, mountain goats, bighorn sheep, antelope, elk, and moose. In South America almost no large mammals remain, probably due to larger human populations and greater distance from the Bering land bridge over which such beasts might have immigrated subsequent to the slaughter. Climate change appears to have been less severe in South America, and as climate had changed periodically before humans arrived without apparent catastrophe, it is likely that hunters played a notable role in bringing about the almost complete disappearance of mega-fauna in tropical America. Hunters also created the large tracts of grassland the Europeans favored on their conquering marches. Fire was the hunter's primary tool, employed less to herd game than to create and maintain grasslands that attracted and nourished the few remaining large mammals, such as deer and peccary, making them more frequent, not to mention easy, targets for human consumption. Throughout tropical America, the Europeans encountered grasslands that by all climatological rights should have been dense tropical forest.

However, when humans began to put down roots, literally and figuratively, nature and culture began to meld into an uneasy alliance in which each began to shape the other in earnest. Hunters and gatherers chased nature's bounty from place to place. Farmers who made permanent homes had to learn, by long trial and error, how to coax nature into consistent local abundance. And the American farmer created, depending on climate, a wide variety of agricultural techniques that still impress for their adaptive sophistication, high productivity, and transformative power. America's first farmers developed agriculture without old-world technology: they lacked metal tools to clear the forests, plow the ground, or harvest their crops; they lacked the wheel (which was known but not implemented) to move bulky goods; and, most significantly, Indians lacked large domesticated animals to assist them in their work or to produce manure to fertilize their crops. The llama and alpaca are the only exceptions, but they were restricted to one narrow region of the Americas and were not much stronger than a man. The success and impact of agriculture in the American tropics was more a matter of imaginative techniques than powerful technologies.

The farmer's essential natural resource is soil. Dirt may seem a dull topic, but fertile soil is the root of civilization, and the civilization, ancient or modern, whose farmers cannot competently manage the soil, soon unravels. Some locations have been blessed more than others, but most virgin soils offer yields that compensate a farmer's labor. However, planting crops in the same field year after year depletes the soil of critical nutrients, primarily nitrogen, phosphorus, and sulfur. Depending on the soil's quality, it might optimistically offer satisfactory yields for 20 years with no addition of fertilizer, but the viably productive period is usually much shorter.

Maintaining soil fertility has been a central challenge of civilization. Before we look at American strategies to maintain fertility, consider very briefly the European approach as a point of reference. In Europe, annual fallowing, that is, letting the soil rest in alternate years, was a common practice until the seventeenth century. The European farmer's field produced for one year, but the crop so exhausted the soil that he had little choice but to let it lie fallow the next year, setting livestock to graze the stubble and manure the ground with their droppings. A year on, a year off – securing one crop every other year in any particular field – European farmers devised a sustainable means to feed themselves. Sometimes they planted a field two years before letting it lie fallow, but compared to some indigenous American strategies, European farming was neither sophisticated nor terribly productive.

Europeans who visited the shores of what is today Rio de Janeiro universally described its inhabitants, the Tupi, as extraordinary physical specimens. Tupi bodies, male and female, were remarkable for more than their oft-described nudity. Jean de Léry, the French Calvinist who lived among them in the mid-1550s, noted that in comparison to Europeans, "they are stronger, more robust and well filled-out, more nimble, and less subject to disease," and he added that they aged as if they daily drank from the Fountain of Youth.[4] Modern research bears out the impression. Skeletal remains from this region and time are, until the twentieth century, the healthiest human specimens of the western hemisphere.

The Tupi were the first and most numerous indigenous peoples the Europeans encountered in Brazil. Beginning in about A.D. 400, they too had come from elsewhere to push out the previous inhabitants to dominate Brazil's entire coastline, living in large villages of about 600 persons that were often in a state of open warfare with their immediate Tupi neighbors. Many Tupi tribes shrewdly enhanced their military advantage over their rivals by trading with the metal- and gun-toting Europeans who frequented the coasts in search of brazilwood. For four centuries, the Tupi and the Portuguese engaged in a vibrant cultural exchange that involved intermarriage as well as the mutual exchange of technology, ecological knowledge, and agricultural practice. Today, many of Brazil's geographical features and natural objects, especially rivers, trees, plants, and animals, retain their Tupi names.

Extremely warlike, the Tupi relished battle and consumed their captured enemies in cannibalistic feasts. However, Tupi health was not the result of access to human flesh. The Tupi high-protein diet derived from coastal Brazil's incomparable mangrove forests, tidal woodlands that provided habitat for oysters, crabs, fish, and birds. By simple gathering and fishing, the Tupi had as much protein at hand as any culture. But they also planted manioc, maize, and other crops that supplied the greater share of their calories. Tupi males felled the forest, let the slash dry, and then burned it, concentrating the nutrients stored in the forest's woody tissues on the soil in the form of ashes. This system, known as swidden, or slash and burn, offered tremendous initial yields to Tupi women who did the actual cultivating. Manioc, a root crop similar in appearance to the yam, offered more calories per hectare than a European farmer could have hoped for and had the added advantage of storing well right in the ground where it was planted. However, after a period of about five years, crop yields in the cleared plot declined drastically. If the farmer stayed put, she and her children would go hungry, so the men of her village opened new fields by clearing more forest.

At that point the cycle started again, but rather than advance into virgin forests, the village usually relocated to forests that had been felled and burned some 20 or 40 years earlier. In other words, this was a

[4] Jean de Léry, *History of a Voyage to the Land of Brazil*, trans. J. Whately (Berkeley: University of California Press, 1990), 56–7.

fallowing system not unlike that of the Europeans, but done on a longer scale. Here a field was worked for half a decade and then abandoned for two or more decades before it was recleared and planted. What the Europeans did every year or two with the help of animals to restore fertility, the Tupi did over decades using the forest's own vegetative recovery to regenerate the soil's growing capacity. The system supported a considerable population, maybe 150,000 in the environs of Rio de Janeiro, consisting of hundreds of village groups. Swidden could not support dense cities but still made a considerable impact on the land. In addition to corn, beans, squash, and manioc, the Tupi also cultivated cotton. The French traded Tupi cotton in the early sixteenth century, and in one recorded case laded 5.5 tons onto a single ship, evidence of the power of Tupi agriculture to produce more than just food. To European eyes, the forests appeared virgin, and although for the most part intact, most coastal forests had been felled, burned, and abandoned many times over the millennium of Tupi presence. The forest was certainly less complex and less diverse as a result: its mix and distribution of species had been altogether altered. It is likely that less disturbed forests remained on the steepest hillsides and in the buffer zones between village territories. But nature had a very different face due to swidden, a strategy employed not only by the Tupi, but by many cultures that inhabited American forests, both tropical and temperate.

Across the breadth of the lower Amazon, Indians who lived in denser settlements than the Tupi found requisite additional means to manage fertility in a tropical forest, a habitat that without human intervention offered little in the way of food beyond fish in the rivers and elusive game in the forests. In fact, in some areas, both fish and game were scarce, a stark reality discovered by more than one outsider. In 1914, former president Theodore Roosevelt joined Brazilian explorer Cândido Rondon for a descent of the River of Doubt (now the Roosevelt), one of the Amazon's last unexplored tributaries. Despite Rondon's unmatched experience in jungle travel and able preparations, it was a hellish adventure: one man drowned, Roosevelt's son Kermit nearly drowned, a laborer was murdered, and the killer was left to die in the forest. Roosevelt himself suffered an acute leg infection, and his contracting of malaria may have shortened his life. For 48 arduous days they saw no human habitation and soon ran out of food. The river, which was choked with rapids, offered few fish, and with no Indians to offer them provisions, the party was reduced to subsisting on the hearts of palm trees. By the time they completed their 2,400-kilometer descent, Roosevelt had lost 57 pounds.

Members of Francisco de Orellana's expedition in 1542, the first Europeans to descend the Amazon, also nearly starved to death. In fact, hunger spawned the journey. Mired in the Peruvian jungle seeking El Dorado, Gonzalo Pizarro had sent Orellana downstream to find food. Orellana's men resorted to gnawing on belts and shoes boiled with herbs, and several reportedly went mad after eating some unidentified roots. Then they arrived in the lands of the Omagua whose territory stretched 300 kilometers along the river and to an unknown distance inland. The hungry Spaniards attacked the city of Machiparo, chasing out its inhabitants, and were astonished by their good fortune. They found food stores sufficient to feed a thousand people for a year, they claimed, both corn and thousands of penned, river turtles. With these provisions and others they stocked their vessel and continued their descent. But the provisions were soon exhausted, and Orellana's men suffered hunger intermittently during the entire eight months of their passage. But note, from that point down river, they went hungry for lack of friends. Their reputation for theft and plunder preceded them, and village after village hurled deadly objects at them as they floated by. Only when their hunger became acute did they risk repeating their raids on the abundant indigenous stores.

The difference between Roosevelt's and Orellana's experience is explained by differences in human presence. More people lived in the Amazon in 1542 than in 1914. There were no populations producing food along the River of Doubt during Roosevelt's passage. Even the noted lack of game along the river was probably due to a lack of human manipulation of the landscape. By contrast, those peoples living along the river centuries before had shaped the Amazon so it would produce human food in abundance. Nature alone generally does not provide. New England's Pilgrims, Lewis and Clark, Cabeza de Vaca, all strangers in a new land, even with all of nature before them, would have potentially starved to death if not for the presence and hospitality of indigenous peoples.

But how did the Omagua and other Amazonians support their substantial populations, which were much larger than those of the Tupi, in a landscape that for years we have believed was plagued with thin, leached, unproductive soils? Swidden was common, but that alone would have been insufficient to sustain their dense towns. Amazonians developed a number of unique strategies. One, flood agriculture, was the same technique that sustained and empowered ancient Egypt. Like the Nile, Amazonia's rivers flood predictably. While most cultures are forced to farm the same soils year after year, the Amazon's annual flood supplied new fertile soil to the intensively farmed riverbanks with no effort on the farmers' behalf. As the waters rose, Andean silt deposited itself in layers on the broad floodplain; as the floods receded, the virgin sediment received seed. Unlike the Nile, the Amazon's waters fall rapidly, allowing planting to take place early enough to secure two crops per year, and its waters rose slowly enough to allow a paced harvest. Farmers harvested two crops per year, year after year.

Another soil strategy has been uncovered only recently. Throughout the Amazon, modern farmers and researchers encountered soils that were inexplicably out of place. Dotting the Amazon's typically thin, usually pale, mineral soils were strange deposits of deep, black, fertile earth. Scientists theorized that these formations must have been the decomposition of volcanic rocks, the beds of former lakes, or some other unknown natural process. Archeology got a rather late start in Amazonia due to the negative assumptions about the nature and extent of civilization in the heart of the tropics. Why dig where one expected to find nothing? But once archeologists got their hands dirty, they found the unexpected. Mixed within these black soils were broken pots, the remains of shellfish, animal bones, and other related human trash. There was nothing natural about this soil's origin. It was a human creation. The indigenous peoples, going back 2,000 years, created fertile fields by concentrating their wastes, that is, by recycling the nutrients of their culture back into the soil, including the ashes of their fires, rotting vegetation, animal remains, probably human excrement, and significantly, charcoal, which has been shown to be the Amazonian's key invention that locks recycled nutrients in the forest's thin, easily leached soils. The results were fertile fields 2 to 3 hectares in size and half a meter deep, although some as large as 100 hectares and as deep as 2 meters have been encountered. Confirmed indigenous black soils (*terras pretas*) are scattered across the region. The strategy required a great deal of human effort, but for a culture up against poor natural soils and a presumably closed frontier, it was a suitable adaptation. The result is still appreciated today. Black soils form the basis of many of today's cash crops, but today's papaya and mango farmers, while inheriting a windfall, have not inherited the wisdom of their antecedents' soil management strategies, which were not only sustainable but in fact improved soil productivity over time.

Lastly, Amazonians, and many peoples living in America's tropical forests, engaged in a variety of forms of agroforestry, managing and manipulating forests for food and other resources. As farmers cleared forests, they left standing the trees they most valued. In the Amazon, farmers might plant their corn and manioc among native brazilnut trees, rubber trees, medicinal plants, and a large variety of palms that provided fruit, oil, alcohol, fiber, timber, and roofing material. When they abandoned a field, they continued to encourage the growth of these trees, and palms thrived in the disturbed plots of ground. They also scattered new seeds about, including cashews. The result was an intentional forest. By careful management, forests became less wild and more capable of producing the commodities that humans prized. Agroforestry was common to many rainforest agricultures. The evidence is apparent even today in the Maya city of Tikal where *ramón*, or American breadfruit, grows profusely out of the ruins. While *ramón* is found wild throughout the forest, it never forms common stands as in Tikal, and it generally yields only once per year. The dense population of *ramón* around Tikal produces year round showing the Maya's capacity to select for valued traits in their agroforestry.

It has been estimated that 12 percent of the Amazon basin consists of forests that are in part manmade. The preponderance in these areas of palm, nut, and fruit trees that are important to humans far exceeds what nature would have produced without intervention. Hence, just as Orellana's men relied on indigenous farms to feed themselves, even Roosevelt's starvation diet of hearts of palm was probably left to him by the indigenous peoples who formerly lived along the River of Doubt. These findings have encouraged some to call the Amazon's forests a human artifact, a garden rather than a wilderness. The claim, one can imagine, is controversial, for many still hold Amazonia as the prototypical virgin landscape, Eden's last holdout. But the assertion can no longer be discounted out of hand. After 500 years, Amazonia still bears the marks of a civilization that was demographically as successful and better distributed than the one that currently inhabits it.

Despite the marks the Tupi and the peoples of Amazonia printed on nature, these were hardly legible compared to what Europeans encountered in the highlands of Mexico and Peru. When the Spanish conquistadors first crested the passes leading into the Valley of Mexico, they were astonished at the view. A broad, shallow lake graced the valley floor, and splendid cities with jutting white pyramids dotted the lake's shores and islands. Wondering if this all was not some dream, they descended into the city of Iztapalapa and marveled at its palaces and streets. Bernal Díaz was confessedly impressed with the city's watery gardens, "a marvelous place to see and walk in," full of flowers, fruits, and trees, as well as a wide variety of water birds treading its shallow shores. This was no wilderness, but a garden, a human landscape worthy of conquest. The next day, the conquerors embarked on the southern causeway that carried them over the lake to the Aztec island capital, Tenochtitlán. That morning, the causeway, 8 meters wide, was clogged by crowds who had come to see these bearded men riding strange beasts. The lake itself teemed with canoe loads of residents out to take in the spectacle.

The lakes' causeways, features worthy of much Spanish comment, numbered in the dozens and were particularly concentrated in the southeastern portion of Lake Texcoco, where they radiated from the island capital toward the mainland. (See Map 3, which only represents those causeways and dikes documented in early sources.) Not only did the causeways make the island Aztec capital appear something out of a chivalrous fairy tale, but they ominously threatened to cut off the Spaniards from reinforcement and from escape. But the strangers misjudged the causeways' primary function, which was neither transportation nor defense. For men for whom transport was by horse and wheeled vehicle, they could not help but assume the causeways were there to bridge the lakes. Far more causeways and dikes connected Tenochtitlán to the mainland than labor and resources could justify or security would reasonably permit if transport were their primary function. Three, at most, would have sufficed, particularly since most goods and people arrived in the city by canoe. The causeways' chief functions were agricultural and hydrological, and any benefit they provided to transport or defense was secondary to that of water control.

The Aztecs' chinampas, often referred to erroneously as floating gardens, were the most fully developed form of raised field agriculture in the Americas, impressive for their sophistication and extent. They may have been the most advanced, but they were not the only form of wetland farming, nor were they the most extensive. The Maya, the Inca, many pre-Inca groups, and the Amazonians engaged in raised field agriculture as a means to create sustainable crops in swamps and lakes. Still visible today are 5,000 square kilometers of raised fields in Colombia and 1,200 square kilometers in the vicinity of Lake Titicaca. The Aztecs only built 120 square kilometers.

Long before the Aztecs appeared in about 1300, the inhabitants of the Valley of Mexico formed chinampas by creating raised fields in the wetlands along the lakes' shorelines. They layered lake mud, aquatic plants, and rotting vegetation on a light skeleton of structural reeds to a height of about 1 meter above the water and then anchored the

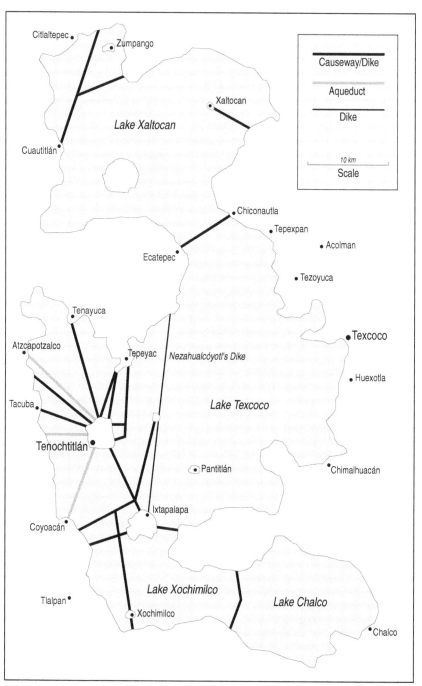

Map 3. Major Aztec hydrological works in the Valley of Mexico, circa 1500. Drawn by author.
Source: Adapted from Angel Palerm, *Obras hidráulicas prehispánicas en el sistema lacustre del Valle de México* (Mexico City: Instituto Nacional de Antropología e Historia, 1973), 243.

platform's perimeter with rapidly growing willows. Fields were a few meters wide and around 70 meters in length, surrounded and connected by a rectilinear grid of canals offering easy canoe transport as well as habitats for fish and waterfowl. The result was one of culture's most charming agricultural landscapes, colorful fields of flowers and food bounded by carefully spaced trees and animated waterways.

As the system held many agricultural advantages it was adopted around the valley basin whenever possible. By bringing crops to the water rather than water to the crops, as in traditional irrigation, it reduced labor: the roots were irrigated from below by capillary action of the layered matrix. The water surrounding the fields also created warmer microclimates that combated frost, a sometimes devastating threat in this valley at more than 2,200 meters elevation. Fertility was sustained by the constant addition of new soil dredged from sediments in the surrounding ditch network, and also by composting much of the society's castoff material, including human excrement. Díaz described enclosed latrines that were built over the city's canals. Canoes tethered below each stall caught the waste, which was then taken directly to the chinampas for application to the soils. The use of human manure and careful composting ensured a nearly complete recycling of the valley's nutrients.

It was an extremely productive system. Farmers could get three to four crops per year and never had to let the land rest fallow. Over a two-year period in which Europeans reaped one crop per field, Mexicans, with the help of their typically mild winters, might harvest eight. And when done carefully, raised fields, like black soils, improved in fertility over the years. Chinampas could support 15 people per hectare in the fifteenth century. Chinese agriculture, one of Eurasia's most successful, which was also based on human excrement, supported fewer than three people per hectare in the same century.

By the conquest, chinampas had spread from their origins in the valley's southern lakes to fringe most of the valley's lake and island cities, including private chinampa house gardens within the capital. The expansion was possible due to the Aztecs' centralization and technical expertise. Chinampa agriculture suffered from a number of potentially catastrophic threats, most of them related to water. The most insidious was salt. The Valley of Mexico was not a typical valley at all, but a basin whose lakes had no outlet. The Aztecs and some Spaniards believed there was a drain near Lake Texcoco's middle as they could not explain how an enclosed body of water, fed by numerous rivers and springs, did not eventually fill the basin. Evaporation, of course, kept the lake at a moderate level, but it also concentrated salt in the water, and chinampas had to be protected from salt infiltration. Drought, a more serious threat, if of short duration, could be managed by hand irrigation from the ditches. Farmers might irrigate entire fields by hand, which may explain why they built them narrow between the canals. But a prolonged drought brought famine. Flood, on the other hand, was the most catastrophic threat, for if it managed to submerge the crops, they were an immediate and total loss. In 1450, the basin was hit by a major flood followed by three years of drought. The result, in addition to thousands of sacrificial victims mustered to appease Tlaloc, the god of rain, was starvation and out-migration. Many sold themselves and their children into slavery to towns on the coastal lowlands that had not been as affected by the drought.

Hence, water that was too high, too low, or too salty invited hunger and death. Water control was the reason for the causeways the Spaniards found so remarkable. The Aztecs, principally during and after the reign of Moctezuma I, embarked on a massive hydrological program that included dams, dikes, river diversions, causeways, and sluices that protected the fields from water's threats and allowed the chinampas to expand into new areas. The largest such project was the dike constructed by 20,000 men under the direction of the poet-engineer Nezahualcóyotl, lord of the city of Texcoco. Nezahualcóyotl's dike spanned Lake Texcoco in 16 kilometers, separating the lake's salty northwestern half from its fresher southern reaches where the Aztec capital was located. The dike created a large sweet spot permitting the expansion of chinampas in and around the city itself. Additional sluiced dikes maintained water at the appropriate level for each sector, served as buffers in threat of a flood, and helped store water in dry times. Some dikes were topped with roads, the origin of the causeways, and two (possibly three) of the major dikes, those from Chapultepec and Churubusco, also supported aqueducts which not only brought potable drinking water to the island capital but are believed to have also regulated fresh water levels in the city's chinampas. The complex system of some 95 known water control mechanisms, including more than 50 kilometers of dikes, causeways and aqueducts, did not always prevent disaster, but imperfect as it was, it was among the world's great hydrological systems. Chinampas were not the only form of agriculture in the Valley of Mexico (Cortés, in a 1522 letter to Charles V, observed that "not an inch" of the broad valley remained "unplowed"), but they are the chief explanation for its considerable demographic success, one of the world's densest populations. The Aztecs had created a flourishing, uniquely lacustrine empire, not one based on a natural harmony but on nature's harnessing.

Likewise, the Incas and their predecessors went to arduous lengths to reshape nature, the very mountains they lived on, to "supply by art what was wanting in nature," as Sarmiento de Gamboa put it. As Pizarro's army marched into the highlands of Peru, they faced some of the most daunting terrain. With each pass they set new European altitude records and found the air so thin that without horses they easily exhausted themselves in battle against the barrel-chested natives. This was not an easy place to make an empire, but the Inca, like the Aztecs, built on their predecessors' successes to create a productive agriculture.

Their primary adaptation to a steep environment was terracing. Pedro Sancho, Francisco Pizarro's secretary, who had no term for agricultural terraces, described them as steps climbing the mountains and called them *andenes*, or platforms. The name came to be applied to the entire range, the Andes, which one might literally translate as the terraced mountains. It is an apt name. From Venezuela to Argentina, they are still plainly visible, the most obvious human mark on ancient America's landscape. In Peru alone there are some 6,000 square kilometers of terraces, and in the region of Lake Titicaca in Bolivia there are another 5,000. Nearly all terraces are precolonial, and about half are now abandoned, most since the time of the conquest. Some slopes, such as those of the Colca and Urubamba valleys, are substantially terraced, and we now know that many of the Andes' jungled, eastern slopes, such as those of Machu Picchu, were also terraced but have been covered and torn apart by rainforest trees over the last centuries.

Terraces took many forms. Sloped field terraces followed the valley bottoms in long graceful curves, such as those just north of Pisac on Peru's Urubamba River. Some were primitive cuts and fills. The most spectacular are the bench terraces that the Incas took to an exquisite form. Many, although abandoned 500 years ago, are in excellent shape; the Incas were obsessed with durability and built their walls, for temples, homes, and terraces, with a precision and mass that will survive many civilizations to come. Perhaps the most ambitious and most pleasing example is the terrace complex of Tipon that nestles in a narrow side valley high above the Urubamba River. A series of 12 terraced fields, some as large as football fields, fill the valley transversely, set behind monolithic walls 4 meters tall. The large central terraces are flanked by smaller terraces, running parallel to the valley's walls. Water comes by

Figure 1. The upper half of the 2 square kilometer, irrigated Inca terrace complex at Tipon, Peru, 2005. Photograph by author.

aqueduct and enters the complex in a grand fountain whose waters then cascade down vertical channels in the walls at each conjunction. Large single stones protrude from the walls as stepping stones from one level to the next, casting dark shadows. This monumental construction feels like a ceremonial, public space, too charming and carefully designed to be thought a mere farm, but it served as a corn field as much as any in Iowa (see Figure 1).

Terraces, like chinampas, were carefully constructed. The wall was given a solid foundation and constructed of local stone. Soil, usually excavated from the upper slope, but in some locations, like Machu Picchu, carried up from the fertile river bottoms well below, was placed on top of a layer of clay, to help retain soil moisture, which itself was placed on a foundational layer of broken stone to permit drainage. While the terraces did prevent erosion, their primary function was to permit irrigation in steep terrain. Most terraces are found in arid and semiarid regions, and they are for the most part irrigated. Steep slopes could have been farmed without terraces, but they would have been impossible to irrigate, so terraces expanded not just cultivable land, but the most productive, irrigated land. They offered other advantages: they increased the soil's depth; increased rainfall catchment, particularly where irrigation was not practiced; increased solar insolation, especially on south facing slopes below the equator; and reduced the threat of night frost which was a more serious problem in the valley bottoms due to nighttime, cold air settlement. Terraces, then, reclaimed land that was otherwise too steep, arid, or cold to produce food.

The Incas addressed soil fertility very much like Europeans, but with variations. They used ashes, compost, fallowing, human manure, and fish heads. They had the benefit of two kinds of animal manure unavailable to the Aztecs. The first came from their llama herds; even though llamas produce less manure, and less fertile manure, than cows and pigs, it was used to great advantage across the highlands. The second was guano, the accumulated bird droppings of millennia, which the Incas mined on Peru's coastal islands. The Incas divided up this resource among coastal communities and passed harsh laws to protect it: Garcilaso de la Vega said stone piles served as guano property markers, that quantities were regulated, and that anyone who killed birds or collected eggs during the nesting season received the death penalty. The droppings were traded as a precious commodity along the coast, and there is good evidence that it traveled to the highlands with some frequency, probably to the fields of the royal and divine. It is hard to say if the practice was sustainable, but the Incas dealt cautiously. It took the Europeans another three centuries to rediscover this unique resource, which they completely exhausted on farms across the world in about half a century.

The Andes were a harsh place to make a civilization. Crops, due to drought, excessive rain, or untimely frost, might fail one in every three years. The Incas accepted such natural disasters as a predictable part of life. They compensated by storing large quantities of surplus food, by working collectively in the construction of their fabulous infrastructure and in their fields, and by distributing their communities and kin across an unusually broad range of altitudes and microclimates. Where they could not change nature, they adapted to its limitations.

Of course, more important than mere techniques (terraces, chinampas, black soils, and swidden), Mesoamerica and Peru, independent of the rest of the world and each other, invented agriculture and civilization, and they did it not in the last millennium, but more than four millennia ago. Indians created corn, today's most important world crop by volume, and they domesticated beans, tomatoes, chilis, avocadoes, potatoes, and manioc, among many other foods. If Columbus discovered paradise, it was a humanized paradise, best described as an assiduously tended garden. Significantly, American nature fell between the spontaneous, celestial Eden Columbus sought and the empty, immaculate wilderness that some still strain to see.

Attitudes toward Nature and Consumption

While we have seen that the Indian, even with limited technologies, had notable impacts on the landscape, did indigenous perceptions of nature, which differed markedly from those of Europeans, place cultural restraints on nature's exploitation? What did Indians think of nature, and did it make any difference in how they exploited it? The Pristine Myth portrays the Indian as proto-ecologist: innately or by long experience, Indians understood nature's intimate workings and followed patterns of subsistence that disturbed nature as little as possible. This mythical Indian thought of the land, animals, and plants as affectionate brothers and benefactors. The reality, for the most part, was quite different. Like Europeans, Indians perceived nature primarily as provisions to be extracted and consumed. Animals were meat, hide, fur, sinew, tooth, and bone; trees were lumber, firewood, fruit, and nuts. However, while Europeans exploited nature's resources with a clear conscience, for their

Christian god had given them unchallenged dominion over plants, animals, and "all creeping things," Indians faced nature with trepidation. Indians did not paint the same stark line that Europeans did between themselves and nature. Indians generally placed plants, animals, and even inanimate objects on a more equal footing with members of the human world. But if Indian culture did not perceive itself as standing above nature, it did not see itself in brotherly harmony either, in an alliance of ungrudging mutual assistance. Nature, for Indians, was a power to be reckoned with, equal to or greater than human powers, and their respect for nature was driven not by friendship but by fear.

We have little evidence of what the Tupi thought of their forested territories, but the Aztecs, and even the forest-dwelling Maya, had an almost paranoid terror of the forest which they described as cold, dark, and miserable, a place of hunger and death. Crocodilians, feline predators, and poisonous snakes were feared with reason, and their perceived powers were co-opted by the ruling elite in terrifying images. Farmers cursed birds, insects, and mammals that ravaged their crops, taking after them with rocks, sticks, and dogs (see Figure 2). The Incas sang a harvest song that warned the *tulla*, a local finch, not to eat the ripe sweet corn; if he did, the farmer would clip his wings, pull out his fingernails, and imprison him securely in a cage.

And yet, despite nature's terrors and annoyances, the Indians remained ambivalent, showing a marked fondness for many natural objects. Birds, flowers, butterflies, and even landscapes might be honored in poetry. Many indigenous cultures kept pets, including monkeys, iguanas, dogs, and a variety of birds, for which they expressed intimate affection. The Yucatec Maya even today have an abiding soft spot for bees, songbirds, rabbits, and deer. The Aztecs maintained zoological, botanical, and avian parks centuries before Europeans established such institutions, expressing a surprisingly passionate cultural interest in nature's beauty and diversity. European cities walled out wild nature. Aztec cities incorporated it. But to a great extent both indigenous fear and admiration for nature were the result of their perception of nature's power, that all things were imbued with spirit, and hence were not just natural, but supernatural. Nearly all indigenous groups made apologies to the animals they hunted, the trees they felled, and even to the fields they worked and the seeds they planted. The apologies were to appease nature, to prevent the spirits of deer, trees, stones, and seeds from taking vengeance on those who did them harm. Among the Tupi, the skilled hunter who brought down an animal made his apologies, performed

Figure 2. An Inca scarecrow, mantled in a dog's skin and carrying a dead bird, wields a sling to chase parrots and other birds from field crops.

Source: Felipe Guaman Poma de Ayala, *Nueva Corónica y Buen Gobierno (Codex péruvien illustré)* (Paris: Institut d'Ethnologie, 1936), 859.

specified rituals, and refused to consume the meat himself for fear of retribution. Animals, it was believed, had the power to make successful hunters sick.

Christianity held that nature was created for man by a benevolent god who stood outside of both nature and time. Nature could be conquered, manipulated, and exploited with full divine sanction, with no requirement for ritual or repentance. The Christian god was stronger than nature. By contrast, Aztec cosmology saw the gods engaged in a volatile, unpredictable struggle to hold nature together. Blood sacrifice was not to appease the gods so much as it was to sustain them in their battles against chaos. The Aztecs' gods were the allies of men, but unlike the Christian god who could part seas and move mountains with a nod, the Aztec gods struggled, often unsuccessfully, even with mundanities like rainfall, and hence demanded assistance. Frequent earthquakes, volcanoes, droughts, floods, and hurricanes proved the gods' weakness and demonstrated that nature was capricious and chaotic. Nature, the Aztecs believed, derived from chaos, and was likely to return to it. And history made it obvious that humanity's place in nature was tentative. The ruins of the celebrated cities that surrounded the Aztecs – Cuicuilco, Tula, and Teotihuacán, the last a much more formidable expression of culture's strivings than the Aztec's civilization – were unambiguous evidence of culture's transience. Nature demanded respect and reverence. The Aztecs and Incas, conquerors of other cultures, realized you could not conquer chaos, so they strove to cautiously tiptoe across it.

But did these attitudes cause Indians, in fact, to tread more lightly on the earth than Europeans? A Tupi elder asked Jean de Léry why his French compatriots came so far, at so much trouble, to gather shiploads of brazilwood: "Is there none in your own country?" De Léry explained to the elder that France had no brazilwood and used it to redden fabric, just like the Indians used it to dye cotton cord and feathers. "Very well," replied the elder, "but why do you need so much of it?" De Léry did his best to explain the advantages of material accumulation in terms a Tupi could understand: with all that brazilwood a merchant could buy more axes, scissors, knives, fishhooks, and mirrors than a Tupi had ever seen. But the Tupi elder pressed him: "But this man . . . who is so rich, does he never die?" Europeans were mortal, De Léry admitted, but he explained that all that wealth would be dutifully passed on to the merchant's children. "Truly," the elder concluded:

> I see that you *Mairs* (that is, Frenchmen) are great fools; must you labor
> so hard to cross the sea . . . just to amass riches for your children? . . . We
> have kinsmen and children, whom, as you see, we love and cherish; but
> because we are certain that after our death the earth which has nourished
> us will nourish them, we rest easy and do not trouble ourselves further
> about it.[5]

On another occasion, a family of 30 Tupi capsized their canoe. De
Léry rushed out in a launch to their rescue. The Indians laughed at the
thought of needing rescue as they swam confidently to shore. But when
asked about their seeming lack of concern over the lost canoe and its
supplies, which they were bringing to the French fort, they replied, non-
chalantly, "After all, aren't there others in the land."

The idea of the nonacquisitive Indian is a central element of the Pristine Myth, and it charmed individuals from De Léry to Rousseau. The
Tupi lifestyle offered the intriguing possibility that greed and avarice
were not inherent to human nature but were the by-products of civilization. The Tupi, like many indigenous groups who relied heavily on
hunting and gathering, did live near the subsistence level, that is, almost
their entire economy consisted of providing the basics of food and shelter with almost no luxuries. They did engage in some trade, but this
had a political and military role rather than economic, and they made
relatively few demands of nature.

But as we have already seen, even to subsist, Indians left footprints
still discoverable after many centuries. The Tupi burned and reburned
their forests in order to feed the children they cherished. And they
burned firewood in substantial quantities for cooking, barbecuing, smoking, firing ceramics, lighting, and defending their villages against noc-
turnal predators. Aztec parents taught their children that they must eat,
drink, and dress, and instructed them on how to do so: cut forests, till
soils, and plant crops. Nobody, then or now, ate without piercing the
soil, felling a tree, or spilling blood. Human survival required some minimum of nature's destruction because human hunger always overrode
any fear of retribution from trees, animals, or guardian stones. Indians
did often apologize for the bloody impositions they made on nature, but
in the end, they imposed.

And Indians, like all humans, had at least a latent capacity to consume beyond the basic needs of food and shelter. It was brazilwood itself
that would betray the Tupi's own acquisitiveness, small as it was, for they

---

[5]   De Léry, *History of a Voyage to Brazil*, 101–2.

freely did the staggering labor of brazilwood's extraction, its cutting and lading into waiting ships. The Europeans offered goods – axes, knives, scissors, fishhooks, mirrors, and even dyed textiles – the which some Indians could not resist, and for which they were willing to labor freely and intensely, foregoing their usual activities. Many remained true to the Tupi elder's ideal of material moderation, for once they had their single ax and a handful of fishhooks, they could not be induced to work for more. But the Europeans were adept at enticing them back into service by introducing new and improved products. And the Tupi were not without entrepreneurial spirit. One enterprising woman, who kept a parrot of some linguistic talent, propositioned French visitors with an enticing offer: "If you will give me a comb or a mirror, I will make my parrot sing and dance now, in your presence." The asking price was not paid, and she ordered the bird to be quiet, which it did despite coaxing from the Frenchmen. She might be the New World's first purveyor of ecotourism.

Human culture regularly consumes more than subsistence requires. Once we have sheltered our heads, filled our bellies, and clothed our backs, our eyes seek pleasures and conceits beyond our basic needs. It is one thing to drink, and quite another to be drunk; one thing for an Aztec to be clad in a cloak of humble cactus fiber, and another to be arrayed in feathered finery. Among urbanized societies such as the Inca and Aztec, consumption for the sake of status knew few bounds, even if only a few were allowed to participate. Both the Aztecs and Incas had stratified social systems, and patterns of consumption were overt markers distinguishing the nobility from the peasants. When Moctezuma I established the Aztec's legal code, half of it, and the first half at that, was sumptuary, prohibiting the consumption of certain high status goods to all but the nobility. Aztec commoners could not wear cotton, build houses with more than one floor, adorn their homes with gables or towers, wear fine jewelry of gold or jade, or consume alcohol, all under pain of death. Only the nobility could wear sandals in the capital. Everyone else had to go unshod. Commoners had to wear mantles of crude cactus fiber no longer than the knee, unless their legs had been wounded in battle. Legs that did not flee the sword could be honored with a few more inches of fabric. Less rigid rules applied in the Inca Empire: feathers could be worn by all, and everyone used fabrics of cotton and wool, although the lower classes were restricted to the poorer quality weaves. In some ways, such restrictions may have prevented the mass consumption of luxury goods and were to that extent conservationist, for when permitted, the underclasses imitate their betters.

And it appears that elite attitudes toward nature were becoming increasingly utilitarian, and less otherworldly. Diego Durán's native informants explained that "the Aztecs felt they were Lords of All Created Things; everything belonged to them, everything was theirs . . . upon the waters as well as upon the earth."[6] The Aztec elites' acquisitiveness is best expressed in their enormous demand for tribute goods, the source of nearly all elite consumption since they formed a leisure class that did not produce. Hence, they demanded not only luxury items but also food, firewood, and building materials. Aztec tribute lists run on for pages, so what follows is an abbreviation that still betrays the Aztec economy's diversity and the high level of elite consumption. A large portion of tribute goods were direct extractions from nature. Animals offered in tribute included live birds, such as parrots, eagles, buzzards, and wild geese; ocelots and jaguars brought in cages; snakes delivered in large pots; honeybees in hives; and centipedes, scorpions, and spiders all presumably safely packaged. Moctezuma II even required lice and fleas in tribute. Among dead creatures were deer, rabbit, quail, turkey, weasel, fish, toasted locusts, feathered birds of all colors, and the skins of every animal imaginable. The forests provided boards and beams, bark firewood (reserved for the elite due to its bright flame), charcoal, rubber, resin, torch pine for torches, sooty materials for painting, and even living trees dug up at the roots to adorn noble gardens. Agriculture offered cacao, raw cotton, a vast variety of flowers, an Aztec favorite, corn, chilies, pumpkins, tomatoes, among dozens of other comestibles. And lastly, craftsmen paid taxes in ready-made elite cotton clothing, maguey cactus fiber clothing, which the elite granted their servants, exquisite jewelry of gold, jade, and coral, cotton armor, obsidian blades, swords, shields, slings, stones, bows, and arrows. The Gulf Coast province of Tochtepec, where cotton was grown and tropical forest products were available, paid an annual tribute of 9,600 decorated cotton cloaks, 1,600 female tunics, 16,000 rubber balls, 80 handfuls of quetzal feathers, 24,000 feather bunches, and 200 loads of cacao. Each region paid tribute in commodities favored by its ecological advantage, and as the empire expanded, so did the elite's tributary selection.

The Incas likewise gathered in tributary goods from a wide region and stored the excess in facilities across their empire. The so-called Inca granaries are often thought of as being emergency food storage for

---

[6]   Diego Durán, *History of the Indies of New Spain*, trans. D. Heyden (Norman: University of Oklahoma Press, 1994), 203–5.

hard times, and they may on occasion have served that purpose, but their primary functions were to store food, uniforms, and weapons for the empire's very active armies. Food was stored for difficult times at the community level, not by the state. Storage facilities, in addition to war material, also stored heaps of high status goods, which were used to cement social relations, usually between the central state and local elites. Pedro Sancho counted 100,000 dead birds in one storeroom, all with their colorful feathers intact, in addition to tools, knives, leather shields, sandals, "and everything in such great quantity that the mind does not cease to wonder how so great a tribute of so many kinds of things can have been given."[7] Francisco de Xerez described storage facilities with rich textiles piled to the rafters. Pedro Pizarro, impressed as he was by storerooms of copper bars and gold and silver plate, described at length the astonishing quantities of iridescent hummingbird feathers. These tiny feathers, which came from just the tiny breast of the tiny bird, were fashioned into full length garments. He was bemused that so many could have been harvested at all. To the Spaniards, Inca storehouse goods were for the most part mere curiosities and were passed over; their indigenous allies, however, plundered them entirely. The extant ruins of tens of thousands of Andean storage facilities are hard evidence of the region's productivity and consumption.

With tribute the Aztec elite held feasts of status foods and built palaces of stately proportions. Díaz reported that Moctezuma served 1,000 meals each day to his noble family and friends, sumptuous feasts enjoyed in the comforts of a sprawling palace compound. Nezahualcóyotl's palace grounds covered almost a square kilometer with 40 temples, a ball court, a zoo, and more than 300 rooms, many designated specifically for the stockpiling of tribute goods. The height of conspicuous consumption was noted by the Spaniards in Moctezuma and Atahualpa's habit of changing garments dozens of times per day, suggesting that in status consumption, quantity was as important as quality.

Despite their best efforts, the Aztec elite could not consume, store, or gift everything they received in tribute, and the excess, which was considerable, was exchanged at market along with nontribute goods. Of the Aztec capital's many spectacles, the central market at Tlatelolco was among the most impressive to Spanish eyes. Sixty thousand Indians shopped here daily for hundreds of products, each carefully zoned on

7   Pedro Sancho, *An Account of the Conquest of Peru*, trans. P. A. Means (New York: The Cortés Society, 1917), 159.

the plaza and strictly regulated. There was nothing in Europe to compare for scale, and even the best-traveled soldiers, who had visited the markets of Rome or Istanbul, had never seen a market "so well laid out, so large, so orderly, and so full of people." In Tlatelolco's grand market one could purchase lumber, bricks, paint, tools, firewood, pottery, cookware, utensils, home furnishings, bedding, mattresses, jewelry, clothing, furs, butchered meats, fish, eggs, fruits, vegetables, tobacco, spices, medicines, paper, bales of cotton, thread of many colors, cakes, and candies of honey and of chocolate. One could also sit down to a meal in an open-air restaurant or get a haircut. The market was a suburban mall, supermarket, and big-box home improvement center all rolled into one. Some cities had specialized markets. According to Díaz, Aztec slavers sold more captives in the slave markets of Azcapotzalco and Itzocan than the Portuguese offered Africans at Lisbon. The Acolman market specialized exclusively in edible dogs. Even 50 years after the conquest, Durán observed in Acolman some 400 dogs of all sizes being selected for the day's meal. Despite their numbers and the piles of dog manure for sale, a local told him with some lament that that day's market was the smallest he had ever seen.

And shopping itself had become a cherished cultural pastime. Durán supposed that if he asked an Aztec woman if she would rather go to heaven or to the market, she would shrewdly answer "heaven; but let me go to the market first." One woman, whom Durán knew personally, always appealed to her old age and frailty as excuse for never attending mass, and she had to be carried bodily to confession. But she walked to every market under her own power, and in fact one day finally died of exhaustion from joining the shopping throngs "doing nothing but walking around, gaping, their mouths open, strolling from one end [of the market] to the other." "Can anyone deny that this is a vice?" asked Durán.[8]

Religious beliefs about nature were themselves motives for extending consumption beyond the basic demands of subsistence. Settled agriculturalists universally performed animal blood sacrifice to aid the gods in preventing nature from veering into chaos. They also "sacrificed" forests. Divine consumption was of such scale that it needs to be included in the sustainability equation. The Incas sacrificed animals in a wide range of ceremonies. Each morning priests slit the throat of a white llama while

---

[8] Diego Durán, *Book of the Gods and Rites and Ancient Calendar*, trans. F. Horcasitas and D. Heyden (Norman: University of Oklahoma Press, 1971), 275.

its head was turned toward the sun. Its body, rather than being eaten, was reduced to ashes on a brazier, the smoke rising to please the sun. This alone amounted to 365 killings per year in each community that practiced it. Sacrifice also accompanied the agricultural cycle. In addition to the blood of guinea pigs offered by commoners, the state dispatched 100 brown llamas at planting to encourage the rains, and 100 more of all colors during the maize harvest. The sacrifice that best illustrates an objective of this animal holocaust was the practice of animal starvation. When drought, frost, or flood threatened hunger in the human population, the Incas corralled black animals, usually llamas, but also dogs, and withheld food until they died. The creatures slowly withered and were probably not eaten, serving no direct purpose in preventing human hunger, but serving a starkly allegorical one in which animals suffered so that man might not. Lastly, the Incas also offered material goods to their gods and ancestors, particularly precious textiles, which were reportedly burned in large numbers, just like the animals that had supplied the wool.

The Aztecs too sacrificed a variety of game to sustain their agricultural gods. Without large domesticates like the llama at hand, they tended to be smaller and of a great variety, but unlike the Incas, the Aztecs seem to have freely consumed their offerings. They did offer food to their gods, burning it, or commonly setting it upon the lakes or in the mouths of caves that were believed portals to the underworld. The gods were also honored by perpetual fires that consumed considerable areas of forest. Both the Aztecs and their indomitable Tarascan neighbors maintained hundreds of fires, eternal flames, in temple precincts. The Aztecs required firewood as part of tribute, but the Tarascans took ritual fires so seriously they entrusted only royal officials the task of collecting firewood. They constructed massive bonfires whenever they prepared for war, and, in fact, the Tarascans explained the Aztec's fall by faulting them for neglecting their ritual fires.

The gods also required shelter, sometimes on a monumental scale. Mesoamerica's pyramids, which housed the gods at their tops, required enormous quantities of labor and resources, particularly the lime plaster that bonded the stone and covered the edifice. The plaster itself consumed immense quantities of firewood for its manufacture. And among the Aztecs, temples were constantly being enlarged. Tenochtitlán's main temple, which was just over a century old in 1519, the Aztecs rebuilt on top of itself, more accretion than rebuilding, seven different times. The city's second temple at Tlatelolco had as many accreted layers. Each community, just as in Europe, appears to have striven to outdo their neighbors in honoring the local pantheon with monumental religious structures. To that end, Europe's cathedrals took centuries to build. By contrast, Mesoamerican temples were rebuilt several times per century. The Incas were more efficient in building monuments to their gods and ancestors, constructing low, precisely laid stone walls that did not require mortar or plaster, and which they roofed in timber and thatch. But they spared little in a temple's adornment. The three Spaniards sent to Cuzco to collect Atahualpa's ransom pried 3,500 gold plates from the walls of the Coricancha, or Temple of the Sun. The temple was literally wallpapered with sheets of gold measuring nearly a meter in length and about a finger in thickness. Each weighed in the range of 2–5 kilograms, and even at an average of 2 kilograms each would have totaled some 7 metric tons. When more Spaniards returned to the Coricancha later, they were pleasantly astonished by the quantities of gold still in the temple's many rooms. The Temple of the Moon, part of the same complex, was similarly upholstered in silver plate, and precious metals in such quantities suggest more than a trivial mining sector. The gods, like humans, consumed flesh, stone, and opulence.

People Eating People

The presence of cannibalism in the Americas has been raised as evidence that indigenous agricultural systems were not up to the task of sustainably feeding human populations. Cannibalism is well documented: of the three cultures we have chosen to examine, two, the Aztec and Tupi, routinely consumed human beings, the former on an almost incomprehensible scale. In the Aztec case, it has been argued that a dense, expanding population that had no large domesticated animals must have depleted the landscape of its wild sources of protein; hungry for protein, the inhabitants began to engage in extensive ritual warfare whose primary objective was not to win ground but to harvest human flesh. The victors marched their victims to the top of the local temple and sacrificed them to the gods in a gory, oft repeated narrative: bloodied priests removed the victim's beating heart with a deft thrust of an obsidian blade and hurled the heartless body down the temple's precipitous steps. Then, in an eventuality not commonly recounted, priests at the temple's base butchered the broken bodies and distributed arms and legs to the kitchens of honored families. The trunks were reportedly delivered to feed creatures in the nearby zoo and aviary; the skulls, whose contents were also consumed, were retained for display in the temple precinct.

Cannibalism's protein thesis partakes of the dated assumptions about the low productivity of indigenous agriculture. But people ate people for reasons other than a need for protein. The Tupi, as we have seen, had more protein than most contemporary humans, which was reflected in their vigorous physiques, and yet they still ate each other, an act as disturbing to Europeans as it was biologically unnecessary for the Tupi.

In the Aztec case, the protein thesis greatly underestimates the nonhuman protein available to the Aztecs. While Mexicans had no large domesticated animals, they had domesticated some creatures of middling size, namely dogs, turkeys, and Muscovy ducks. Among the Olmecs, dogs were eaten more than any other mammal, wild or domesticated. And while archeological digs of Aztec valley settlements do show declines in deer remains over the centuries, deer accounted for the largest volume of animal protein consumed right up to the conquest. The remains of dogs and turkeys increase over time, suggesting a slow shift toward domestic sources of protein, but wild sources predominate. Also found are the remains of rabbits, whose reproductive capacity can stand up to the highest human pressures. The shells of mud turtles are common, but fish remains are not found as their soft bones do not endure. However, we know from historical evidence that the lakes were a major source of fish and fowl both before and well after the conquest. At the beginning of the sixteenth century the Aztecs harvested more than a million fish each year, primarily the *blanco*, and dried them for market. Likewise, birds were widely hunted, especially on the lakes. In dog-keeping societies such as that of the Aztecs, the bones of many smaller game animals are often underrepresented in archeological digs because the dogs consume them, including the bones of other slaughtered dogs.

More important than the sources above, particularly for the masses, are all those creatures that fell into the European's queasy category. Protein is fairly abundant everywhere if you are not terribly picky about a food's appearance and texture. For westerners, protein is the flesh of mammals, birds, and fish, but the Aztecs ate almost every edible protein, including snakes, lizards, wasps, flying ants, and insect larvae, critters the Spanish derogatively labeled *animalitos* and which they refused to accept in tribute. A daily handful of dried ants is more than sufficient protein for an adult. The red worm *ezcahuitli*, harvested from the lake and roasted in loaves was a particular Aztec delicacy, one even the god of war, Huitzilopochtli, called "truly my flesh, my blood, my substance." *Ocuiltamalli* was a tamale made of worms. Even today some of Mexico City's residents consume salamanders, beetles, dried crickets, and the eggs of mosquitoes.

In addition, the Aztecs had two significant vegetable sources of protein that were nearly lost and forgotten but have recently reappeared in health food stores. Chia, an oily grain seed similar to sesame, ranked only slightly behind corn and beans in the Aztec tribute payments. It is 20 percent protein and was popular in soups and drinks. Chia was also religiously important. The seeds were ground into a dough from which life-size images of the gods were fashioned and displayed. The edible images were then divided and consumed. Due to its pagan embodiments, a practice too close to divine transubstantiation for comfort, Spanish priests discouraged its production and consumption, and it almost disappeared from history. Quinoa, a highly nutritious grain of the Andes suffered the same near-disaster for similar reasons of religious association. The most unusual source of Aztec protein, *tecuitlatl*, the algae spirulina, grew profusely on the surface of Mexico's valley lakes. It is 60 percent protein and contains all eight essential amino acids: alone it might have satisfied the Aztec's protein needs. Díaz described families who gathered this green slime in nets, layered it on the shore to dry, and then cut it into small bricks which were sold at market. He noted it looked like bread and tasted like cheese, but most Europeans did not acquire a taste for it. The peoples living around Lake Chad, in Africa, who have almost no sources of meat, still rely on it as their sole source of protein.

Even had the Valley of Mexico been bereft of all these delicacies, the Aztec staples of American corn (eight varieties) and beans (twelve varieties) were together potentially sufficient as complete sources of protein. Corn alone provides seven of the eight essential amino acids. One of the seven, tryptophan, corn binds such that the body cannot assimilate it, but Mesoamerican women, much to civilization's benefit, had learned to slake their corn with lime which releases the tryptophan. Corn only lacks lysine, but beans supply it in abundance. Corn and beans combined, as they were traditionally prepared in a variety of dishes, formed a complete protein whose consumption, in sufficient quantities, required no additional meat. Even those Aztecs who got little or no meat had the local potential for a complete, vegetarian diet.

If not for protein, then, why eat each other? The Tupi ate their war captives out of vengeance, a basic religious concept. Enemies had eaten their brothers, and now they would get retribution by eating an enemy's brother. The Aztecs and Incas sacrificed humans (the Incas generally did not eat them) for the same reason they sacrificed birds and llamas: to sustain the gods. There may have been additional political and tributary motivations for human sacrifice, but cosmology, not hunger, remains the primary explanation for the many cultures that practiced it. Religion was not a cover for the butchering humans for food. But if cosmology explains Aztec human sacrifice, it does not explain Aztec cannibalism. Why did they eat the bodies of sacrificial victims? The Tupi ate warriors in part to internalize their strength. But the Aztecs ate both men and women. For the Aztecs, a likely explanation is simple practicality. Why let good food go to waste? Unlike Europeans, Indians had no taboos against consuming human flesh. The Indian perceived humans and animals as spiritual equals. If it was acceptable to eat a deer, a sentient creature with spirit and power, why not a human. If one sets aside Christian conceptions of the body, burial, and resurrection, cannibalism appears quite rational as an ecologically efficient means to dispose of the dead. A corpse is a public health threat, and Aztec sacrifice produced thousands of them. Deep burial, the European solution, occupies space, demands substantial unproductive labor, and does not recycle nutrients effectively. Cremation requires considerable fuel. Appalling as it is, anthropophagy is the cheapest, safest, and most efficient form of dealing with a corpse. Another explanation is yet simpler: the elite, who benefited from an essentially free source of calories, acquired a taste for human flesh. They ate human flesh in part because it tasted good, as did the Tupi. It was reported that Moctezuma II sacrificed daily in part because he and his guests wanted human flesh at their meals. Bernardino de Sahagún's Aztec informants claimed that an indolent wife, who would not grind corn, cook, or spin thread, was sold "to the traders who buy slaves for food, and thus she would end on the sacrificial block of the idols."[9] Here, food seems an important justification for sacrifice, in addition to the cosmological, and it is likely that an appetite for meat, not a need for protein, reinforced Aztec practicality.

Whatever its motivations and justifications, Aztec sacrifice had significant environmental consequences. Estimates of human sacrifice in Mexico range widely: one well-respected researcher places it as high

---

[9]   Bernardino de Sahagún, *General History of the Things of New Spain: Florentine Codex*, trans. A. J. O. Anderson and C. E. Dibble (Santa Fe, NM: School of American Research, 1950), 238 [Book 4, Chapter 28].

as 250,000 per year, and many agree that it could easily have been in the range of 20,000. The Aztecs asserted that in one four-day bloodletting in the mid-fifteenth century they sacrificed 80,400 persons for the main temple's rededication. The figures boggle, but the Aztecs had the evidence. At Xocotlán, Bernal Díaz found a pile of skulls "so regularly arranged" he counted its length, width, and height to estimate a product of more than 100,000. Aware of his reader's incredulity at such a number he repeated it. Díaz noted his count did not include the *tzompantli*, the rack that displayed yet more skulls arranged on horizontal poles that pierced each skull's shattered temples from ear to ear. Likewise, Andrés Tapias counted 136,000 skulls at Tenochtitlán's main temple. The numbers suggest some startling contentions. First, cannibalism made a notable contribution to the Aztec food supply. Raising humans for food is not a terribly efficient use of resources, but as many of the victims came from outside the central valley, it was a net gain for the dominant region. The Aztecs did not need human flesh for protein, but they did not reject it. Second, human sacrifice must have inevitably hindered population growth. Not only did it remove thousands of people directly from the living, but as most of the victims were young, it reduced overall fertility. If there were indeed more than 100,000 skulls displayed in single cities in a valley whose population was 1 million, sacrifice's impact on the Aztec population must have been substantial, even if the skulls represented a sacrificial distribution over many decades. Reducing numbers and fertility were not at all the intent of sacrifice, for both the Incas and Aztecs had no Malthusian preoccupations; if anything they were pronatalist, promoting births by honoring women who birthed many children. However, every human dispatched to the sky gods was one less mouth to feed of its generation, and many fewer in the generations that followed.

The Question of Sustainability

If the peoples of the Americas leveraged their human capital to reshape nature's landscapes, it does not automatically follow that their relations with nature were unsustainable. Sustainability, the genius to manipulate, alter and exploit nature to meet human material needs without compromising your children's ability to do the same, is a cultural honor far easier to define than it is to bestow. Did Indians merit the honor of sustainability? If the New World was old in 1492, was it also moribund, in ecological decline? The question of indigenous sustainability is much contested, but it appears that after millennia of living on the land, indigenous peoples had learned empirically how far they could push, at least in the area of agriculture. They did not always get it right: sometimes they prioritized productivity and luxury over sustainability. Some cultures obviously crashed, and their failure to achieve sustainable lifestyles may have played a role. For the most part, however, Indians expected the future to be very much like the present and generally farmed in one year with an eye focused carefully on the next. By the fifteenth century, most Indians, like most Europeans, had settled into sustainable patterns of producing food.

In other areas, Indians were not blind to the negative impacts they had on nature and at least in some cases adjusted to conform to more sustainable systems by the practice of conservation. The Aztecs and the Incas were aware that critical natural resources – soils, forests, water, and wildlife – could be depleted. We have seen their empirical conservationism in agriculture. In forests, we have some evidence of protected reserves and reforestation. The Aztecs, or at least the Texcocans under Nezahualcóyotl, protected forests, although the extent and motives are open to speculation. Reserves may have been similar to those of Europe whose chief object was to create exclusive hunting grounds for the elite, or they may, in fact, have been to set aside timber reserves for future use. But whatever the motive, if protections were of any extent, the benefits to the population would have been expressed in healthy tree stocks, wildlife habitat, consistent springs, and reduced erosion. Nezahualcóyotl's forest reserves initially precluded any extractive activity, but regulations were relaxed in the interest of poverty relief that permitted peasants to enter the forests to collect deadwood for fuel.

Andeans appear to have invested in the reforestation of their mountain slopes with the native alder tree. Lake sediment cores from Peru's southern Andes show that there were few trees in the region before about A.D. 1000, the pollen record dominated by weeds and grasses with significant evidence of soil erosion. However, thereafter, erosion rates decline and the appearance of alder pollen rises dramatically. Chroniclers reported that the Inca emperor himself oversaw alder planting and imposed stiff penalties for unauthorized cutting. Researchers argue that even if a warming, wetter climate played a role in the expansion of alder trees, forest restrictions must have been important in their protection. Inca populations were large, and without some regulation, the forests were likely to have been consumed as quickly as they recovered in a region of so few trees. Notably, alder pollen declines sharply after the conquest, and today, alder can be found only in remote ravines.

Centuries in a land of few trees had also made the Andeans stingy with fuel. They developed a small, ceramic woodstove for cooking and heating that was many times more efficient than open fires. Incredibly, the Spaniards burned more fuel in a day than the Indians did in a month, observed Bernabé Cobo in the seventeenth century. One wonders if the seemingly insignificant invention of the ceramic woodstove correlated with the regeneration of the region's forests at the turn of the millennium, or even the appearance of the Incas as the region's cultural leader. History has turned on lesser innovations.

In the arid highlands, water was possibly the most important limiting factor to Inca and Aztec development. The Incas tapped deeply their rivers, lakes, and springs to irrigate arid mountain valleys and desert coasts. It is unlikely that they understood the role of forests as watersheds, but they unwittingly benefited from their forest policies. The Aztecs also appear to have tapped all available sources of water for agriculture in the Valley of Mexico, including the diversion of major rivers, for in times of drought, they had no excess reserves. Possibly, the most important Aztec water conservation measure was the widespread use of human excrement on agricultural fields. By recycling human waste back to the soil the Aztecs avoided the intractable scourge of sewage that has plagued the basin since its conquest. The Spaniards, only after a few decades, turned Lake Texcoco into a cesspool and repurposed the dikes and causeway from water control to pollution control devices. The dikes now served to prevent the city from being flooded with its own filth. Aztec practice benefited soil fertility, but it also maintained the valley's sensitive basin lakes as viable ecosystems in support of healthy fish, bird, and *animalito* populations.

We have little evidence of Aztec wildlife conservation, but the Incas showed a strong hand in wildlife management, restricting hunts to particular seasons of the year and dividing and rotating the hunting grounds on a four-year cycle. They prohibited outright the hunting of vicuña. Rather, they captured these swift creatures, sheered their fine wool, and released them unharmed. This was a marked contrast to the Spaniards who set their dogs after the vicuña. Spanish wool gatherers found it simpler to kill vicuña in order to sheer the wool, and despite belated attempts by the crown to stop this wasteful practice it continued into the twentieth century, guns replacing dogs to devastating effect. The annual Inca hunts were mass, ritualistic events, the nobles directing the commoners to flush and drive the game into pens. In the first hunt to which the Spaniards were invited, 10,000 men encircled a huge area near Jauja, beat the animals into an enclosure, and slaughtered 11,000 head of game. Male deer and guanacos, among other game, were killed and consumed, or turned into jerky. Females still of birthing age were released, as were the very best male specimens for breeding. Inca officials kept careful records of the hunt and presumably used them in their management strategies.

A stout attachment to place benefited indigenous conservation and sustainability. Most settled Indians had tied their cultural achievements so solidly to particular environments they could not imagine one without the other. While modern culture retains some remnants of this pride of place, we for the most part can no longer grasp its full meaning. We have become too mobile to achieve the attachment to the land that a person who knows all her ancestors and all her grandchildren live with their feet on the same limited soil in sight of the same reassuring landmarks. There was much that was incomprehensible about the Iberians to the Indians, but one of the greatest mysteries was why the strangers were wandering about in the first place. According to Gómara, Inca peasants referred to the Spaniards as sea foam, fatherless, homeless men who never rested long enough to form families or to plant crops. Spaniards appeared kinless, without origin or destination, characteristics that to the Incas were utterly unhuman.

Both the Aztecs and the Incas recognized the landscape itself as sacred. The Aztecs saw the bodily parts and functions of Tlaloc, the god of rain and earth, in the earth's curves, caves, peaks, and springs, and ritual tied them materially to named natural features that could not be easily abandoned. The cardinal directions, and for the Incas nearly all directions, had distinct sacred meaning and were associated with powerful colors and symbols. Both cultures venerated natural landmarks and honored their entombed ancestors. One could not imagine living elsewhere, without the benefit of generations of topographical meaning or the ancestors' resting places. The Aztec capital's location had been indicated by their god of war, Huitzilopochtli. As prophesied, an eagle perched on a cactus devouring a snake was the sign that this was to be their new homeland, an augury of tremendous import for a tribe that for generations had been wandering. The eagle bowed his head and said "O Mexicans, it shall be here!" No matter that it was in a swamp in the territory of others. The land they dredged up from the bog was sacred, and this was reflected in the city's care. The Spaniards, in whose minds cities and filth were inseparably linked, were bewildered by the cleanliness and orderliness of Tenochtitlán. Trades offensive to gods and men, such as leather tanning, were banished far from the city, and the daily sweeping, washing, and repainting of the city and its edifices were acts of devotion. Streets, canals, homes, and large public spaces were not the haphazard mess familiar in Europe's medieval cities. They were laid out carefully by central planning to be not only functional, but beautiful, proportional, and clean.

Indians also venerated food, particularly corn, the real Aztec and Inca gold. They correctly understood that corn was the foundation of their civilizations, the sustainer of flesh and blood, and they honored it as sacred material. By contrast, Europeans had by this time largely desacralized both food and place. Flour and wine became holy only when they were transformed into Christ's body in the Eucharist; and places were sacred only if the feet of the virgin or the saints had rested there. For the most part, the Iberians saw the earth and its features as transitory and focused their geographical attentions instead on an unearthly heaven. Perhaps the greatest distinction between European and Indian beliefs about nature was in their perceptions of nature's future. The Indians prayed and sacrificed to avoid natural catastrophe, to save their terrestrial homes in perpetuity. The Europeans prayed for millennial cataclysm, for the end of their mortal existence redeemed by their ascension to heaven, and for the destruction of nature itself which could not, in their eyes, merit salvation.

Perhaps, as has been suggested, the Incas and Aztecs were at the limits of nature's carrying capacity under existing populations, current technologies, and the prevailing climate. The Valley of Mexico may, in fact, have overshot its carrying capacity, for tons of food – corn, beans, and human flesh – flowed to the city in tribute. If the arms of Aztec power, which enforced the heavy demands of tribute, had been summarily lopped, many at the center would have gone hungry. It is the nature of both empires and cities to carry negative balances of trade with their hinterlands, and like all true empires, the Aztecs and Incas lived beyond their means by conquering beyond their bounds. Eventually they might have faced the threat of their own successes. Tributary demands, for example, increased faster than subsistence because with more commodities – food, clothing, palaces, servants – the nobility reproduced itself faster than the general population. With more resources, elite men married numerous wives and fathered a lopsided proportion of each society's children. Moctezuma II had as many as 1,000 wives, and while accused of not being able to keep them all satisfied, 150 were reported pregnant at any one time. Children born to noble men, whether to the first or secondary wives, inherited their father's status and rights to receive trib-ute, which redounded to their own health and procreation. The skele-tons of Maya elite, for example, are on average 10 centimeters taller than those of peasants, blatant evidence of unequal consumption.

The Incas were beginning to feel these pressures before the conquest. In a most unusual custom, the Inca king inherited nothing from his father except his title. Dead royalty, who were housed in mummified state in sumptuous palaces, did not subscribe to the adage that "you can't take it with you." Even in death, they retained possession of all their lands, llama herds, and treasures. And believe it or not, they con-sumed them. The royal mummies were nourished by burning their food before them, and during festivals, the mummies' drinks, after being pre-sented to them in gold pitchers, were poured down the same channels into which the rest of the partiers urinated. Of course, even a glut-tonous, dead Inca king consumed limited victuals and alcohol, but in addition to property, the mummy retained to himself his *panaca*, that is, his descendants except the children of his successor, whose role it was to honor his mummy. These too had to be luxuriously fed, housed, and ser-viced in perpetuity, and the numbers that had to be maintained might expand with every generation. And particularly pious, living Inca kings, like Huayna Capac, gifted their dead fathers yet more land and wealth. Huascar, who warred to secure the Inca throne at Huayna Capac's death, complained that it was the dead who had the best of everything in the Inca realm. The refusal of the dead to bequeath their property to the rightful heirs forced the living ruler to conquer for himself, from scratch, those lands and goods beyond the empire's borders that were his right. In an increasingly bizarre situation, the Inca peasants were forced to share out an ever larger portion of their food and labor to sustain not only the living ruler's immediate family, but also his dead ancestors and their living descendants.

It is impossible to ultimately judge the sustainability of America's cul-tures at the end of the fifteenth century. Any judgment, positive or neg-ative, is ultimately unfair since the long-running experiments of Amer-ican cultures were nipped by the conquest. Their trajectories were fore-shortened by a drastic cultural and natural break that illustrates that the human relationship with nature is never static. Cultures change, or are changed, sometimes for the ecological better, sometimes for the worse. And nature itself changes, sometimes handing out new, substantial ben-efits to humans, sometimes painful liabilities, and in a few cases, utter destruction.

As I have suggested, environmental history is concerned with more than just the survival of the human species. What is at stake is the survival and success of human culture and civilization. If ancient American history makes one fact obvious, maybe even more so than the ancient old World, it is that while humans as a species have doggedly survived sometimes frightening natural odds, high human culture – cities, technology, art, architecture, all subsumed under the term civilization – has crashed, repeatedly, irreversibly, and often abruptly. America's many ruins – Olmec, Teotihuacano, Toltec, Maya, Chimú, Moche, Nazca, Wari, and Tiwanaku – to name only a prominent few, testify to human culture's evanescence. Burdened under profound dust or rank vegetation, their fractured walls and scattered stones whisper compellingly: "Can you tell the cause of so great a fall?"

Every stone repeats the question, but as much as we pick and prod at them, they refuse to speak the answer plainly. In recent years environmental arguments have waxed in popularity, joining a host of antecedents, to explain the demise of ruined American cultures. Environmental explanations, with their potential to offer a moral lesson with current relevance, hold a tempting instructive appeal. It may have been environmental overshoot – urban sprawl, deforestation, erosion – that brought down mighty states like the Maya or that of Teotihuacán, for even their home improvements indict them. One Maya living room in El Mirador has a broad cement floor 9 centimeters thick, a quantity of cement sufficient to destroy many square meters of forest to obtain the fuel necessary to pulverize the essential limestone. For reasons of vanity, status, convenience, or aesthetics, the same El Mirador floor, in a major remodel, was refinished with a new 21-centimeter layer of cement. There is more than ample evidence that indigenous cultures avidly consumed timber, fuel, water, and soil nutrients, and sometimes faster than nature could replace them. But in the end, we can have no certainty that poor environmental behavior explains, or even played a role, in a particular culture's demise. Political, military, social, and economic factors may alone explain American ruins. The declension narrative, the stories of human culpability in the devastation of nature and, hence, culture, is highly seductive, for even when we admit we are at fault, what were really claiming is that if we changed our behavior, then we would be in control, as if it all depended on human will and action. The reality is that cultures sometimes fail for ecological reasons well beyond their control. Even if nature can be plainly implicated in a culture's collapse, it does not necessarily follow that it can be attributed to human errors of

material greed or ecological ignorance; sometimes nature presents challenges that have nothing to do with a culture's environmental relations.
Disease, climate change, earthquake, and hurricane have caught cultures off guard, and sometimes the lessons of environmental history are
rather starkly amoral, impersonal, and practically useless. As savvy as we
have become, keeping our eyes on hurricanes long before they hit shore,
watching and preparing, however carefully, for such threats as avian flu
and earth-bent meteors, nature has more tricks than human culture can
ever entirely predict. Spending billions to evade avian flu, money I think
well spent, will not protect us from such imponderable plagues as were
HIV and Ebola when they first appeared. And building dikes to protect
homes below sea level from category five hurricanes, money I think ill-
spent, will be useless when nature disregards our categories and sends
along a storm that by all rights must be ranked a six, seven, or higher. It
is incumbent upon us to assess and prepare for every potential risk, for
much is at stake, but sometimes, despite the most sophisticated coun-
ters, culture gets sucker punched.

   Of all Latin America's ancient ruins, only Cuicuilco has left unassailable evidence that the environment was the central cause of its
demise. We know very little else about the city, despite its accessible location within the expanding urban footprint of modern Mexico
City. Who were its inhabitants, what were their origins, what language
did they speak, and when was the city founded? Most scholars agree
Cuicuilco is the earliest known, major city of Central Mexico, preced-
ing the metropolis of Teotihuacán which was to become its rival or
successor. Twentieth-century urban sprawl covers much of the former
ruin, but digging has unearthed many of the trappings we associate with
ancient Mesoamerica: ball courts, sky gods, pyramids, and an accomplished, sometimes whimsical art. At the center of an extensive, planned
urban zone stood a modest pyramid 20 meters tall, unusual for its circular shape, centered in a large plaza. Surrounding this, there is evidence
of terraces, irrigation canals, and shallow retaining pools for agriculture.
At its peak, Cuicuilco may have had 20,000 inhabitants. Its dating is
still debated, but most agree its foundations were laid on or before 700
B.C., and that it was entirely abandoned by A.D. 300, a span of thousand
years.

   How do we know nature played the primary role in the city's
destruction? Today, the central pyramid, which has been excavated from
its tomb of solid rock, is surrounded by the Pedregal de San Angel, a lava
field 10 meters deep extending over 80 square kilometers. In an event

that some date to A.D. 76, three years before Vesuvius destroyed Pompeii, the Xitle volcano cut short Cuicuilco's cultural trajectory, smothering the city in molten rock and locking away fertile farms. Lava flowed from both Xitle's main volcanic cone to the south as well as from a perfectly circular lateral vent to the city's north, still much in evidence on the national university campus. It would appear there was no escape. However, it is likely that the disaster took the form of a series of eruptions over a few decades; some believe the inhabitants fled to join or found the city of Teotihuacán to the north, well out of reach of the valley's southern volcanoes. Cuicuilco is now a large ecological park, eerily quiet in the midst of the bustling city. Tenacious vines, cactus, and agave scrabble to survive on the gray, undulating, lava substrate. Sometimes nature conquers, and the story proffers no morality play, no declensionist narrative. For all we know, Cuicuilco's inhabitants were America's most ecologically sensible, harmonious, and friendly culture. But in the end, nature did not care.

In 1492, America was abundantly populated and its landscapes substantially humanized. Amerindians were remarkably successful biologically, filling two continents with diverse cultures who elbowed up to one another in nearly every latitude. American cultures had also created a succession of flourishing, transformative, agricultural systems, evident even today in their layered ruins. For the moment, we know more about the role nature played in indigenous successes than in their failures, but their histories, so punctuated by collapse and decline, should move us, the latest Americans, to caution.

CHAPTER TWO

NATURE'S CONQUESTS

And still the horses had not sated their thirst, to the frightening astonishment of the Indian women; and they said to the Spaniards, "in truth, our lords, if these animals eat so much as they drink, there is not enough in all of our lands that can sustain them."[1]

Columbus and his colleagues, I have suggested, did not discover a new world in America; they happened upon another old world. The discoverers did, however, consummate an abrupt, forced marriage between two hemispheres that after decades of gestation and a prolonged, difficult labor gave birth to something new. A wide variety of peoples hailing from three major landmasses – Eurasia, Africa, and America – melded to form cultures that were racially and culturally distinct from anything that had come before. Of this crucible was born Latin American civilization, a cultural hybrid. The Eurasian and African arrivals, however, carried more than cultural baggage; they also impregnated America's landscapes with new plants, animals, seeds, and germs, making of the Americas something of an ecological amalgam. The Old World's biological baggage, much of it stowaway, muscled in and grafted itself on to the lives and landscapes of America's existing ecological foundations. By the hundredth anniversary of this complicated union, the title "New World" finally made an apt description of both the cultural and natural consequences of the penetration of one hemisphere by another.

All agree that the conquest of the Americas was just such a seminal event, one of the hinges on which swings the modern world.

[1] Bernabé Cobo, *Historia del Nuevo Mundo* [1653] (Seville: Sociedad de Bibliófilos Andaluces, 1867–1907), Ser. 1, Vol. 19, 2nd ed., 350, my translation.

We cannot help but continue to argue about its consequences, ultimate meaning, morality, and even about what methods were most significant in its accomplishment. But we never think to question the identity of the winners. This, we say, was a European, largely Iberian, victory. But let us set aside human vanity for the moment. If we give nature its rightful place on history's stage, we must consider nature a contender for the honor and spoils of this conquest. Without denying the power of guns, the advantage of steel, or the significance of human divisions and alliances in the conquest of empires, without ignoring the guileful deceits of Cortés, the unrestrained ambition of the Pizarros, and the undeniable sadism of some of their companions, in the end it was nature, not the inhumane, but the nonhuman, that effected most of the creative and destructive processes that refashioned the New World, its hybrid cultures and its amalgamated natures. For the next couple centuries, nature shifted notably toward America's center stage.

PESTILENCE

The central cultural reality of the conquest of America was human death. In the century after 1492, some 50 million Indians vanished, more than 90 percent of America's once vigorous populations. That left only 5 million survivors, an unprecedented human disaster that staggers the imagination. America, an entire hemisphere, lost all but a remnant of its human inhabitants. And as we move in for a closer look, the tragedy only worsens. In the Caribbean, a region that held as many as 7 million Indians, mortalities reached 99 percent, as on Hispaniola, and fully 100 percent on many smaller islands. On the Mexican mainland, deaths exceeded 99 percent along the main arteries leading to the Aztec highlands. The city of Zempoala, formerly housing some 100,000 citizens, had only 25 native inhabitants by 1550. Not all those who disappeared had died, but when a city or region lost its critical mass of inhabitants, the remnant sought viable homes elsewhere. The Spanish governor in Vera Cruz related a local reality that could be accurately generalized for much of the Americas. Already by 1580, the precontact size and vitality of the indigenous population was a memory fading.

> According to tradition of the oldest residents of this land, at the time that the Spaniards came, there were many places and large Indian populations within six leagues [25 kilometers] all around this city. These have become so diminished that many have become completely depopulated, leaving no trace except the memory of a name; and others now have so few

residents and people that, compared to what was, the extreme to which they have been reduced is sad to see. . . . In this notable way the natives of this district have declined since the Spaniards mastered the land; and each day the towns continue to disappear, two or three places joining together into one in order to better to preserve themselves, in such a way as one cannot expect anything but that those remaining will come to a total ruin and destruction.[2]

Pedro Cieza de León echoed the tragedy for Peru, lamenting that the Andean valleys that many remembered as being heavily peopled were in his day, 1540, all but deserted. By 1653, Bernabé Cobo and his contemporaries had already forgotten the substantial indigenous presence, and Cobo went to erroneous lengths to show how the lack of rainfall in the Andes created a small Indian population that was easy for Pizarro to conquer. In the forests of the scattered Tupi villages, within a century, 95 percent of their inhabitants had vanished. In 1724, the Portuguese governor of Pará, near the mouth of the Amazon where Indian depopulation came a century or more later than elsewhere, bemoaned the disappearance of the Indian peoples and called it God's punishment on the Portuguese for enslaving them, as if a just God punished European sinners by inflicting death on the very people they had victimized.

An even closer look, if we could see it, would expose the tormented faces of anguished fathers, mothers, and children as they helplessly witnessed their communities and families implode. Most deaths came within the first decades of the encounter, and those who outlived the first waves of destruction must have contemplated the horror of annihilation: all that was friend and familiar were reduced to corpse. One death piled upon another so quickly that the living must have numbed and despaired of life. The cataclysm, the end of the world that Indians by blood sacrifice had so piously sought to evade, descended upon them without pity.

The reality of the cataclysm is no longer doubted, but the causes have been debated for centuries. Las Casas' view from the mid-sixteenth century, that the destruction of the Indians came from the direct action of Spanish sword, gun, and garrote, has been among the most influential historically. The so-called Black Legend, inspired by Las Casas and enthusiastically embraced by Protestant Europeans during the Reformation, pinned blame on the Catholic Iberians' crusading sadism. Alonso

---

[2] Quoted in Andrew Sluyter, *Colonialism and Landscape: Postcolonial Theory and Applications* (Lanham, MD: Rowman & Littlefield, 2002), 63.

de Zorita, still in the sixteenth century, refined Las Casas' theory of Spanish cruelty to more indirect methods such as overwork, relocation, excessive tribute, and coerced military service. There is little question that both theories, direct and indirect, explain a multitude of appalling murders. But extreme cruelty and violent extortion are well documented over a notable Iberian cross section throughout the entire colonial era, even after the point at which Indian populations had begun to recover. Warfare, cruelty, harsh labor, agricultural disruption, and population displacement, particularly moving men to mines far from their wives, all worked together to reduce Indian numbers and fertility. Even the successful competition by Spaniards for native women served to block indigenous reproduction: on Hispaniola, by 1514, 35 percent of Spanish men had married indigenous women, and many more formed more casual relationships.

Toribio de Motolinia, who in 1540 looked to the ten plagues of the biblical Exodus, was among the first and few who identified epidemic diseases as a central cause of the American holocaust. Probably more important than the clash of guns and steel with bows and stone, or the uncontested cruelty of the conquistadors, was the clash of trillions of virulent microbes against millions of human bodies. Conquest and disease are ubiquitous features of human history, but rarely have their consequences been so catastrophic. If steel and cruelty were often the vanguard, as they have been in nearly all conquests, what made this conquest unique was that old-world microbes followed close on the conquistadors' heels, dispatching substantial fractions of the previously unexposed populations.

We often construe the Iberians as the agents and promoters of this microbial introduction, as if smallpox, influenza, measles, and a host of other bacteria and viruses were somehow an additional European weapon, or even an ally, but these are not accurate metaphors for they assume that microbes took sides. Germs did not cross the oceans innocuously in trouser pockets. They traveled in human tissues, killing as they went. It is more accurate to see diseases as the agents of their own dispersal. Microbes infected European bodies, consumed their cells, and then manipulated their hosts to transport them to other bodies, usually by inducing coughing and sneezing, or producing skin lesions that oozed infected blood and fluid. For the first time, host bodies were transported to two new continents, something over which microbes had no control but on which they sensationally capitalized. Those hosts that survived ocean crossings and continental journeys coughed and oozed on unsuspecting Indians. Millions died often horrific deaths. One snapshot from the Aztec point of view in besieged Tenochtitlán suggests the excruciating death by smallpox.

> It was [the month of] Tepeilhuitl when it began, and it spread over the people as a great destruction. Some it quite covered [with pustules] on all parts – their faces, their heads, their breasts, etc. . . . They could not walk; they only lay in their resting places and beds. They could not move; they could not stir; they could not change position, nor lie on one side; nor face down, nor on their backs. And if they stirred, much did they cry out. Great was its destruction. Covered, mantled with pustules, very many people died of them.[3]

Germs infected humans indiscriminately, regardless of their geographic origin or even the state of their immune system. Only in killing did they discriminate. But the Europeans and Africans did not go unscathed. Smallpox was as easily contracted by Iberians as by Indians, and while it killed more than 90 percent of the Indians it infected, it had always killed a third of Europe's urban citizens and a greater fraction of rural folk whose exposure to the virus was less frequent but more deadly. Deaths among Europeans in America must have been more common than in Europe with so many infected Indians about them to return their unwitting gifts. Moreover, many more Europeans died when malaria and yellow fever hitchhiked to America in bodies involved in the African slave trade. If the Europeans had had any say in the matter they would have left the ravages of old-world endemics and epidemics at home to live happier, less tragic lives with America's blessed isolation to defend them. But they had neither the knowledge nor power to stop the microbes' own empire building.

Still we like to think the Iberians, at least those who escaped an early death by pestilence, benefited as a result of the indigenous holocaust, but few Iberians of the time would have agreed. Maybe in nineteenth-century North America the only good Indian was a dead Indian. For sixteenth-century Iberians, a good Indian was a living Indian, one who paid his tribute loyally and offered her body demurely. The Iberians were seeking tributary subjects, not genocide, conquering to rule, not to ruin. It is true that the demise of the indigenous populations opened the ground for European settlement; but it is arguable that all world cultures would have taken greater benefit and experienced less cultural

---

[3] Quoted in Alfred W. Crosby, "Conquistador y Pestilencia: The First New World Pandemic and the Fall of the Great Indian Empires," *Hispanic American Historical Review* 47 (August 1967): 336.

destruction if the Iberians had gotten what they wanted: millions of new subjects for the kings of Spain and Portugal, not a land dotted by mass graves. There would have been more commodities to trade, more people to which to market them, a more complete Columbian exchange of useful foods, materials, and ideas, particularly in Europe's direction, an abundant American labor, and no need for the deadly African slave trade. It is also more likely that indigenous agricultural systems, well adapted to their soil and climate, would have better survived; some might have even been adapted to the Old World. Without germs, without an American holocaust, the entire human species, Indian, African, European, and Asian, would have been better off.

We can continue to flatter ourselves, or we can contemplate that Córtes, Pizarro, and their successors were pawns in a much bigger, more consequential battle than American conquest. Nature, not man, took the best advantage of continents divided, and it conquered on all fronts. The microbial victory was akin to the Spanish attacks on Mexico and Peru, both of which took advantage of human divisions. Expressions of human culture, as complex as war or as simple as a kiss, redounded to the germs' expansion and growth. It is exaggeration to say that the conquistadors left as many pregnancies in their camps as they did casualties, as one scholar has aptly described an important biological aspect of the conquest, but this cycle of intimacy and violence played right into the microbes' hands. Disease prospers best in human wars that bring previously unconnected humans together who promptly open each other's immune defenses with cutting wounds and illicit encounters.

From the point of view of a virus or a bacterium, the conquest was a high point in its still largely unwritten history. A single bacterium in a healthy host can become a billion in an eight-hour workday. In fact, most of America's invading microbes were too successful: their rapid multiplication exceeded the host's capacity to sustain the germs' population growth. Microbes that consumed human cells too quickly choked on their own wastes and died with the host. The fortunate ones leaped to a new body, new territory, to experience another few billion generations of fevered glory, but eventually, after a few flourishing decades, there were too few susceptible bodies remaining to sustain their epidemic successes. Only after microbes had their own demographic collapse did humans even begin to slowly reconquer a nature that had nearly overwhelmed them.

The microbial victory was almost complete. The human population of Latin America was a pale shadow of its former self. Of Latin America's original population of some 50 million, even by 1750, there were only 12 million people of any origin, less than a quarter of the precontact population. And Latin America still had at least a century to go before it would begin to break even numerically. Over the more than three centuries of colonization, immigration from Europe was small. Spanish arrivals numbered a meager 700,000, the majority during the early silver booms; Portuguese immigrants numbered 525,000, most of them arriving in the early eighteenth-century gold rush. This total, about 1.2 million Iberians, exceeded English, French, or Dutch arrivals to the Americas by a wide margin, but it could not fill the land emptied by disease. Before the nineteenth century, Europe simply did not have excess population to spare.

The most significant immigrants numerically came from Africa, and microbes starred in this drama as well. With Indians dying in multitudes and European immigrants in short supply, the conquerors looked to Africa for manpower. They also turned to Africa because disease continued to kill, particularly whites and Indians, on the humid, lowland plantations of sugar and tobacco where malaria and yellow fever had infiltrated. The Africans that had lived for centuries in the tropical homelands of malaria and yellow fever survived these plagues much better than Europeans perhaps for the same reason that Europeans survived influenza better than Indians, an inherited genetic immunity. However, this was not a racial immunity. Black Africans from regions where these diseases were absent lacked the genetic defenses and died in rates very similar to whites. Hence, African slaves were taken largely from regions where tropical fevers were endemic, and they made plantation America viable. In Havana's first yellow fever outbreak in 1649, 536 whites died, but only 26 blacks. Even in nineteenth-century Antigua, where 96 percent of the population was black, 84 percent of yellow fever deaths were among whites. And in Jamaica, fever killed 10 percent of the white soldiers annually but only 0.08 percent of black soldiers. Despite the fact that black slaves suffered inequitably from the diseases of malnutrition, not to mention from physical mistreatment and harsh labor, they still survived better than better-fed whites. Slaves endured life better despite being denied membership in the human culture, being denied even family, and being treated as if they too were among nature's beasts, nonhuman. About 7 million Africans were forced to Latin America by 1800, outnumbering all white immigrants by more than five to one, and in some regions coming to dominate local populations by very wide margins. Nature profoundly shaped the New World's cultures.

None of this is to say that disease was the central factor in the Iberians' military successes. Even without smallpox and other Eurasian plagues, it is quite possible that swords, armor, guns, and horses could have overturned empires and placed Iberians as America's new rulers. But without disease, America's conquest would have turned out differently, probably more akin to the Iberian experience in Africa and Asia where Europeans remained a tiny elite minority engaged in coastal trade and other minor activities, but leaving local cultures largely intact, relatively unchanged. Due to disease, America was more than a mere political extension of Europe's empire. It became a New World.

Biodiversity's Gains

If humans, regardless of origin, were harmed by the extraordinary deaths and dislocations of American conquest, nature, as a result, experienced something of a reprieve from human impositions. Population is not the only determinant of environmental change, but in no other period does population, or the lack of it, explain nature's transformed reality. For most of the colonial era, the human population of the Americas fell well short of one quarter of the precontact population. In 1650, possibly the nadir of American demography, all humans of all origins could only muster 10 percent of the 1492 population. Much of the landscape fell silent of human voices. As a result, soils, forests, waters, and wildlife that had been mined, logged, dammed, and hunted for millennia, under constant indigenous pressures, got a sudden reprieve. With fewer people, the land's evolution was driven by natural processes instead of human aspirations. This change formed an elemental aspect in making the New World new.

Much of nature's rejuvenation is difficult to document and it is in part assumed. However, there is evidence of forest regeneration in a variety of locations. The town of São Paulo, founded on a broad, treeless plain by the Jesuits in 1561, was in less than 30 years set about by trees on all sides. Officials ordered the inhabitants to clear the forests that surrounded, even invaded, their fortified stockades in order to improve the town's defenses. Without Indians to periodically burn the Paulista grasslands, the forests returned with a measured vengeance. The story repeated itself in Rio de Janeiro in the early seventeenth century. The open fields of Central America also reverted to forest, just as they did after the Maya collapse five centuries earlier. The abandoned fields of the indigenous dead, fertile and open to the sun, were particularly susceptible to invasion. The Amazon's banks that had been farmed with flood agriculture were quickly colonized by trees well adapted to the river's seasonal inundations. The Omagua and their neighbors literally vanished within a century, their traces so covered by vegetation they were not uncovered till recently. Most of the terraces in Mexico and Peru were abandoned, as were all the raised fields of the Yucatan and South America. Former raised fields became artificially undulating grass-lands or forests, depending on rainfall. Swidden fields across the region were allowed to follow the long pathway of succession, mounting larger trees and greater diversity over the succeeding centuries without human disturbance. The Americas were more heavily forested in 1800 than they had been in 1500.

Wildlife also appears to have gained by the microbial destruction of humans. With the Omagua's disappearance, river turtles in the Amazon were no longer penned as food nor had their nests raided for eggs. Jaguars gained as their only predator, man, diminished. Birds, hummingbirds included, no longer suffered darts to satisfy the vanity of a population that esteemed their feathers. Fish that spawned in rivers proliferated as numerous irrigation dams fell into disrepair and fish no longer had to evade the humans that so frequently concentrated on their spawning grounds. Surely, where the colonizing Europeans concentrated, human pressures continued, but culture redirected the demands. The European impact was real, as we will see in the next chapter, but it differed from the indigenous impact and was substantially limited in its geographic breadth.

Nature's regeneration was the primary source of the Pristine Myth. For those immigrants who came a century after the conquest, the New World was a greener, wilder place than it had been. There were immea-surable forests, abundant wildlife, and few people, just as they reported. When British settlers arrived in North America, at Jamestown, Ply-mouth, and other beachheads, the indigenous inhabitants had already been diminished, and much of nature had revived. Europeans did not have to reach to every corner of America to host the microbial front. Sometimes, microbes took the vanguard. Pestilence ravaged both con-tinents well in advance of the Iberian conquerors, fully unrecorded. If smallpox arrived in the Inca empire years before the Spanish arrived, traveling thousands of kilometers, crossing the Panamanian Isthmus, traversing numerous climate zones, and ascending soaring altitudes, what was to prevent it and other infectious diseases from extending elsewhere, especially when Europeans were showing up at will all over the coastal margins and penetrating to the continents' very hearts well before the sixteenth century expired? Hernando de Soto and his ever-changing set of companions in conquest could alone have introduced diseases on a hemispheric scale. In 1514, at age 14, De Soto arrived as a common soldier to conquer Panama; at 24, he invaded Nicaragua and Honduras; at 31, he was the first European to meet the Inca Atahualpa in Peru; at 35, he paid a large sum to join Almagro's conquest of Chile, but he was turned down; so at 41, as Cuba's governor, he sailed to Florida seeking conquest in what is today Georgia, the Carolinas, Tennessee, Alabama, Mississippi, Arkansas, and Oklahoma. In 1542, he died on the Mississippi, and his men buried his body in the river to hide their mortality from the Indians. After a lifetime of violent confrontations and passing through dire straits too numerous to count, De Soto himself died of a simple fever. It is possible that simple fever, or another that accompanied his band, began the pestilential wave that decimated the indigenous cultures of the American Southeast after 1540.

Not all nature benefited by the human catastrophe. Those plants and animals whose fortunes had risen with the success of indigenous cultures – fruit and nut trees, palms, some varieties of game, and native domesticates, such as turkeys, dogs, and llamas – suffered declines without their human assistants. Llamas, butchered by Spanish conquerors, declined drastically. Likewise, many soil features in fact degraded, erosion becoming common in the years just after the conquest. Sediment core samples from lakes in former indigenous agricultural regions document this. It is possible that the combined cow and plow of the Europeans played a role in disturbing hillside soils and vegetation, but it appears more likely that it was the failure of the Indians' sophisticated agroecological systems, particularly terraces, having broken down without human maintenance, that dispatched much of the local soils. A portion of "nature" was a human artifact that fell into ruin without its creators.

When in the vanguard, microbes eliminated many of the humans who would have obstructed or contested the arrival of a host of other alien introductions. The biological conquest of America is more accurately seen as the replacement of Indians not with Europeans or microbes, but with cows, sheep, pigs, chickens, and hundreds of other new nonhuman species, in addition to the resurgence of native wildlife. An animal's or a plant's capacity to transform a landscape derives from its immense power to self-replicate, just like germs, something no machine, no matter how powerful, can match. Eurasian domesticates and "weeds" replaced the human dead and may have even displaced some living humans, but they did not have the same mortal impact on American nature that Eurasia's microbes had on American peoples.

Columbus imported most of Europe's large herbivores already on his second voyage in 1493. Many of them found a superb ecological niche. The total numbers imported in the first century from Europe were tiny, but their reproductive capacity was fantastic in these conditions. They browsed America's rank vegetation with few natural predators or competitors due to the ancient mega-faunal extinctions. Unlike Iberians, in part because so few came, domesticates initially did not bring their diseases with them which enhanced their formidable reproductive powers. With so much fodder available cows were calving commonly at the age of one, whereas in Europe this did not occur until the third or fourth year. Already at the end of the sixteenth century, Samuel de Champlain observed what he thought were infinite numbers of cattle strewn across the northern grasslands of Mexico.

As in the case of microbes, European livestock did more to make the New World new than those who brought them. Gonzalo Fernández de Oviedo, who wrote the first natural history of the Americas in the first half of the sixteenth century, believed that cattle and other large livestock were primary agents in the improvement of American nature, their constant movement and heavy breathing thinned the air, dispersed the vapors, and further pacified what to Oviedo was an already tame continent. It is uncertain whether cattle were the cause of any American species' extinction, but their role as introducers and distributors of new seeds and weeds, in their manure, and as modifiers of the existing plant species mix are uncontested. Their presence greatly influenced the types and distributions of plants across broad sections of the Americas. In Mexico, it is believed that cattle turned some grasslands and farms into scrub and thorn. In the pampas they introduced a variety of new grasses and weeds, most prominently the cardoon thistle which in the pampas' deep soils grew more than 3 meters tall. The thistles only exploded in occasional years, but their presence, stretching to the horizon, overwhelmed nearly everything else. Most animals, native and invasive, thrived on it: the leaves were favored by dozens of species; and when the thistle went to seed in billowing clouds of fluffy cotton, sheep, horses, and rheas took it as a delicacy. Nineteenth-century horsemen, however, hated this mass of prickly vegetation that was impenetrable to the eye and nearly so to the body. The thistle presented a fire hazard greater than the natural vegetation. If the fields took fire, neighbors came together to prevent the flames from reaching homesteads, and the most effective means to create a firebreak was to kill a few sheep and drag them behind horses to flatten the thistles upwind of the house.

However, livestock and weeds experienced a history that in some ways parallels that of the invading microbes. As they arrived in a new area, their numbers grew quite rapidly. But their rising numbers consumed the resources unsustainably and their populations leveled off, or in some cases crashed to more modest levels. Predatory humans, jaguars, wolves, and wild dogs, all benefited by livestock explosions, as did American and Eurasian pests such as ticks, which helped reintroduce the animals to disease.

The debate continues over the impact of livestock on New World vegetation, soil, and water resources. Ranching, particularly of cattle and sheep, but also pigs, became the most extensive economic activity in the Americas reaching from Northern Mexico to the Amazon and Patagonia. Cows did replace people. The Vera Cruz lowlands became a landscape whose human silences were interrupted by the lowing of cattle browsing beneath ruined pyramids. In some vulnerable areas like the Caribbean, livestock depredations incurred irreversible damages to vegetation and water resources, permanently ruining the soils for indigenous farming. In such cases, ranching became the only viable activity.

In other regions, the impacts, while noted, were more modest. Vegetation was modified and redistributed, but livestock did not entirely degrade the land. Pollen profiles from the period do not evidence universal weed outbreaks nor active devegetation. The Iberians introduced ranching practices that had been sustainable in Spain, some of which fit America's ecological spaces surprisingly well. For example, from the swampy Marismas of southern Spain, ranchers introduced flooded pasturing systems to the Vera Cruz and Panuco lowlands, areas that Indians had previously exploited for chinampa-like raised fields. In the rainy summer season, when the lowland grasses flooded, cattle were driven to green mountain pastures. Come the dry winter, they were herded back down to the coasts where the receding rivers exposed a lush wetland vegetation. At Christmas, the mountain pastures were burned, to rid them of ticks and tarantulas, and the cycle recommenced. Flood ranching also took hold in the Amazon and Paraguay River basin. Transhumance, the practice of alternating seasonal pastures, was practiced widely, even by the Inca llama herdsman before the conquest, and protected pastures from permanent degradation. Ranchers, such as Mexican president Santa Anna, continued these practices well into the nineteenth century.

New animal and plant species added to American nature more than they subtracted. Human disease dealt a direct blow on American cultures because humans on both sides of the Atlantic were the same species. Beasts and weeds did not encounter themselves, that is, their same species in America; microbes are species specific and generally cannot cross the species barrier to other plants and animals. Hence, while Eurasia's plants and animals muscled their way in, pushing native plants and animals aside, they could not annihilate them in the way that human microbes did humans. It is possible that some few species became extinct, but this was less likely in the tropics than it was in the temperate pampas or North America. The tropical forested lowlands of coastal Brazil, the Amazon, and Central America, put up an effective resistance to Europe's temperate weeds and animals. Only in the Caribbean's tiny island ecologies can we assume substantial species' loss. In stark contrast to the human experience, where people were catastrophically reduced as a species and their cultures destroyed, American nature, both flora and fauna, experienced a net gain and probably achieved greater, not less, biodiversity by the encounter.

An Enriched Platter

Nature's fortunes varied in the conquest. Some parties – cows, sheep, tropical forests, and some native wildlife – gained; others – llamas, brazilwood, native grasses, and quinoa – lost. However, postconquest humans, those survivors of the lethal plagues, made considerable gains by the creation of this new, biologically diversified world. What the conquest did for the most part was not smother and degrade American species, especially those valuable to humans, but added thereto. To the preexisting suite of useful resources that the Indian painstakingly compiled over millennia, the conquest interspersed the terrain with a highly selected set of goods that had been the most beneficial to the European's biological success. European wheat and turnips joined corn and potatoes; African sweet potatoes joined manioc; and Asian bananas and rice joined peanuts and pineapples. In addition, by the introduction of livestock, America gained a fabulous selection of meats that had previously been unavailable. A few Eurasian introductions backfired, but on the whole, for humans, the New World was literally the best of both worlds.

We largely talk about the Columbian Exchange as it stood to benefit Europe by the introduction of corn and potatoes, but that was a long time coming, and in fact far fewer foods transferred to Europe than came to the Americas. For example, from America's fauna, Europe received squirrels, muskrats, and turkeys from North America, and guinea pigs from the Andes, but not much else. The Americas by contrast received cows, pigs, sheep, horses, goats, asses, chickens, geese, cats, and rats, and new varieties of dogs, ducks, and honey bees. Even camels made the crossing, although their stay was short-lived. Indians and African slaves habitually consumed cane sugar centuries before it became a staple carbohydrate of Europe's working classes. Also significant was the Iberian practice of dispersing American crops, such as potatoes, cacao, pineapples, tobacco, and local varieties of chili peppers, beans, and corn, over greater ranges in the Americas than had the Indians, making the intra-American exchange nearly as important as the Columbian Exchange.

The biggest, and first, beneficiaries of the exchange were the peoples living in the Americas, Indian and Iberian. Within a half century of the conquest, possibly no people had as much food, in both variety and quantity, as did humans in tropical, colonial America. Not only were there numerous crops and domesticates available, there was an abundance of empty, fertile farmland and pasture, far in excess of the population's subsistence needs due to the demographic catastrophe. Throw in the tropical blessing of multiple crops each year and you have a relative agricultural paradise. The Indians' sustained numerical recovery after the mid-seventeenth century was in part due abundant foods.

Food ways, that is, cultural food preferences, are extremely conservative. Oviedo observed that the Spaniards found no foods in America resembling those inherited from their fathers. Almost universally, Iberians preferred not to eat corn, potatoes, and quinoa, and whenever possible consumed more familiar foods, imported direct from the metropolis or planted in America. Unfamiliar native foods were the impetus that brought European foods in the first place, but it was easier done in temperate lands and highlands where European crops might adapt. But even here, Europeans often had to condescend and were lucky to have indigenous calories as substitute, even if they begrudgingly partook. In the lowland tropics, however, Europeans had little choice but to adopt indigenous foods, like manioc, other root crops, corn, peanuts, and pineapples. In less than a generation, Iberians in the lowlands ate much like their Indian neighbors.

Indians were as circumspect as Europeans in adopting new foods and they generally rejected European fare entirely. Pero Vaz de Caminha described the first Portuguese encounter with the Tupi in 1500, which included a bit of sampling of the Europeans' ethnic cuisine.

> We gave them food: bread, cooked fish, sweets, pastries, honey, and dried figs. They did not want to eat hardly any of it; and if they did taste something, they immediately spat it out. We brought them wine in a glass; it was all they could do to put it to their mouths. They did not like anything, and they did not want any more.[4]

Vaz de Caminha found notable the lack of domesticates in Brazil. When shown a sheep, it made no impression on the Tupi; when presented with a chicken, they became agitated and were reluctant to touch it. However, with time Indians across America came to recognize the value of adopting some additional calories and particularly new sources of protein. Cows were often beyond their means to acquire and required considerable cultural experience to manage and breed, but many Indians adopted pigs, occasionally sheep, and preeminently chickens, prized for their eggs. Wheat, wine, and oils, however, were largely rejected except by those Indians and mestizos who sought a place in European society through appropriate displays of consumption.

The Portuguese, finding many of their home crops unsuitable to Brazil's soil, heat, and humidity, introduced crops and trees from their tropical Asian and African contacts with notable successes: mangos, coconuts, yams, okra, citrus, and eventually rice. The now ubiquitous banana was the most notable introduction from Asia. When Jean de Léry observed it in 1550s Rio de Janeiro, its already widespread use by the Tupi caused him to presume it a native plant. Indians and Europeans rapidly distributed the banana throughout the Caribbean basin and South America's Atlantic coasts. The banana, which comes in many varieties, rivals, if not surpasses, manioc, and hence all other crops, in calories produced per unit of ground. Alexander von Humboldt was duly impressed by the banana's benefits and estimated that it produced 130 times more calories per acre than wheat, and 44 times more than potatoes. Additionally, the banana, before its diseases followed it to America many centuries later, was the kind of plant you could set and forget. Plant a few at monthly intervals and one had a constant food supply with very little effort. A few days of labor fed an individual for a

---

4 Pero Vaz de Caminha to King Manuel of Portugal, May 1, 1500, Biblioteca Nacional, Rio de Janeiro, Biblioteca Digital, digital image of original, my translation. http://bnd.bn.pt/ed/viagens/brasil/obras/carta‗pvcaminha/index.html.

whole year. It was not just for exotic effect that a French artist sketched slave quarters in Brazil prominently planted with bananas about the foundations. This was the lowland tropics' sustaining tree of life.

Considering the chaos of conquest, surprisingly few people went hungry in early colonial Latin America. There is no documented American famine in the sixteenth century. By contrast, in the same century, France had 13, and Spain struggled to import food adequate to feed itself. America was relatively well stocked and essentially self-sufficient. American crops had not only higher yields and greater variety, but also greater consistent variety over the year's course. While Europeans suffered from seasonally restricted diets during the austere winter and early spring, meals reduced to the monotony of dried beans, bread, turnips, and salted pork, Americans in the tropics had fruit, melons, and fresh vegetables year round. Bernabé Cobo was delighted as he traveled the countryside to see crops in every stage of maturation all at once, an impossibility in Europe where farmers had to march in lockstep with the seasons.

Even among the Indians, it has been shown that caloric intake was greater after the conquest than it had been earlier. Meat was consumed in unprecedented quantities, particularly by the poor. The explosion of domesticates free ranging on verdant grasses had made meat so widely available that the Indians, who could not afford wheat bread, ate more meat than Spaniards through the sixteenth century. It was so essential to their diet that Pope Pius III exempted Spanish Americans from the Catholic fasts in 1562, a sanction that lasted well beyond the 30 years after which it was supposed to have expired. The Indians themselves perceived that food was more abundant. In an attempt to discover why the Indians were dying, the crown, in about 1580, had the sense to ask the Indians their opinion on the matter. In a broad survey of over 190 Indian communities, nearly every village answered that food was a primary cause of their sickness and death – not the lack of it, but its excess. They argued that before the conquest life was more Spartan and less luxurious: they ate less food, consumed less salt, and drank less alcohol. Precontact moderation, they believed, had granted them health and reproduction. They also insisted that life before the Spaniards was more hygienic (they had bathed more often and wore fewer clothes), that indigenous medicine men were better healers than the Spanish bleeders, and that the Christian prohibition against polygamy had limited their birthrates. But it was an excess of food that Indians most commonly faulted for their precipitous numerical decline.

Many societies have found it expedient to legislate food ways: the French, the Chinese, and even the Aztecs outlawed the consumption of status foods to the lower classes. In Europe and the Incan Andes, the poor were effectively prevented from consuming certain game by excluding them from forest preserves; but not in colonial America. With food so abundant, the rich and poor, white and Indian, had no legal restriction on their choice of foods, and even hunting was open to all as almost no attempt was made to protect wildlife. It is lamentably ironic that in sixteenth-century America food and death so abundantly coexisted.

Responding to Alien Natures

The encounter of each culture with the other's nature was full of surprises and bewilderment. For the Indians, their first encounter with the Old World was frequently not with man but beast. The sudden appearance in the village of a pig, cow, or horse, all of which broke ranks with their Iberian masters and wandered unshepherded, must have caused a considerable stir among a people who knew their own nature so intimately and attached to beasts so much spiritual power. Not accustomed to adding to their lexicon, they could find no distinct names to catalog them. Horses, often first seen with strange men on their backs, the Aztecs referred to as *maçatl* (deer), and the Maya called them tapirs of Castile. Charmingly, the Aztecs referred to sheep as *ichcatl* (cotton).

The Indians were exposed to a relatively limited number of new plants and animals. The Iberians, on the other hand, were overwhelmed. More than anything, they were stunned by the scale of American nature. The forests stretched interminably; the mountains towered; the rivers deluged: there was nothing in Europe for comparison. Thousands of new animals and plants had to be named, explained, and tested for utility. Some specimens had at least some general similarities with European flora and fauna, but many were bizarre. Cactus, in its 900 varieties, had no old-world counterpart. Hummingbirds were almost magical, as were fireflies, which with one in the hand a priest could read predawn prayers from a tiny breviary, according to Las Casas. Flowers, from thousands of varieties of orchids to the single stunning passion flower, got nearly as much attention as precious stones. Jaguars, coyotes, rattlesnakes, crocodiles, manatees, parrots, and monkeys, the host of the Neotropical bestiary, provided popular material that American writers described enthusiastically to their curious European readers.

As exotic as America was to the Iberians, it bizarreness fell short of expectations. The discoverers so expected to find their myths confirmed in America – headless men with eyes in their chests, giants, pygmies, Amazons, unicorns, centaurs, mermaids, dragons – they occasionally saw them despite their eyes. António Pigafetta claimed he saw plants that walked like men. And actual contact often did little to dispel the myths: in 1498, John of Holywood insisted America's inhabitants had blue skin and square heads. Otherwise, European responses to American nature were rather ambivalent: on the left they saw paradise; on the right they saw hell, two familiar categories. Coming from a land that not only lacked the tropics' lushness, but that would become increasingly unsettled by national and sectarian violence, it is no surprise some Europeans strained to see an American paradise in nature. Oviedo encouraged his readers to leave behind the troubles and dangers of the Old World by immersing themselves in his four volumes on New World nature. If you could ascribe pride of workmanship to divinity, Oviedo asserted, God must have been most pleased with his American creation. And for Oviedo, American nature was almost entirely benevolent toward humans, native and Spaniard alike. The cats did not meow; the dogs did not bark; and the lions, unlike those of Africa, fled in fear from men. Even bizarre natural productions were eminently useful: the stomach stones of crocodilians, he contended, had no rival in the cleaning of the Spaniards' steel weapons. The Franciscans, who led out in Indian conversion, saw the New World's discovery as a central sign of Christ's imminent coming. The world had to be joined before it could end. As they saw it, the New World was just the place where religion could get a new start, in new lands and new hearts, and they worked to build utopian communities that could welcome the millennial reign rather than be destroyed by it. If the world began with Eden, which they assumed was located in a yet undiscovered corner of America, why should it not end there? The Garden myth died hard: as late as 1656, António de Leon Pinelo, a celebrated scholar, published his *El Paraiso en el Nuevo Mundo* which placed Eden at the center of South America; an authoritative map delineated the four rivers, by new names, the Amazon, Magdalena, Orinoco, and La Plata, that the bible reported had origin in Eden. The very flora and fauna testified of Eden's presence. From where but Eden could have escaped such stunning flowers as orchids and such dazzling birds as macaws and quetzals? Some took the passion fruit, with its lusty succulence and spectacular flower, as the very fruit by which Eve transgressed.

American nature's devilish side received as much attention. The Jesuits, a more grounded and materialistic order than the millenarian Franciscans, provided sober, largely accurate, descriptions of the Neotropics. However, at least in Brazil, they tended to emphasize nature's terrors and dangers over its paradisiacal qualities. José de Anchieta, in 1560, described the land of the Tupi as containing a malevolent nature unknown in Europe. Here, storms were horrifying in their frequency and intensity: lightning shattered the atmosphere, winds uprooted enormous trees, and rains crashed to the ground. In a litany of frightful hazards, Anchieta listed the constant danger of poisonous snakes, spiders, and foods, stating how little time each required to kill, the chilling roars of feline predators, and the endless annoyance of biting ticks, chiggers, and mosquitoes. He insinuated that a godless people must have brought these curses upon themselves, for Christian Europe had none of them. God, Anchieta seemed to say, punished the pagan with a malevolent nature.

However, one European response was universal. Above all else humans want to know nature's utility. The first question regarded what was edible, and Europeans sampled American food plants and animals widely to determine their palatability. Anchieta consumed ants, grubs, manatee, anteater, and various fruits with little apparent queasiness, and Jean de Léry tested much of the Tupi diet which he favorably reviewed. The second question was whether or not nature could be packaged, processed, traded, shipped, and turned to profit. Once Indian cultures had been despoiled of their precious metals and riches, the Iberians cast their covetous eyes toward nature: brazilwood, animal skins, parrots, monkeys, and cochineal, among dozens of other extractives. And only after a full half a century of this kind of biological plunder did the Spanish begin to extract America's mineral resources on any scale.

Iberian attitudes toward nature differed markedly from those of Indians. Perhaps among the most symbolic expressions of this was the Iberian insistence on separating oneself from the ground, placing oneself above the earth. Indians, it was pointed out, betrayed their lack of civilization because they sat on the ground, ate on the ground, and slept on the ground. They often did not wear shoes, so their bare feet made contact with the soil, and they even ate out of earthen pots, vessels formed from dirt. To the Iberians, this was beneath human dignity, and the conquerors would neither stoop nor squat. They insisted on eating out of metal pots or porcelain plates, wearing shoes, sleeping in beds, dining at tables, and sitting in chairs, all at a comfortable and symbolic distance from the ground. Even clothing, blatantly unnecessary, even a hindrance in much of tropical America, served as an Iberian's personal boundary between self and nature. For Indians, the boundary between culture and nature, human and earth, was blurred. For Iberians, the division was stark, and they made it a point of honor not to cross it.

However, one wonders if the Iberians began to worry that no matter how many cultural barriers they employed, America's soil was rubbing off. For one, hundreds of Iberians, particularly Portuguese men, dropped these barriers entirely under a tropical sun. They shed their clothes and went unshod into the forest to live with the Indians, turning savage in their compatriot's opinions. More significantly, American birth, even into shoes and beds, carried a substantial stigma. The peninsulars, Spaniards born in Spain, looked down on American-born creoles from the beginning, although the creole was racially, culturally, and religiously no different than a Spaniard born in Spain. Ridiculous pride of place may be the simplest explanation for this prejudice, but congenital contact with American nature seems to have formed part of the basis for a social discrimination under which the American-born creole chafed. It would not be the only time that one group would use a variant of environmental determinism, too intimate contact with a cursed or inferior nature, to set themselves above another.

However, in their attitudes toward consumption, the Iberian elite were in most respects similar to their Aztec and Inca social counterparts. The goods given consumptive priority differed in content but not intent. Both enjoyed clothing that identified their status. Both sought to build residences to their social enshrinement. Both consumed luxury commodities of precious stones, metals, and foods that they accumulated to excess whenever possible. And both spent heavily in pious activities and religious constructions to honor their gods. Barring the role of overseas trade, which I will address in the next chapter, the elemental difference between consumption before and after the conquest was the catastrophic decline in the number of people consuming at any level.

Conceptions of property were also more similar among Iberians and settled Indians than they differed. Of course, among the Tupi the story was very much like North America, two cultures whose ideas about property were so at variance there could be no middle ground for mutual comprehension or compromise. In these situations, Iberians and Englishmen, who judged the Indians as no better than animals running about, or worse, as idlers unwilling to work and improve the land, resorted to the Roman precedent of *res nullius* that granted legal rights to those who used and improved the land. From the European perspective, neither the Tupi nor the Massachusett had established land ownership with the appropriate signs of permanence. Among the Aztecs and Incas, the justification of *res nullius* could not apply under any stretch of interpretation. Here, Indians settled the land visibly and improved it in the permanent construction of cities, homes, walls, and roads. Farms, whether raised fields or irrigated terraces, were more substantial improvements than Europeans themselves had created in Europe.

The settled natives' conception of property, while differing in specifics, was entirely comprehensible to Europeans. Indians usually did not hold land as individuals, but as communities, or as kin groups, but they worked their apportioned plots and enjoyed the fruits of their labor as individual families. Among the Incas, larger kin groups assisted individual families in such tasks as planting and harvest, part of a long collective tradition that helped the Incas accomplish so much in so little time, but the product of their labors accrued to individual households. The exact nature of animal ownership is not well understood among these groups, but it is likely that such mobile property as turkeys, edible dogs, guinea pigs, and some llamas were held exclusive to households. Likewise, the Aztecs owned slaves as personal property that they bought and sold outright.

The settled Indians' permanence and evident sense of property greatly complicated European settlement. The king took a strong hand in protecting the lands and villages of his new Indian subjects and prohibited Spaniards from living among Indian communities. He also, contrary to almost all contemporary thinking, denied the conquerors the power to enslave settled Indians. The crown was often late and not always successful in its attempts to protect Indian persons and property, but its efforts explain in part why many Indian cultures and languages remain intact in Mexico, Central America, and the Andes even after 500 years.

The Indians also maintained commons, usually forests, that were in most respects similar to European commons. At first, Indians seemed willing to share the common forests with the invaders as long as their impositions were not excessive. The Indians had used forest commons largely for firewood, lumber, and the hunt. So did the Spaniards, to which they added pasture, letting their cows and pigs run freely to graze the forests' vegetation and mast, that is, acorns and other fallen tree nuts. Of this there were indigenous complaints of damage and, possibly, of competition by livestock for resources on which local game also depended. By the time the demographic collapse had run its course and natives began to recover, many Indian groups lost access to their personal lands due to Spanish usurpations, and all that remained to them were the commons. Unable to produce food to support themselves, many Indians turned to the production of firewood, lumber, and tree bark for tannin to earn cash to exchange for food. Now, it was Spanish ranchers who complained that stripped oaks produced no acorns and that Indian logging and fueling removed so many trees they exposed the soils to rains that eroded them down to gravel. But there was no rigid ethnic divide: some Indians ran cattle and pigs, and some Spaniards cut lumber. And every race consumed pork, beef, and firewood. The human comeback was beginning to reimpose itself on nature. Surprisingly, of the competing impositions on the forest, Spanish forms of grazing live-stock seemed to offer the more sustainable forest use.

In another case of common resource possession, it was Inca prece-dent that held. The Europeans saw all ocean resources as common. No individual could own or control a coastline's marine populations; fish, seals, and shellfish were open to all, first come, first served. The Inca saw it differently. As on Inca land, the coasts were divided between coastal communities, each of which excluded outsiders and managed the local resources without interference. In 1566, the Spanish declared a common fishery that obliterated the traditional lines communities had drawn to bound their waters, but crown officials changed their minds almost immediately due to confusion, protests, and the potential for violence. Until the eighteenth century, local communities sued others in court for invading their fishing territories. In this case Indian approaches to the commons probably served sustainability best. Commons are less likely to suffer the tragedy of overexploitation when they are controlled com-munally by locals with a vested self-interest in maintaining sustainable stocks.

One small difference of opinion, over the utility of lake water, ably demonstrates how cultural experience shapes one's perception of nature. The Iberians' attitude toward stagnant water led, eventually, to one of the most notable human transformations of the New World landscape: the draining of the Aztec's basin lakes that sprawled some 8,000 square kilometers. For the Aztecs, the lakes of the Valley of Mexico were a bounteous gift. They were the primary source of food: fish, shell-fish, wildfowl, *animalitos*, and spirulina were extracted directly, and the lakes' shallow waters and broad shores provided both water and fertile sediment for the cultivation of critical chinampa crops. The lakes also provided an excellent transportation network with 200,000 canoes laden with commodities slipping over the lakes and into the canals that dissected the Aztec capital. The lakes were the foundation of Aztec civilization, a blessing from the gods for which to be grateful. Despite the lakes' occasional hazards, the valley, to the Aztecs, was a glass half full.

For the Spaniards, the valley was a glass half empty – and they wanted it dry. Draining the lakes became an obsession for which the conquistadors and their descendents struggled for 400 years. The lakes were an ongoing annoyance and frequently a disaster. Sensible citizens questioned the wisdom of building the Hispanic capital of the New World on a low, swampy island and suggested its relocation to higher ground to the west. But Cortés insisted. The location's cultural value to the Aztecs was too great to be abandoned. Building atop the Aztec's divinely designated capital legitimized Spanish claims to conquest. But political capital came at a high price. The city's soils were saturated with water. The water table could be reached with just a few minutes digging by hand. Before a burial, graves had to be baled of water and coffins weighted with rocks to prevent the interred from buoying out of the wet ground. The Spanish built tall, heavy, stone buildings that immediately began to sink. The Aztecs had built heavy stone pyramids, but broad foundations must have helped float them on the landscape. The cathedral, by contrast, one of the world's largest, was built on narrow stem foundations that slowly displaced the sediment beneath and sank into the earth. Visitors remarked on bell towers and palaces that teetered far out of plumb, a problem exacerbated by the excessive twentieth-century use of ground water but with earlier origins. Some conceded and built less imposing homes, but others went to the expense of driving wooden piles as foundation.

The Spanish were bewildered by the presence of these salty lakes so far from the oceans and with no outlets, and some accepted the proposition that they were remnants of Noah's flood. For Europeans, waters that were warm, turbid, stagnant, and brackish, which accurately described the basin lakes, were unhealthy, and to the lakes they attributed fevers, constipation, dysentery, and even hernias. Some of these diagnoses may have been true, particularly as the Spanish discharged their raw sewage into the lake. They even presumed that the lakes, which became fetid on hot days, made the very air injurious. But the most convincing reason to eradicate the lakes was the threat of flood. After the conquest, the Indians continued to attempt to control the lakes' waters for agriculture,

Figure 3. Looking east over Mexico City in 1628, the year before the Great Flood overpowered the distant San Lorenzo dike and inundated the city for 5 years.

Source: Juan Gomez de Transmonte, "Forma y Levantado de la Ciudad de Mexico," in Atlas Cartográfico Histórico (Mexico City: Instituto Nacional

but it became increasingly difficult without a water-competent central government and less necessary as the dead abandoned the chinampas. It is possible that the Spaniards exacerbated the city's tendency to flood. Increased erosion after the conquest, whether from abandoned indigenous fields, Spanish livestock, or the felling of 25,000 trees per year for piles, added considerable silt to the lakes' bottoms. This reduced the lakes' overall storage capacity raising the water level one unit for every unit of sedimentation. For a few decades, the Spanish were fortunate: the lakes behaved most of the time and the occasional minor swelling in water level was dealt with by donkeys driving pumps to put water back beyond the city's dikes. But in the meantime, the indigenous mechanisms and constructions that had been used to control the rare floods fell into disrepair. When the first postconquest flood came in 1555, the city was taken unawares. Indians were consulted, and some of the ancient waterworks were restored, but another half century without a deluge left them again in neglect. Two minor floods came in 1604 and 1606, and then another as bad as 1555 in 1607. The streets filled with water; low houses, most of them of adobe, dissolved at their foundations. Some of the wealthy stuck it out on the upper floors of stone buildings, but the poor had to relocate temporarily.

At this latest disaster, city officials gave the matter their full attention. Relocation was reconsidered, but now powerful citizens held valuable urban real estate that they were not about to abandon. In vain, another prize was offered to anyone who could find the lake's mythical drain. Indians were again consulted to repair the old systems. However, most agreed on the need for a more permanent fix. The conclusion was to drain the lakes. Some residents believed that the city was an artificial island surrounded by an artificial moat, created by the Aztec dikes. If these were removed, a relatively simple deconstruction, the city would return to its supposed natural, noninsular state.

But Enrique Martinez, the engineer placed in charge, realized that the dikes were essential, and also that it would require a much larger undertaking to remove the water; he proposed a drainage system, half canal, half tunnel, that would extend 13 kilometers north from Lake Zumpango, giving the basin an artificial outlet that pierced the valley's northern ridge of mountains. Westerners had not attempted such a grandiose work since Roman times when the emperor Claudius had dug a 5.5-kilometer tunnel to drain Lake Fucinus. Thousands of Indians, forcibly recruited, excavated the canal and tunnel in only 11 months, an astounding accomplishment. The tunnel portion, more than 6 kilometers in length, 2 meters wide, and 3 meters high, reached

45 meters below the surface. When Humboldt examined the works and subsequent improvements in the late eighteenth century he pronounced them one of history's engineering wonders.

Despite the project's monumental scale, it was of little avail. The heavy rains of 1609 showed the tunnel's capacity insufficient. The canal's walls tended to cave, and the tunnel was easily clogged. And it would never suffice to drain the highest body of water in the valley, Lake Zumpango, when the city was surrounded by the lowest, Lake Texcoco. Martinez himself admitted that the other lakes would also require outlets for the system to function properly. Adrian Boot, a Dutch engineer and Catholic convert, pronounced the whole project a waste of time and recommended rather that the city build better dikes to protect itself and to maintain the city's useful canals. But a former Calvinist arguing for an indigenous approach to water control held little appeal even though he correctly warned the citizens that to drain the lakes would destabilize further the city's building foundations.

Still officials temporized as floods failed to come for another couple decades. But in 1629, the rains commenced again, saturating the ground in preparation for something big. Beginning on September 21st, a torrential downpour, possibly a hurricane turned tropical storm, descended upon the valley nonstop for an ominous 40 hours, as estimated by local officials. Residents awoke to 1 or 2 meters of water in the streets that continued to rise. In short order, the only dry land at city center was a small patch near the cathedral that came to be called "Island of the Dogs" as all the city's canines converged their for refuge. It was an unprecedented disaster that looked as if it might become permanent. The rains continued, not for a few months, but on and off for five full years during which time the flooded city was nearly uninhabitable. It is probable that even Aztec works in good repair would have been overwhelmed by this deluge. The Dominican, Alonso Franco, wrote that the city appeared a graveyard of wrecked ships with its damaged buildings poking chaotically from the placid water.

> Her houses and churches, though of stone, looked more like ships than buildings resting on the earth. They seemed to be floating upon the water, and as with waterlogged ships, which need to pump incessantly, in the houses and churches the pumping went on day and night.[5]

[5]   Quoted in Louisa Hoberman, "Bureaucracy and Disaster: Mexico City and the Flood of 1629," *Journal of Latin American Studies* 6 (1974): 214.

By the end of September, only 400 of the city's 20,000 Spanish families remained. Of the city's estimated 8,000 houses, 7,000 were a total loss, their foundations dissolved to clay. Many sought refuge in neighboring cities while others were forced to live in makeshift camps on higher ground. Those who could not escape the city took up residence in the cathedral. Nearly every economic activity except canoe building ceased. The church did its best to function. Wealthy families that stuck it out were allowed to fashion altars on balconies and rooftops where circuit priests in canoes could administer mass. The viceroy ordered the image of Guadalupe to be carried to the cathedral in a floating procession of 200 canoes, accompanied by himself, the nobility, priests, and the pious to make petitions to the virgin for relief. A few people pressed on, building raised sidewalks and relying on canoes, hoping the water would recede soon. But even without additional rains, they had to await the long process of the lakes' evaporation as the monumental drainage ditch proved useless again.

With time, the tragedy only worsened. Food, much of it still produced on chinampas that must have universally flooded, was in short supply, and many starved despite city-sponsored relief efforts. With the population in a weakened state, trapped in the city, disease began to make its rounds. At the end of five difficult years, two thirds of the city's buildings had been destroyed. The archbishop estimated that 30,000 Indians had died (probably including Africans of which there had been 5,000 in the city), and he accused the viceroy of neglecting the city's flood works out of prejudice against or lack of concern for the lower classes of all races. To the accusation, the viceroy replied that it was not his fault that creoles were easily so drowned; he also smirked that if the water had been alcohol, the common people's predisposition for drink would have saved the city.

When the waters receded, still the Spanish would not concede to relocate. The city was rebuilt, for the second time, just as after its initial conquest. Dikes were improved and work continued on the drainage project. Martinez, who was initially jailed for criminal incompetence, was released, and began to convert the tunnel into open canal, a project not completed till 1789. And it would be yet another century before the lakes were successfully drained.

Two different attitudes toward water resulted in starkly different approaches to the Valley of Mexico's environment. But we must be careful not to attribute this to monolithic cultural attitudes toward nature that can be split easily between European and Indian. After centuries of experiment and experience during which their culture evolved within a particular landscape, the Aztecs had learned to effectively manipulate the valley's resources to maximize the production of food and ease the movement of goods. The Spaniards attempted to do the same, but according their own perceptions of how nature ought to be organized. They did not have the benefit of the Aztec's long familiarity with local water and landscapes. In ignorance, the Spaniards imposed a more costly and less efficient system. Relationships to nature come out of particular historical experiences as much as broader religious and cultural traditions. If it had been Incas that conquered the Valley of Mexico, they might have abandoned the lakesides the Aztecs so valued to settle and intensively terrace the surrounding hills. If it had been the Dutch or the Venetians who conquered Tenochtitlán, it is likely that today's Mexico City would still be an island surrounded by dikes and water, and connected to the lakeshore by multilane motor causeways.

Despite a remarkable cultural ignorance about the ground they were occupying, the Iberians, in a remarkably short period of time, solidified their hold over a region many times larger than the Europe they came from. By the end of the colonial era, the Spanish had founded more than 900 cities from California to Patagonia. However, nature, not culture, managed most of the New World transformations. Cows, pigs, rats, and weeds remade America's natural complexion in a remarkably brief period. By contrast, it would take four centuries for humans to drain Mexico's lakes. And while microbes annihilated 90 percent of the human population in a century, the human species also took four centuries to recover its preconquest numbers. Population collapse was the most significant environmental event of the conquest, and throughout the colonial period, there remained large gaps between settlements. Emptied of her indigenous peoples and unoccupied by her new rulers, America, for the first time in ages, embraced broad frontiers that vegetated undisturbed.

CHAPTER THREE

THE COLONIAL BALANCE SHEET

Every time I goe up to the plantation, it makes mee more and more
to love the countrey for to see how bravely the canes grow, and how
the slaves goe tumbling down the trees.[1]

Once the Iberians had plundered Indian gold and exhausted themselves
in useless searches for El Dorado, they had to face the upsetting reality that America had little else to offer of tradable value. Indian commodities for the most part could not be sold in Europe. Even elite status
goods – feathered tunics, jade figurines, jaguar pelts, noble weapons –
while they made quaint gifts to kings and friends, did not constitute
viable items of trade. Some native products, like cacao and cochineal,
had potential, but it would take time to develop new European tastes and
markets. And mines of any consequence were not to be discovered until
some 50 years after America's discovery. Columbus had sailed west to
find the treasures of the East, but America had gotten in the way. For half
a century, it remained an obstacle to material gain. The truth was that
settled Indians and invading Europeans were commercially more alike
than they were different. To that point, neither produced commodities
that found eager buyers beyond their immediate regions. Both Europe
and America focused their attentions on growing food on densely populated landscapes, agricultural systems that were largely sustainable and
had been for thousands of years. And both engaged in local trade. But a
globalizing commerce that had just begun to connect diverse ecologies

[1] William Whaley, Jamaica, January 20, 1672, quoted in David Watts, *The West
    Indies: Patterns of Development, Culture, and Environmental Change Since 1492*
    (Cambridge, England: Cambridge University Press, 1987), 284.

would revolutionize local production, and it would do it in America before it did so in Europe.

Many factors combine to explain the New World commercial revolution. One was the culture of conquest itself: Iberian men had not risked their lives crossing oceans and conquering continents to simply settle down and subsist as they had in Europe. If Pizarro had wanted to remain a swineherd he would have stayed in Extremadura. The conquerors would settle for nothing less than lordships, if not in legal title than at least in practice. But again, the reality was not what they had anticipated. The conquistadors managed to replace the indigenous elite, to be waited on hand and foot, which was the victors' privilege, but the Indians could only bestow on their new lords traditional tribute goods: corn, firewood, spirulina, and feathers, hardly fitting spoils, and even these mundane tributes were shrinking with the ever diminishing Indian population. The victors' dignity could only be fully gratified by the consumption of Europe's status goods. But with the plundered, precious metals spent or squandered there was nothing left with which to buy them. The only way colonials could begin to consume those goods conspicuous to their newly assumed status was to find in America something of value for which Europeans would gladly trade. Until they did, Spaniards would continue to live like native lords, eating corn and wearing cotton; and the Portuguese would continue to shed European clothing and culture altogether, abandoning God and civilization to cohabit with Tupi women, as a much-chagrined church described their degeneration.

The search for tradable commodities was a colonial obsession, a search that forced itself upon the conquistadors who had little other choice. And it paid off, eventually, in the second and third generations. In some cases, the Iberians found native products, such as tobacco, indigo, cacao, and cochineal, that they could exchange for Europe's familiar foods and sumptuous religious objects, or, more commonly, Asia's assorted textiles and fine household goods. For Spanish America, the most significant trade good was silver, discovered in fabulously rich mines in Mexico and Peru, for traders all over the world welcomed hard cash. For Portuguese America, it was the introduction of an unusual grass, sugar cane. These two commodities, in their colonial spaces, would shape the landscape as much as had weeds and germs for they were quite different in scale and impact than any economic activity that had come before. They were not sustainable over the long term, as our story will bear out, and the marks they left on nature and culture were deep and enduring. In fact, their impacts were global: in short

order, American silver became the preferred medium of exchange for
world trade; and, in time, sugar would evolve from an indulgent condi-
ment to sweeten elite palates to a staple carbohydrate to fuel the industrial working class. However, if silver and sugar's scars ran deep, they
were of limited geographic coverage. It was both colonial America's tiny
populations and colonialism's multifarious commercial restrictions that
permitted many of America's ancient natural wounds to heal.

Consuming Sugar

Sugar, maybe even as much as hard cash, was a welcome commodity in
Europe. Indeed almost no culture has rejected sweetness. The human
tongue, as resistant to change as it is, craves sugars, whether in fruit,
honey, or soft drinks. But until the fifteenth century, the sources of
sweetness were few, weak, or expensive. Only with the introduction
of potent sucrose, processed from the succulent stems of sugar cane,
did sweetness become viable as an item of significant consumption and
trade. From its origins in New Guinea, sugar cane traveled across Asia
to the Mediterranean to give Europeans their first taste. The Portuguese
introduced the canes in the mid-fifteenth century to their newly discovered Atlantic islands, Madeira and São Tomé, and the spike in production on the islands caused the price of sugar to drop significantly
in Europe. So at Brazil's discovery in 1500, market conditions for sugar
were not ideal. But in the rabid colonial search for goods of trade, it was
soon planted, by 1516, in the former fields of the Tupi.

Sugar is one of agriculture's most ravenous activities, for in addition
to burning forests for fields and depleting soils of their fertility, practices
typical of many crops, it also destroys forests well beyond the plantation
in gathering immense quantities of firewood. Sugar's extraordinary powers of plunder, in fact, made Brazil a colonial success. On the Atlantic
islands, despite that some, like Madeira, had never been inhabited and
had a wealth of virgin soils and thick forests, local resources were too
limited to sustain sugar for more than a short century. Madeira, the
translation of which is "Wood" in Portuguese, was named for its single, all-encompassing forest, which the fifteenth-century poet Luis de
Camões described as the island's greatest renown. The island was volcanic in origin, blessed with excellent soils and abundant fresh water,
but the voracious sugar mills methodically stripped the island bare. An
observer in the early seventeenth century could find not a single tree
on the colony's entire 740 square kilometers, the island's namesake

essentially eradicated. By 1550, Madeirans had no choice but to abandon sugar for lack of firewood and began to cultivate their famous wine grapes in sugar's stead.

Why, one wonders, did Iberians, who had a largely sustainable agricultural relationship with Europe's nature, a tradition more than 6,000 years old, abruptly abandon it for such short-term, devastating activities on arrival in these new worlds? Certainly, acquisitiveness played a role, but that character flaw was common to Iberians, Incas, and Aztecs, regardless of period. As we have noted, attitudes toward consumption differed between elite Iberians and Indians largely in their preferences, not in scope. There are a variety of elements that combined to produce plantation monoculture, yet another rather novel element of this New World. The most important was a single, ancient technology whose reach and grasp exploded in the fifteenth century. The ship, the global link of the early modern world, made possible the New World's discovery, but it was also large enough and reliable enough to make the commercial connection between the earth's continents permanent. It, more than differing cultural attitudes toward consumption, was an essential factor in transforming New World nature. The ship did not introduce trade to the Americas. Even the Tupi traded on a small scale, and the Aztecs and Incas traded goods significant distances, even over local seas in a few known cases. The ship, then, simply increased trade's reach, and that changed everything. Before the ship globalized commerce, trade was rarely more than a regional phenomenon. Producers had markets that were limited in size because they were limited in reach. The ship potentially made the whole world one's market. And America got in on the ground floor of globalization because the discovery and commercial linking of Europe to Africa, India, America, and China, essentially in that order, all took place within a few decades. Now, American producers of even heavy or bulky goods, such as sugar, tobacco, brazilwood, and even raw timber, no longer had to limit their production to what their immediate neighbors could consume. They would produce, if possible, for the whole world, which resulted in a significant intensification of resource use. And it should be kept in mind that this global commercial revolution that Europe introduced to the New World was about as novel to Europeans as it was to the Indians.

The consequences of the conquest and Columbian exchange also played central roles in the nature of New World economic activity. The death of millions of Indians opened up broad frontiers to agricultural expansion. In both Europe and preconquest America, one had to manage the soil carefully because the farmer inherited a limited piece of ground from parents and had to make do. There were no frontiers. In postconquest America, vacant lands were so abundant that all the effort and cost of reinvesting in a particular plot's fertility, in manuring, or in fallowing, made little sense when there was abundant fertile soil well on this side of your horizon. Likewise, with the introduction of new foods and animals, and the productivity of tropical agriculture, suddenly there was enough food available that farmers found monoculture worth the risk. Where food or land was scarce, monoculture, even in food crops, was a dangerous experiment: if your single crop failed, you went hungry. Planting a variety of crops was a food security strategy. But with food in abundance, monoculture, even in noncomestibles, was seen as a calculated investment rather than utter stupidity.

An additional attitude that exacerbated the shortsighted use of natural resources was the colonialist's disinterest in making the colony a permanent home. Colonists of most national stripes, be they in Peru's silver boomtowns or Barbados' sugar fiefs, saw the colonies as a temporary job, a place to get rich quick and then depart as soon as possible for civilization in Europe where one's wealth could be flaunted in front of people who could fully appreciate and envy it. Few succeeded in that goal, but the attitude remained pervasive. Oviedo criticized those colonists who neglected careful agriculture in favor of trade, mining, and pearl fishing; they treated America like a stepmother, he said, when in fact she had nourished them better than their European mother. But they proved the assumption that one will care little for the land that one refuses to call home. Sustainability demands no consideration away from home.

With Madeira's degradation, Brazil, with forests of continental proportions, soon became the most important producer of sugar. From only five sugar mills in 1550, Brazil boasted nearly 500 by the century's end that together produced some 10,000 tons each year. And Brazil, after the devastating Indian epidemics of the mid-sixteenth century, had substantial land and forests to exploit with little effort in conquest. The Portuguese, always adaptive in the tropics, adopted indigenous agricultural systems. The sugar plantations, which combined technology and slaves in what may be the first truly modern agriculture, in reality practiced Indian slash and burn, but did so on an incautious, grand scale. Brazil's coastal Atlantic Forest, a treasure of unique plant and animal species inhabiting the crowns, trunks, and leaf litter of massive, flowered trees, experienced the first incursions of a violence that would extend and intensify over the next five centuries. African slaves, like Indians, but with the benefit of iron axes, felled the colossal lowland forests, let the slash dry for a period, and then set it all aflame. They planted the ashy fields in perennial canes and then collected the harvest for a period that ranged from usually 10 to 15 years. When yields fell to unprofitable levels, the slaves were sent off to repeat the cycle of devastation.

What set limits on sugar's production in Brazil, however, was not a lack of fertile land but the difficulty of acquiring firewood. Sugar was not a simple agriculture like wheat or corn. Harvested cane required considerable processing, and some have described the business as a proto-industry. Once cut, the canes' juice had to be expressed by a large, complex mill powered by water or oxen. The sticky, green liquid flowed from the mill to the furnace house where it was successively boiled in copper kettles over roaring fires to evaporate the water and remove impurities, leaving only a thick molasses that was placed in inverted conical forms to crystallize into varying grades of sugar. The final product was a conical loaf of sugar that shaded from deep brown at the cone's point to brilliant white at its base. During the nine-month harvest, slaves worked 24 hours per day in shifts, often seven days a week. And the fires of the furnace house were the very center of the operation, burning without pause during the entire season, if one could only keep them stoked with firewood. Fire became the metaphor for a successful mill. At Bahia, the colonial capital in northeast Brazil, defunct mills were written off as "*fogo morto*," literally "dead fire," and one colonial cartographer used a rising column of smoke as symbol on his map to identify Bahia's mills. André João Antonil, a Jesuit sugar miller in Bahia, described the mill's multiple furnaces as "truly devouring mouths of woodland, a prison of perpetual fire and smoke, a living image of the volcanoes Vesuvius and Etna, and almost of Purgatory and Hell themselves."[2]

Each mill in the sixteenth century consumed about eight cartloads of firewood per day, but as production increased, mills came to consume 15–25. By the mid-eighteenth century, Bahia's 180 mills combined to consume 3,300 cubic meters of firewood daily, exceeding even the notorious fuel consumption of industrial iron foundries in contemporary Europe. Firewood accounted for 15–20 percent of a sugar mill's operating costs, matching, and often exceeding, the cost of acquiring slave labor. The lack of firewood was the most commonly reported reason for stoppages at the mill. However, it was not for absolute lack of

---

[2]   André João Antonil, *Cultura e opulência do Brasil, por suas drogas e minas* (São Paulo: Companhia Melhoramentos, 1976), Book 2, Chapter 8, my translation.

the resource; Antonil admitted that Brazil, and Brazil alone, had sufficient forest fuels to feed Brazil's sugar fires for years to come. Millers did attempt to restrict the construction of new mills to a half league from other mills, arguing there was insufficient fuel for higher mill densities, but their concerns were really more about limiting competition than any sincere anxiety about the resource. Firewood shortages were a reflection of labor and transport difficulties, not the lack of trees. In fact, much of Brazil's firewood did not come from the forests that surrounded the mills but from distant mangroves that provided an excellent, dense fuel that was easily accessible to water transport. The mangroves, which grew all along Brazil's sugar-producing estuaries, had an unmatched tenacity and grew back at prodigious rates, especially when their roots were left intact. But as fuelwood cutters had to go progressively farther up and down the coast to harvest firewood, the costs of the firewood business increased.

Brazil's fertile frontier and abundant forests inspired waste. Planters did not carefully cultivate the soil nor improve its fertility, but callously abandoned used fields for the next forest plot that they in turn felled for its virgin substrate. Firewood was not conserved nor consumed efficiently. The mill's furnaces were essentially closed bonfires, fueled with recently cut logs that in their green condition were as much as 90 percent moisture by weight. Fuel was also reportedly burned in massive logs whose diameters were too large for a slave to put his arms around. With tiny populations and outsized resources, Brazilian planters showed virtually no interest in the conservation of soils or trees.

Brazil's decadence as a producer of sugar in the mid-seventeenth century cannot be explained by environmental decay, as was the case in Madeira. In 1630, the Dutch, aching for a piece of American sugar production, invaded Pernambuco, capturing Brazil's preeminent sugar zone. They held it almost 25 years, but due to a local resistance movement the Dutch never managed to make the land profit as had the Portuguese. Colonial patriots thwarted Dutch attempts to woo the population with freedom of religion and tax breaks, and Brazil's colonists eventually organized themselves, without crown support, to push the Calvinists back into the sea. Tellingly, the common password of the resistance was "*açúcar*" (sugar). Despite the resistance's success in 1654, Brazil's sugar economy was significantly damaged. Not only did direct destruction of sugar fields and machinery play a role, but the long war virtually destroyed both Spain's and Portugal's merchant fleets. For decades, Brazil had little means to get its sugar to Europe during a period when both sugar's price and Europe's cravings were on the rise. Before the occupation of Pernambuco, it had been the Dutch who had carried much of Brazil's sugar to Europe, but now they took both their ships and what they learned about sugar production in Brazil to the Caribbean.

For the next century, Brazil found it difficult to compete with the Caribbean as the Dutch, British, and eventually the French established plantations on many of the region's smaller islands. These rising nations had more investors and better shipping, and not only were they closer to Europe's markets, now with their own sugar colonies, they protected their home markets by blocking Brazil's sugar entirely. Thus began an explosion of sugar production on the non-Spanish islands of the Caribbean. Britain led on this new frontier, having taken control of Barbados, Jamaica, and a number of other small islands that the Spaniards, busy with silver on the mainland, made too little effort to defend. British men swarmed to the Caribbean. By 1642, while there were only 49,000 British in all of North America, there were 80,000 in the Caribbean, 37,000 of them crowded on the tiny island of Barbados. In the 1630s, sugar had begun to displace Barbadian tobacco, and African slaves began to displace the white, mostly indentured population. By 1680, only 17,000 whites remained, but with 37,000 black slaves on hand, Barbados had become the New World's most densely populated and valuable real estate.

But it was more than the little island could bear. Within 20 years, planters bragged they had deforested the entire island, submitting every available square foot, about 80 percent of the island's landmass, to cultivation. The Barbadians' success spawned imitators, and the deforestation of many of the Lesser Antilles followed apace. By 1700, nearly all the small sugar islands – St. Kitts, Nevis, Montserrat, Martinique, Guadalupe – took the form of reverse tonsures, shaved bald but for little tufts of forest left on their mountain crowns. The more exuberant an island's forests, the more eager were the planters, for dense forests they believed uncontestable evidence of the soil's fertility.

As on Madeira, the inevitable consequences of sugar expansion came quickly to these little islands. When the soil's fertility declined, planters had no frontier onto which to expand or relocate. Moreover, deforestation exposed the soils to rain and heat which leached the soil's nutrients, and sugar, a perennial grass that was not easily rotated with other crops, further sapped the soil's flagging strength. The governor of Barbados reported that plantations, only after 30 years, produced one third less sugar per acre. Others claimed it was half. The only early response was to let fields lie fallow, and planters from 1680 to 1700, in fact, reduced the area planted in sugar by one third.

The removal of the trees also resulted in massive erosion, especially in hilly terrain like that of northern Barbados. It got so bad a farmer could not trust his land to stay put. Barbados' trees had anchored a fertile layer of soil, 10–12 inches thick, to its gravelly foundation, but now, without roots, the earth began to move. Griffith Hughes, a resident, said the land often "ran away." He described one rainy season in which a tenant farmer's entire field, full of mature crops, slid off his property and plummeted from a cliff into the ocean. In compensation, an adjoining field of sugar owned by his neighbor, a Mr. Foster, skated down to "richly" cover the poor man's recently exposed land, the canes still upright and intact. Mr. Foster was left with a field of chalky gravel. More commonly the soils flowed slowly, like glaciers. It was not unusual to see single standing trees change position over the course of a year.[3]

As can be imagined, the rapid clearing of these small islands' forests was an irredeemable disaster for the plants and animals that resided there. The islands, in many cases, had had their species already diminished by the dense Indian settlements in previous centuries, but sugar's impositions were strikingly more devastating. Scores of plants, mammals, reptiles, and birds were unique to each island, and an uncounted number of species, possibly ranging in the thousands, without their forest habitats, disappeared forever without the slightest human notice. On Barbados, a few deletions were noted: the palmito palm, the mastic tree, the wood pigeon, a few species of conures, the yellow-headed macaw, and one variety of hummingbird – all vanished. No monkey species survived sugar's colonization, and of the 529 noncultivated species of plant found on Barbados today, only 11 percent are native to the island.

With the forests gone and soil disappearing in sheets, the Caribbean planters, lacking Brazil's frontiers, were forced to adapt and innovate. Without local firewood, planters looked abroad, first to other islands, then to Suriname, even to England from which they imported coal for a period, and finally to North America. But this was expensive, potentially making their sugar uncompetitive, so they introduced two significant furnace innovations. The British developed a furnace called the Jamaica train in which a single fire, rather than six bonfires, heated all

3 Griffith Hughes, *The Natural History of Barbados* (London: 1750; reprint, New York: Arno Press, 1972), 21.

six kettles by means of a flue and chimney. The savings in fuel were significant. Then, by 1680, with new, woodier varieties of sugar cane, Barbados' planters were able to burn bagasse, the spent cane, reducing further the need for firewood imports.

Fertility and soil degradation were not so easily addressed. Planters fought a losing battle by ordering their slaves to haul soils that had eroded downhill back up to their fields of origin, a withering occupation one observer compared to the toil of ants. Some built walls and terraces to retain the soils, but this was only occasionally successful, and many eroded lands were abandoned by 1700. Some observers claimed that one third of Barbados was so eroded as to be unrecoverable. Caribbean plantations practiced monoculture in the extreme; planters would neither rotate their crops nor waste labor in keeping livestock. Without manure, fallowing was the only option in dealing with infertility. By 1665, trade itself began to supply the manures the island lacked, and some were willing to pay a pretty penny for imported dung, but that too would prove uneconomical. In time, a few small farmers, not engaged in sugar planting, acquired cattle and began to ranch them not primarily for meat, hide, or milk, but for manure, a commerce without European precedent that thereafter became of central importance to the island's scratching by as sugar producer for another century.

In a rather short period, whether on limited islands like Barbados, or continental masses like Brazil, sugar culture devastated nature, destroying forests and displacing soils. Where there were no frontiers, farmers were forced to return to more sustainable practices, if it was not already too late. On Barbados and some few other islands, sugar became more sustainable over time, but in a world sugar market, sustainability alone was no salvation. Export monoculture is compelled to compete, and small islands could not long run with Brazil or, at the end of the eighteenth century, with the larger Caribbean islands. On newer sugar plantations of the French Caribbean, 30 slaves could produce as much sugar as could 100 on Barbados. Maintaining fertility and yields per acre was a labor intensive operation. Barbados produced 15 units of sugar per slave in 1650, but only nine per slave in 1700. They compensated by adding more slaves, which kept production up. But as Saint-Domingue, Hispaniola, Puerto Rico, and Cuba came on line as sugar producers, with fresh soils and untapped forests, the smaller islands' need for additional laborers made them less competitive. But it is interesting to note that while many contemporaries liked to blame the slave, or the slave system, for the rapid destruction of nature, nature's destruction created conditions under which yet more slaves were imported, counteracting nature's stinginess with human bondage and sweat. And astonishingly, where colonists and slaves failed to maintain sugar culture, as on Antigua, nature began a new phase of forest regeneration, again obliterating the evidence of culture's fleeting presence, but the recovering forests were botanically less diverse, and notably silent for lack of animal life.

DEADLY SILVER

Unlike sugar, which was introduced to much of Latin America's tropical lowlands, silver's direct environmental impacts concentrated narrowly around a handful of highland mining zones. But never had so little territory supplied so much wealth. During Iberia's colonial American rule, 85 percent of the world's silver came from Latin America, principally Peru and Mexico, as did 70 percent of its gold, most of that from Brazil's interior highlands. Even by 1660, after a single century of American mining, Spain had received 16 million kilograms of silver, three times Europe's entire former reserves. The eight peso ("piece of eight") coins, minted at Mexico City and Potosí, became the medium of exchange in ports from London and Amsterdam to Manila and Bombay, and more than half of all the silver mined in America was used to balance a global trade deficit with China through the ports of Canton and Macau, sometimes directly across the Pacific out of Acapulco or more commonly after having passed through many prior hands in Europe, Africa, and Asia. Nevertheless, a substantial portion of Spanish silver and Portuguese gold remained in America where it financed colonial administration, built cities, and established rich churches, creating demand for all kinds of colonial economic activities. The major colonial cities developed in response to precious metals, either at the mines themselves – Potosí, Zacatecas, and Ouro Preto – or along routes of the mines' supply and bullion's egress – Lima, Panama, Havana, Vera Cruz, Buenos Aires, and Rio de Janeiro. The Iberian colonial system, global commerce, and Europe's coming industrialization all revolved around the abundance of America's mineral wealth.

The city of Potosí, America's first boomtown, crowded like a squatter's camp beneath the Cerro Rico, an almost perfectly conical mountain riddled with the richest veins of silver ever encountered. Discovered in 1545, the mines, at more than 4,000 meters, made an unlikely place for human civilization to thrive. But the camp quickly transformed itself into the world's highest city, and by 1660, the population teemed inconceivably at 160,000, larger than Seville, Madrid, or Rome. Too high for trees or agriculture of any consequence, nearly everything the inhabitants needed, for survival and indulgence, was imported. Timber was dragged at great effort from the Andes' eastern slopes; wheat, horses, and wine arrived from Chile; and goods from Europe, status items that would legitimate a grubbing new elite, as well as mining tools and machinery, arrived legally from Panama and Lima, and illegally by way of Buenos Aires. Visitors described a city madly and uncharacteristically disorganized for a Hispanic municipality. Stunning personal fortunes, sufficient to pave the streets with silver ingots on public occasions, propelled extravagant consumption, and the resulting garbage piled so high at the edge of town as to compete for attention with the city's 86 opulent churches.

For decades, the quality of Potosí's silver ores was such that miners were satisfied with the Inca technique of smelting with the *guayra*, a stone or ceramic vessel that was charged with fuel and ore and set afire upon a windy ridge that served as bellows. The extreme heat melted the ore, separating the silver from the dross. Fuel was in short supply, but miners scavenged wood from lower altitudes and even collected the local grass. Mining, and the dense urban entities that surrounded that pursuit, deforested most mining zones. Alder pollen, so common in core samples in the late Inca period, virtually disappears again between 1550 and 1650. The lack of fuel later forced some mines to close, particularly those of Mexico's arid north. As early as 1550 Antonio de Mendoza, Mexico's first viceroy, told his successor that Mexico would run out of timber before it ran out of silver. Zacatecas and Potosí struggled on, paying for wood from distant forests carried by mule train.

The solution to the problem of fuel scarcity arrived in the form of mercury, a metal as rare and almost as precious as silver itself. Mercury, the alchemists' sublime metal, had a number of unique properties that bordered on the magical. Most unusual, it was a liquid at room temperature, seemingly alive rather than inert, hence its popular name quicksilver. Some considered it the materia prima from which all other elements were created. Liquid mercury is so heavy that a cannon ball can be floated on a shallow pool of it, not unlike a beach ball on water, and as it responds predictably to changes in temperature and pressure, it was used in barometers, thermometers, and the pendulums of clocks, tools of the new magicians of science. Its most valued trait, however, was its seemingly mystical affinity for gold and silver to which it readily bonded forming an amalgam, a property that made it possible to extract precious metals from their ores with little or no fuel. The new method, called the *patio* process because it was typically performed on a large, paved space, was introduced to Mexico in the 1550s and to Potosí by 1572.

For amalgamation to be effective, silver ores had first to be pulverized. So only a decade after mercury's arrival in Peru, 120 stamp mills, driven by water, were constructed along Potosí's main stream. Residents also built a large network of dams above the city forming more than 20 reservoirs that increased the mills' capacity to process ore year round. Eight-meter waterwheels powered heavy trip hammers that crushed the rocks in what must have been a terrifying racket that heralded the coming industrial age. The mill's product, powdered rock, was so fine the Spaniards called it flour. This they mixed in stone tanks containing a solution of water, salt, mercury, and a bit of iron filings. Two weeks or more later, depending on the ambient temperature, the tanks were dredged for the amalgam that had formed, which was about 80 percent mercury and 20 percent silver. Its high mercury content kept it soft and moldable, unlike the modern dental amalgam that we implant in our teeth that contains 52 percent mercury to about 33 percent silver and small quantities of other metals. Workers shaped the amalgam into cones of about 45 kilograms, coincidentally similar in shape to loaves of sugar, and placed them in furnaces where the mercury vaporized and was partially recovered for reuse. What remained was a conical chunk of pure silver riddled with tiny voids where the mercury had been.

Silver processing, what had been a primitive operation destructive of forests, had become an industrial process with far more insidious consequences, for mercury's magic came at a cost. Mercury is a significant human poison that had long been suspected of sickening those who worked with it: it made hatters mad and alchemists toothless. Mercury poisoned miners at various stages of the mining process. On the patio, Indians mixed the floury ore and mercury in the tanks of water with their feet, absorbing mercury through their skin. Later, animals mixed the solution with their hooves, but men still had to enter the vats and remove the amalgam by hand. At the recovery furnaces men might breathe mercury's concentrated vapors directly. At greatest risk were those who worked the mercury mine at Huancavelica, Peru, America's only viable source of mercury. Forced to labor in the tight confines of narrow, sweltering mine shafts, the miners breathed a noxious cocktail of ore dust and highly volatilized mercury that entered the bloodstream through their lungs and through the perspiring pores of their skin, reaching every bodily organ. An assignment to work in Huancavelica was a death sentence, recognized as such even by crown officials who, as a result, shut the mine down briefly in 1600. In this early period, as many as two thirds of all mercury miners died, usually within a few years of their entering the mine. Some referred to the mine as a "public slaughterhouse," and indigenous mothers were reported to have crippled their children to disqualify them from work at Huancavelica.

The reasons for such drastic language and precautions were horribly obvious to local mining families. Mercury poisoning was a slow, debilitating death. Many of the symptoms were psychological: depression, personality changes, memory loss, and irritability. Physiological symptoms included bleeding gums, loose teeth, acute fatigue, and monotonic speech patterns; victims lost the ability to modulate their voice. The most commonly reported symptoms were lack of muscle coordination and uncontrollable tremors. For some, spasms were so unrelenting and violent that, unable to sleep, they became exhausted to the point of death. Moreover, they were entirely helpless, relying on others to feed them. The only treatment, other than total removal from the mine, was bleeding, a catchall remedy for early modern disease, but that in this case may have done some small good. If a miner was bled at the heel a quantity of the heavy mercury that had settled in the feet might drain with the blood. Some miners recovered, if they were removed from the environment early, but many thousands were worked to their deaths and buried with their coworkers. In the grave, after the flesh had decayed, their white bones rested on shimmering silver pools of incorruptible mercury, damning forensic evidence against their employers. All who lived in the mining districts were also exposed to a variety of heavy metals, mostly in their water. Mine shafts and tailings, heaped about the hillsides, leached zinc, lead, copper, and arsenic, all of which entered local streams and ground water, and eventually human tissues.

Silver was more important than Indian lives, so the deadly work continued. Only after 1642, when a major ventilation shaft was completed at Huancavelica by order of the crown and at great cost, did mortality decline, but even thereafter as many as a third of mercury miners would still succumb to poisoning and other lethal factors associated with deep shaft mining. It is difficult to say how much mercury may have affected those not directly involved in mining. Its quite likely mercury, which was poorly handled and transported in sheepskin bags, found its way into local streams and soils. In any case, silver and mercury mining were like epidemic diseases, more significant as destroyers of human beings than as transformers of the landscape. Nature, by comparison, got off easy with a few mineshafts and local deforestation. Overall, silver mining in Spanish America is responsible for the deaths of hundreds of thousands to mercury poisoning, silicosis, cave-ins, carbon monoxide, explosions, poor treatment, and overwork.

Gold and diamonds, discovered later in the mountains of Brazil's interior, were less detrimental to human beings as the miners worked above ground in placer deposits, but for the same reason the mines' environmental impacts were more apparent. Smelting was largely by fire, so deforestation was general. If gold bearing soils were covered in trees, miners set fire to the forests to expose the earth. Miners diverted entire rivers to get at their auriferous gravel beds and they built massive sluices to separate the gold, chopping up the land with canals and grade cuts. They excavated potential deposits with such abandon that across the mining zones rivers ran muddy and a once forested land became pock-marked, mineral tailings so strewn across the landscape that only the toughest of stunted herbage could again take root. In addition to the tens of thousands of miners, including Brazil's largest regional slave population, farmers and ranchers followed the gold rushers to make their own ecological impacts through slash and burn agriculture and pasturing. This large, often itinerant population, bounding from one strike to the next, transformed land on a scale and pace beyond what their predecessors had done on the sugar plantations. The change was so complete that foreign scientists who visited the formerly forested mining zone in the early nineteenth century just assumed it had always been a barren, sterile plateau.

Handcuffed Colonists

Despite the intense transformations of mining and planting, it is still more accurate to see the colonial era as one of nature's recovery and regeneration rather than its grand despoliation. The catastrophic decline of human numbers associated with the conquest remained a central factor in nature's trajectory at least until the nineteenth century. There were notable technological introductions associated with the conquest, particularly in the form of metal tools; and water power, a significant advance, was introduced to express sugar cane and crush silver ores. However, most labor was still accomplished by simple hand tools, and there were far fewer hands now available to wield them.

Despite the coerced toil of numerous Indians and the enormous import of Africans, the colonial labor force paled by comparison to the manpower that had been available before the conquest.

Moreover, we need to keep in mind that colonial documentation concentrates itself in the areas of Iberian settlement offering a tolerably clear view of the impacts of mining, planting, logging, and ranching, but the view should not be generalized much beyond the bounds of Iberian cities and farms. Throughout the colonial era, Indians, although greatly diminished in numerical force and impact, still controlled and defended vast territories: Patagonia, northern Mexico, the North American West, and Amazonia, among many other enclaves, large and small. Nor should we exaggerate the Iberian's impacts. Even Warren Dean, who in the harshest terms condemns Portugal's avarice and ignorance in destroying the ecological treasure that was Brazil's Atlantic Forest, acknowledges that colonial sugar planting was probably sustainable due to the relatively small number of humans engaged in its production over an extensive, forested landscape. The Atlantic Forest began to disappear in earnest only in the nineteenth century with the arrival of coffee, more slaves, and many more European immigrants.

Metropolitan restrictions on colonial immigration were among the most important demographic factors limiting environmental change in the colonies. Iberia's kings wanted to populate their colonies, but only in regions they could defend and police, and only with people they could trust. That meant that settlement in remote areas, including coastal zones that might engage in contraband, was discouraged. More importantly, it meant that non-Iberians were barred from Spanish and Portuguese colonies with rather few exceptions, such as for foreign Catholic priests. The Dutch West Indies Company invaded Brazil in part because Dutch citizens had no possibility of emigrating there legally to grow sugar. And the 80,000 British that crowded onto the small Caribbean islands, far more than had gone to British territories in North America, did so because the tropics, from which they were generally barred, offered better economic opportunities. Hence they stole the islands from the Spanish. Some few foreigners did get through and made lives in Iberian colonies, but it was uncommon and dangerous. On occasion, officials summarily purged all non-Iberians. In 1617, royal authorities expelled all foreigner residents from Brazil's northeast, married or single, with or without children, despite pleas for common decency from local officials. Without these restrictions on foreign immigration, which were driven by xenophobic mistrust and religious sectarianism, Iberia's colonies might have been substantially better populated by a broad cross section of nationals from the European continent, and by the additional slaves they would have imported to work for them.

The limits of environmental change in colonial Latin America were not entirely dependent on demography, however. Economic policy was also central. If Europeans introduced America to global trade, it was by no means free trade. In colonial America, the invisible hand that Adam Smith identified as the economy's unerring guide was cuffed. Artificial barriers restricted the flow of trade, and monopolies limited economic choices. Obviously, just as foreigners were denied the right to settle Iberia's colonies, they were also denied the right and opportunity to trade there. The main justification for possessing a colony was that the metropolis could channel the colony's trade and commodities exclusively to metropolitan ports, enriching the state through taxes on trade, which were remarkably high, and enriching the nation's merchants by eliminating foreign competition. Colonial producers had the whole world as their market but that world could only be reached through metropolitan middlemen. The power of the middleman attached itself to his exclusive role as buyer and seller in colonial markets. Without competing bids, the prices offered for colonial sugar, tobacco, cacao, indigo, and even the exchange rates for silver and gold, were substantially lower than they would have been in a system of free trade. Artificially low prices reduced colonial incentives to produce where returns were marginal. Moreover, the prices for imports were excessive, bleeding off colonial capital for goods that again, under a more open trade, would have been consistently cheaper. Of course, the monopoly of colonial trade could not be perfectly enforced; contraband was common, as popular with Iberia's colonists as it was with the foreigners with whom they conspired. But there is little question that overall Iberia's exclusive trading policies, which were enforced with vigor and harsh penalties including death and banishment, limited colonial trade and production. When Spanish monarchs opened more American and Spanish ports for trade after 1778, trade and production of various kinds increased substantially. In just one example, cattle on the southern pampas had been poorly exploited during the colonial era: most were feral and most evaded capture and slaughter, living to die of old age. If they were slaughtered, the effort produced a few prime cuts immediately roasted, but the rest of the carcass was left to rot. Some hides were exported legally, and many as contraband, but prior to 1778, Spain's exclusive hide trade had received only 150,000 per year. With freer trade, permitting more regions to trade directly with Spain, hide exports just to Spain reached 800,000 the following year, and 1.4 million by 1783. All colonial trade, between 1778 and 1796, increased 10-fold, and after 1796 it expanded further as the Spanish colonies were opened to foreign trade. For nearly three centuries, colonial trade had run at a tiny fraction of its potential.

For most of the colonial era, many economic activities were banned in order to protect metropolitan interests. Olive orchards and grape vines were destroyed so Spanish exports of oil and wine to America would not be harmed. Salt production was banned in Brazil so Portuguese salt could be sold at excessive prices, a policy that harmed the potential growth (and, hence, lessened the environmental impact) of ranching, dairying, and fishing. Most forms of manufacturing were proscribed entirely. The result was that many goods would continue to be supplied to America on the back of European nature, reducing colonial economic opportunities but also colonial environmental degradation.

In addition to general bans, the Iberian monarchs monopolized particular colonial economic activities for their exclusive revenue. This involved a list of goods too long to enumerate fully, but examples include mercury, salt, diamonds, whale oil, timber, soap, tobacco, and, in Peru, even glacial ice for chilling drinks. There was nothing novel in royal monopolies. In Europe, kings commonly restricted the commerce in essential goods to themselves: the Duke of Bavaria monopolized the production of beer, and the Austrian emperor ran an exclusive royal copper mine. The intent in each was to eliminate all competitors such that the crown's revenues were enhanced by their ability to control the price of the monopoly good. From the crown's point of view, the best way to make money was not to promote production, but just the opposite: capture the production, limit it, and channel the unnaturally high prices to the royal exchequer. Monopolies of production were quite different from the monopolies of consumption instituted by the Aztecs and Incas. The Indian elite did not intend to reduce production, just concentrate it into their own hands, and the more produced the better, for they could always gift it to cement social and military alliances or build more storage to house it. The Iberian monarchs, by contrast, wanted very much to limit production because in European commerce, unlike indigenous markets, price mattered, and it rose and fell based on supply. In the case of Brazilian diamonds, as we will see, the Portuguese king was more interested in maintaining high diamond prices than in their actual accumulation in his coffers, something the Indian elite would have been unable to comprehend. To the Inca and Aztec elite, consumption, and hence production, was central. To the Iberian elite, profit was the primary consideration. It may seem counterintuitive, but the goal of colonialism was not primarily to increase production and extract as many exotic goods from the colony as possible. Among colonialism's chief goals was to produce profits for the king and his merchant associates at as little cost as possible. In cases where a product had competitors outside the Iberian colonial systems, such as with sugar and silver, high production, highly taxed, was the best means to profit. But in products that had few or no competitors, human greed worked to spare nature rather than spoil it for the trick was to produce and trade as little as possible at the highest price.

Three Brazilian examples, brazilwood, diamonds, and whales, illustrate monopoly's results for colonial production and nature. The first important colonial monopoly was brazilwood, a red dyewood prized by Europe's textile manufacturers. Brazilwood was so important to Portugal's early trade that it christened the colony with the name Brazil, a reality that angered pious churchmen who insisted the colony go by its official name, derived from another tree, Land of the Holy Cross. Indeed, the business itself became the colonists' namesake: a Brazilian, by all linguistic precedent, should be known as a *brasileno*, but calls himself a *brasileiro*, literally a Braziler, one who cuts and deals in brazilwood. Brazilians may be the only nationals named after the agents of a particular trade or occupation. It would be the equivalent if the United States were named Tobacco, after its first major cash crop, and all its nationals Tobacconists.

Brazilwood was a natural monopoly, that is, it was only found in Brazil, and as there were few substitutes (one of them a distant Malaysian tree species to which the name *bresilium* was first applied) there were no real competitors. From the beginning, the crown restricted brazilwood extraction to those it licensed, and over the course of the colonial period, despite their occupational name, very few Brazilians were permitted to profit it by it. Competition, initially, was from foreigners who dared to infringe on the Brazilian coast. The French, English, and Spanish all engaged in direct brazilwood trade with the Tupi, and the quantities they removed were considerable, an average of about 8,000 tons each year in the sixteenth century. During this first century of the trade, Tupi fellers brought down more than 2 million trees in exchange for Europe's iron tools, tawdry baubles, and stuffy clothing. It was this illicit foreign participation that forced Portugal to settle the brazilwood zone after 1530 to defend it from interlopers. The king ordered the death penalty for all brazilwood contrabandists, and while even that severity never fully shut down contraband, by the seventeenth century, Portugal had secured the controlling hand in the trade.

In 1605, the king formalized an already established system of monopoly contracts for the brazilwood trade. Every three years, traders bid on the exclusive right to extract the dyewood from Brazil. The single winning bidder could export only 600 tons of the dyewood each year, a pittance compared to the average 8,000 exported previously. The contractor's entire timber harvest had to be deposited in the royal timber warehouse at which time he was paid a set price per unit of weight. The king, and usually his contractor, profited handsomely, not because they imported large quantities, but by importing little, the price of brazilwood in Europe remained quite high.

In one important sense, the monopoly led to waste. Landholders, such as sugar planters, often had brazilwood on their property, but the monopoly prohibited them from cutting and selling it. So, rather than protect and preserve it for the contractor who might come unannounced to trespass on their lands and take what belonged to the king, planters cut and burned brazilwood before the crown could appropriate it. Once converted to ashes, there remained no evidence of their spiteful crime. However, despite the waste and occasional reports of contraband, the brazilwood monopoly, which lasted until 1859 under the Brazilian Empire, well after independence, inadvertently conserved the resource for almost four centuries. Had brazilwood been a commodity of free commerce, it is quite likely that it would have disappeared quickly from both farms and wild forests. Traders with Indian and slave laborers would have flooded the forests taking every tree within reach, exhausting the resource much as did the miners of silver and gold in the highlands, or the trappers of beaver in North America. Had the beaver the same arrangement with a European king that brazilwood had with its monarch, its story might have been considerably less tragic. Even under the monopoly the resource was much depleted, but this was more the result of an unrelated activity, expanding agriculture, than contractor and contrabandist logging.

Diamonds are another case in point. The much coveted stones had been trickling into Europe out of India for centuries and were so valued they were each given personal names. When Brazil's gold miners discovered diamonds in quantity in the 1720s, there was general rejoicing in Portugal occasioning parties and parades. Not only would diamonds contribute to Portugal's greatness, it was assumed, but they were also believed a good omen: diamonds denoted pureness, strength, and innocence. Europeans also associated diamonds with the world's creation, and the finder of a diamond thought himself near Eden. The Pope and Portugal's allies applauded the happy occasion declaring publicly that Portugal had found the key, the mystical stone, that would "regenerate and felicitate the universe."

Portugal's John V worked tenaciously to ensure that Brazil's diamonds enhanced primarily his own personal regeneration and felicitation. Unlike Brazil's gold, whose price Portugal could not control as there were many other producers, Brazil's diamonds were so abundant that controlling their supply influenced their world price. Within a couple years of their official discovery in 1729, John V drew a heavy line around the diamond region, centered at Diamantina, and ordered his officials to forcibly remove free whites, free blacks, all women, and particularly priests who were notorious for gold contraband, even if individuals and families had lived in the region for generations. The only people to remain were reputable miners and their African slaves, and this was to be enforced by an armed guard that patrolled the diamond district on horseback. The region became a colony within a colony with entirely separate administrative and judicial prerogatives. The king trusted no one: years before the diamond's official discovery, colonists had been mining diamonds secretly in order to avoid paying the king his due taxes, the standard fifth of their production. By 1733, after only four years of regulated, sanctioned mining, so many Brazilian diamonds flooded Europe that the gem's value fell by more than two thirds. This was unacceptable; market forces would not rob Portugal of her just rewards. For the next five years, John V ordered the human species purged entirely from the diamond district, effectively preventing the mining and export of diamonds.

Prices recovered. But to secure them, John V decided that a strict monopoly was in his best interest. Under the current system he could never be sure he was getting most of the diamonds produced, for he could not prevent massive contraband with so many independent miners. Much like with brazilwood, four-year contracts were bid out and the winner, a single miner, worked the diamond fields exclusively with as many as 600 slaves, possibly the largest slave unit in the New World. A painting from the period depicts hundreds of slaves, a uniformed blue army, carrying on their heads baskets of gravel excavated from immense terraced pits. At washing stations, slaves sifted the gravel for the dull crystals under the watchful eyes of their masters. An overseer monitored the slaves' every movement to ensure they did not place the diamonds in their hair, under fingernails, between toes, in their mouths, or other bodily orifices. Masters discouraged theft with severe beatings and encouraged honesty by rewards. If a slave found a diamond of notable size, he was presented with a new set of clothing – or even his freedom, if the stone exceeded 17 carats. But steal they did. Among the most common tricks was to flick a diamond with the thumb into the mouth of a comrade, a technique one visitor observed slaves practicing in camp with beans. It was a notable form of passive rebellion against a slave order some described as the harshest in all Brazil. Diamonds that evaded the slaves' swindles entered the king's strongbox, and the contractor was paid by the carat. Hence, the Portuguese king became the only official supplier of American diamonds to Europe, and it was in essence illegal for any colonist to possess a diamond, regardless of source. Just the same, they were almost the common currency in the region. So, in 1771, due to increasing laxity, rising contraband, and official corruption, the crown again ordered the district cleansed and began to mine the diamonds entirely on its own account, under royal officials with the labor of slaves owned by the king. This exclusive royal operation also continued well into the postindependence period being abolished only in 1835.

The fact that prices in Europe never again fell, as they did in the 1730s, suggests that the crown monopoly was reasonably successful in keeping prices high and in reducing smuggling. The monopoly resulted in a substantial reduction in production compared to the free for all that came before. Before the institution of the 1737 monopoly contracts, some 9,000 slaves were engaged in diamond mining, and as many as 300,000 carats were exported officially each year, not counting illegal stones. After 1737, the number of slaves plummeted to fewer than 600 with an annual production of only 35,000 carats. In the long run, environmental destruction due to diamond mining was probably a wash: whether done rapidly by individuals, or slowly by monopolists, the tearing open of the breast of the land, the diversion of rivers, and the strewing of tailings left indelible marks. Without the monopoly, however, the diamond district would have experienced these changes in a matter of decades, soon busting after its boom. More important for nature than restricted production was that the monopoly barred immigration and even depopulated the landscape. Unlike in the previous Brazilian gold rush, tens of thousands of potential immigrants and slaves did not arrive, did not produce, and did not consume – and neither did their descendents.

Whales also benefited from the Portuguese crown's tendency to restrict certain economic activities to itself. Bay whaling developed in Brazil in the sixteenth century with the arrival of Basque colonists, and it was so successful that by the early seventeenth century whale oil was plentiful and cheap. Two major producers in Bahia with ties to crown officials did not care for the low price of whale oil, so they encouraged the crown to form a royal monopoly, which it did in 1614. Generally, ocean resources were viewed as common goods by Iberian societies, but as the whale was considered a royal fish, due to its size, an exception was made. Now, similar to brazilwood and diamonds, the crown auctioned contracts to exclusive whalers. Whale oil became scarce and expensive, and many whalers had to find other employments. The crown divided the coast into a handful of whaling grounds, each under the control of a single, royal whale station.

The whale contract was riskier than the others we have examined. Each station employed a lookout who sounded the alarm when a whale entered the bay. In winter, hundreds of whales might appear in Brazil's warm, shallow inlets from their arctic feeding grounds to calve, nurse, and breed, spouting all over the bays. In other years, sometimes a few years in succession, few arrived, which could ruin a contractor. Although documents never specify, the primary catch appears to have been the southern right whale, "right," so-called by the English, because its blubbery body floated upon its death. Many other whale species sank upon harpooning, a useless pursuit.

Good years made for seasons of nonstop activity. At the alarm, men, most of them free farmers paid a fee per catch, ran to the beach like volunteer fireman, took up the oars, and gave chase. Spectators came to the beaches and bluffs to watch a spectacle that often began with the harpooning of a new-born calf. Injured, but alive, the calf struggled at the end of the harpoon line. The calf's mother refused to leave its side, often nudging it to the surface so it could breathe, just as she had done at its birth. Her maternal instincts made it a simple task for the whalers to lance her, repeatedly if necessary, for even mortal wounds did not discourage a nursing whale's devotion. The adult whale's heart, once lanced, stained the water a deep red with its final, gushing beats. The whalers, abandoning the useless calf, towed the adult carcass to the whaling station where its blubber was flensed and boiled, reducing the enormous creature to a mere 15 casks of oil used for lighting, soap, and lubrication.

In the seventeenth century, only about 140 whales were taken during an average three-year contract. Numbers increased, but only slightly, in the eighteenth century, largely due to the expansion into Brazil's more productive southern waters. Techniques did not change as the lack of competition provided few incentives for innovation. So, while Europeans and Americans were revolutionizing the business by open ocean whaling, Brazil's monopoly bay whalers, despite the imprudent concentration on female and baby whales, maintained a sustainable system for two centuries.

By the end of the eighteenth century, however, contractors reported ominous declines in the monopoly's whale counts. One observer blamed this on the over harvest of females, chastising Brazil's whalers for this and other wasteful techniques, but the reality was quite beyond their control. New England whalers had begun to harvest the southern right whale well off of Brazil's coasts in waters that the bay whalers dared not go in their small row boats. Soon the Americans entered the arctic to harvest the whales at their feeding grounds, rapidly decimating the breeding populations that had long migrated up Brazil's coasts. Whaling ships, essentially floating factories belching black smoke through filthy sails, had industrialized the process, and some of them returned to port with more oil in a single hold than many Brazilian whale stations could produce in a year. One ship arrived with 2,600 barrels in 1823, the product of about 170 whales. Multiply that by the hundreds of ships just from the town of New Bedford. Monopoly failed to keep up. Brazilians did belatedly attempt open ocean whaling. They captured an American whaler and forced its crew to teach the local whale men how to work on the open sea, but nothing came of it. It was later than they realized; the primary whaling grounds were already shifting to the Pacific and Alaska. In the late-eighteenth century, American whalers had rejoiced in the whale numbers Brazilians had left them in the south Atlantic. By their own records they processed 193,522 whales on the open sea between 1804 and 1817, probably more than Brazil's exclusive monopoly had accomplished in two centuries of whaling.

Nearly all the colonial monopolies, while they enriched a few, served to impoverish the general human population. But inadvertently, they often served to protect nature. If not for the fall of colonialism and the rise of industrial capitalism, the harvest of renewable resources, such as brazilwood and whales, might have been indefinitely sustainable under such rigid and selfish restrictions.

One last monopoly merits mention, although of an entirely different order. Latifundia, that is, the predominance of large, sometimes extremely large landholdings, was a feature for which Latin America has become notorious. It was not a universal phenomena as small farms were common in some areas, but where latifundia was the rule it amounted to a monopoly of the primary means of colonial production, and it resulted, quite unexpectedly, in the preservation of natural resources. Latifundia had the same selfish logic as all monopolies, and the central motivation was not to empower the landholder with the ability to produce more goods on greater acreage. Rather, large land grants served two related purposes. The first was to secure laborers by shutting them out of the possibility of setting up their own independent farms. Land was plentiful. In fact, there was too much of it. What was lacking was labor to work it. By hoarding much, and in some cases all of the cultivable land, landholders hoped the poor would have little choice but to work for their betters. In the lowland tropics, the free poor, however, even without land, usually withheld their labor, and subsisted by planting a few bananas, manioc, and corn on plots granted by the landlord for nonlabor services, such as political and military support. They supplemented their diets with hunting and fishing. The landholder was forced to turn to slavery or other coercive means. These factors further limited immigration. Many potential Iberian immigrants saw no reason to come to America where they could neither get land, due to latifundia, nor find wage work, due to slavery. Hence, immigration to Latin America was of little consequence until the abolition of slavery in the nineteenth century, and then increased substantially only in those countries that still had open, unmonopolized frontiers, such as Brazil and Argentina.

The second impetus for acquiring large tracts of land was to limit competition. Planters wanted the same privilege that the king and his favored merchants enjoyed. The strategy was to acquire as much land as possible, far more than one could actually farm, and prevent competitors from producing competing crops or competing for limited resources such as firewood and water. The Spanish crown had wanted to avoid large landholdings, but circumstances played into the landholders' hands. With Indians dying, land was available for the taking, and the powerful pushed aside weaker claimants. In Brazil, the crown seemed happy to make grants to their favorites that averaged some 44 square kilometers, to which this privileged elite appended yet more acreage by purchase, theft, or marriage. The large landholders generally had neither the capital nor the labor to work all their property, so most of it lay untouched, and untouchable, just as they had intended. Unlike in North America where land taxes forced overreaching farmers to sell the lands they could not make productive, Iberians had no direct property tax. It cost a landholder nothing to hold vast tracts perpetually vacant. As a result, many forests, soils, and waters experienced less activity and exploitation than they would have under a more equitable system of small farms that would have invited more competition, more intense resource use, and more immigrants. Unutilized private land, which was spitefully denounced by the poor, would in later centuries serve as the most compelling motive for national land reform, finally granting the peasants that which had been unjustly denied them. But for four centuries, and sometimes longer, the powerful successfully locked nature away from the disinherited masses. And most fights over natural resources in the twentieth century were largely over their just distribution, not their scarcity.

Iberia's powers did not entirely neglect resource conservation in their colonies. From the late medieval period, both Spain and Portugal had enacted substantial legislation at home to protect forests, game, and fisheries, and some of this found its way to the New World. But as in Iberia, conservation measures were justified by economic interests. As a result, trees got much of the attention. They were necessary for a number of critical activities, such as shipbuilding, mining, and sugar production, and local shortages inspired some action. But wildlife, soils, waters, and fish were for the most part neglected in the colonies either because they were of little economic value or because they were considered so abundant as to need no protections.

Forest policies varied in time and place, depending on needs. In the mining zones, forests were protected, or reserved, for fuel and shoring for mine shafts. In Brazil, Cuba, and the Pacific coasts of Mexico and Ecuador, the king reserved forests, or monopolized particular trees, in the interests of building ships of war and trade. Bahia, Havana, and Guayaquil built some of the largest and most durable ships of the period, and the colonial powers passed literally hundreds of laws to protect those tropical woods, such as guachapeli, tapinhoã, and mahogany, whose longevity as lumber made these ships so coveted. If their intentions were good, their failures lay in the fact that conservation policy never got much beyond the paper upon which the laws were written.

Enforcement was haphazard at best, and few policing institutions or agents were deployed. In Brazil, the finest ship timbers were often stolen away from the royal shipbuilders to be used in private merchant vessels, but many more were poorly employed as fence posts, crude furniture, and even firewood. More comprehensive and progressive forest legislation arrived in both Spanish and Portuguese America right about 1800, but it arrived too late to do much good, for the independent republics to follow rejected them.

One area in which conservation made good was in the commons. Just as in Iberia, common lands, usually forests and waters, were considered the property of all, including Indians and sometimes slaves. Each citizen had a right to take from the commons what was needed for their day to day needs in fuel, in pasture for animals, in fish, and other miscellaneous goods, under a fairly rigid set of traditional regulations. Even here, despite tradition, the powerful often attempted to take the commons for themselves and bar the poor's access. But the kings of Spain and Portugal remained adamant in keeping them open. In Spanish America, the common forests were in some cases the only way dispossessed Indians could earn a living by gathering firewood, logging timber, and hunting for food. Even in places where these activities were prohibited, officials often looked the other way in mercy to the poorest among them. The result was increased destruction, but regulations probably softened the impact some.

Subsistence rights played a more direct role in protecting forests and waters in Brazil. Here the poor – white, black, slave and Indian – relied heavily on the mangrove forests to feed themselves, just as had the Tupi before them. This exceptional habitat supported dense populations of shellfish, particularly oysters easily harvested from the mangrove's stilt roots, crabs, the favored food of rich and poor alike, and more than 100 species of fish, some permanent and others that returned to the mangroves annually to spawn. Due to these food resources, as well as the mangroves as source of firewood, tannin for leather production, clay for ceramics, and lime in the form of massive shell middens, various interests, including planters and religious orders, had attempted to capture the mangroves for their own use to the exclusion of the poor, but again the crown stood firmly behind the poor's right to eat. And when sugar producers intensified their use of the mangroves for fuel, and leather producers their use of mangrove bark for tannin, operations that destroyed fish habitat, officials sided again with the poor and banned outright the removal of mangrove trees and their bark within broad areas around rural towns. This amounted to forest preservation in the interest of fisheries conservation, and in some locations appears quite successful.

As slight and ineffective as it was, colonial conservation policy must have tempered rapaciousness. Some colonists actually obeyed the laws. And traditional commons are rarely tragedies but can serve as effective means to distribute scarce resources equitably and sustainably. A stark point of comparison is found in what came after independence. Latin America's new national leaders, enamored with liberal economic ideas and national advancement, abandoned even the attempt at conservation for many decades. The commons, forests, fields, and fisheries, were converted to private property to enrich the nation by turning out the poor. The kings of Spain and Portugal, despite their failures, were abler stewards of the poor and of nature than their independent, single-minded successors. And in some cases it was the very greed of kings and the avarice of landholders that limited the production of colonial goods and, thereby, the despoliation of American nature.

TROPICAL DETERMINISM

Desolating earthquakes and hurricanes overtake us unawares, and we live in perpetual ambush of inevitable geographic cataclysms. . . . The climate dissolves our determination and incites our rapid psychological deterioration. The heat ages us before our time and too quickly causes us to decompose; its enervating pressure creates our national temperament.[1]

With Latin American Independence, which was largely complete by 1824, dozens of new republics shook off the chains of colonial economic restrictions and monopoly. While struggling to achieve a semblance of political legitimacy and stability, they embarked on a path projected toward national advancement and material prosperity, hoping that without metropolitan barriers to trade, production, and immigration, they might follow the economic leaps being made by the industrializing north. Isolated Paraguay took significant, although ultimately aborted steps, in the direction of self-sufficient industry, but the rest of the region quickly discovered that with the end of their colonial relationship with Iberia, not only were they free to compete in world markets, they were forced to. There were benefits, of course. Manufactured goods – textiles, tools, tableware, timepieces – long coveted, could now be bought at reasonable prices without paying a premium to Iberia's merchants. But Latin America was in no position to compete in the production of industrial goods and would not be until the next century. The region's clearest path to prosperity was one they already knew

[1] Antonio S. Pedreira, *Insularismo* (San Juan, Puerto Rico: Editorial Edil, 1969 [1934]), 43–4, my translation.

well: the export of agricultural, mineral, and forest products. But now these commodities belonged to the nation, not the king, and specific plants, minerals, and animals, those that could be extracted, packed, and shipped, were virtually regarded as fellow citizens of the nation, partners in the venture for development. Almost a century before there were banana republics, there were copper republics, cattle republics, and coffee republics. Fortunately, the industrializing north required just what Latin America had to offer. Northern industrialists demanded Latin America's natural resources – cotton, tin, rubber, copper, and leather – to feed their voracious machines, and called upon the region's agriculture – sugar, coffee, beef, and bananas – to fuel a rapidly expanding industrial workforce that was exiting temperate agriculture at an astonishing pace.

Racist Dogmas

To achieve national development through sustained exports, a variety of environmental obstacles had to be conquered, some of them real, such as frail transportation networks and virulent plant diseases, and some of them imagined. Let us first examine the imaginary, for these were to profoundly trouble the American mind. The new republics' bid for progress faced two damning theories, both of which were deterministic in character and difficult to dispute. One was racism. From the eighteenth century, European thinkers, rationally enlightened and ethnocentrically motivated, had come to hold that there were four races in the world – white, red, yellow, and black – and that each was unequally endowed with the mental, physical, and cultural capacity to create civilization, science, and political order. Not surprisingly, whites, whose theory this was, ranked themselves on top; the others, those whom whites had colonized and enslaved, were unfit, or less fit, for civilized advance. More damning yet, some theorists avowed that mixed races, such as the mulattos and mestizos who frequently made up national majorities in Latin America, were less capable of cultural evolution than even their benighted progenitors. More than in any other world region, supposed inferior races mixed on an unprecedented scale to create yet more feeble human specimens. Latin Americans who accepted racism, and there were many, despaired of ever being able to keep pace with the white nations. The only solution was to intensively promote the immigration of northern Europeans to whiten and improve the racial stock, an idea that turned urgent policy across much of the region. However, many Latin Americans rejected outright these pseudoscientific, self-congratulatory, theories and responded with their own pseudoscience, arguing that it was, in fact, the Indian and the African, and their mixed descendants, who best adapted to the tropics. They also liked to remind the racists of the noble, ancient Indian civilizations who had ably demonstrated the indigenous capacity for cultural development. Mexican intellectuals, for example, responded by glorifying the Aztecs and equating Aztec achievements with those of the Greeks and Romans.

The second theory, environmental determinism, which was intimately linked to racism, was a more difficult dogma to refute. Environmental determinism argued that nature, more than race, decided human cultural success, some climes fostering civilization and progress, others barbarism and decadence. Environmental and racial determinism were really a unified theory for it was believed that different races had indeed been formed by different climates. A figure as eminent as Gottfried Wilhelm Leibniz theorized in the early eighteenth century that as all humans descended from the same original parents, their different racial expressions must be explained by the environment, in particular, the climate. Environment, then, was more momentous than race; an individual's success in life was determined not so much by the color of her skin but by the nature with which she was surrounded. Under temperate climates, Leibniz alleged, humans "improved": their skins remained white (for he assumed the first humans had light skin), and their features remained refined and pleasing, according to his tastes. Those humans who migrated under the tropical sun degenerated, their skin darkened, their capacity for physical and mental activity waned, and the race's very moral fiber began to unravel. Montesquieu put it bluntly in 1748:

> You will find in the northern climates peoples with few vices, enough virtues, and much sincerity and frankness. As you move toward the countries of the south, you will believe you have moved away from morality itself: the liveliest passions will increase crime. . . . The heat of the climate can be so excessive that the body there will be absolutely without strength. So, prostration will pass even to the spirit; no curiosity, no noble enterprise, no generous sentiment; inclinations will all be passive.[2]

---

[2] Montesquieu, Charles de Secondat, baron de, *The Spirit of the Laws*, trans. A. M. Cohler, B. C. Miller, H. Stone (New York: Cambridge University Press, 1989), 234.

In the latter half of the eighteenth century, the Count de Buffon and Cornelius de Pauw made direct attacks on American nature, arguing for America's geographical degeneracy compared to Europe's enlightening climes. The universal presence of dark skinned inhabitants, from Patagonia to the Arctic, they reasoned, had to be explained by a universally enervating nature. Buffon observed, incorrectly, that American nature had produced no large animals, evidence of a weak environment, and De Pauw added that all American beasts tended toward the grotesque: crocodilians, lizards, snakes, and insects. De Pauw reasoned that Indian men's degeneracy was exhibited by their lack of beard, inclination toward baldness, and, most outrageously, by their ability to lactate. De Pauw went yet further to state the most frightening point of all: American nature would enervate all races of man and beast, even white Europeans. Immigrants, he claimed, became shorter and weaker with every generation, and the fiery sun literally burned up the brain's "delicate and subtle organs." Even European dogs lost the power to bark in the New World, he insisted. Guillaume Thomas François Raynal twisted the blade when he pointed out that in three centuries of colonization, America had produced no scientific, literary, or philosophical minds to compare with Europe's lights. Despite being white and European in blood, America's stock, the creoles, had bred no intellect to rival Newton, Locke, or Voltaire. The European Enlightenment's conclusion on the subject was that a degenerate nature damned all American aspirations for civilization.

North Americans responded unsystematically to Europe's condemnations; Thomas Jefferson, for example, shipped Buffon a stuffed moose to prove the size of American wildlife. But it was Mexican priests who produced scores of tightly reasoned texts to refute the Old World's deprecating views of the New. Juan José de Eguiara y Eguren produced his lengthy *Bibliotheca mexicana* in 1756 to prove the breadth and heights of creole intelligence in New Spain. He emphasized Mexico's renowned scholars of mathematics, theology, and history; he paraded out the formidable skills of the everyday American-born priest who spoke dozens of languages and published scores of grammars and dictionaries; and he noted the strength of Mexico's universities and many libraries: all the products of acute, intelligent minds unaffected by tropical nature. José Joaquín Granados y Gálvez argued that Spanish America was pious, had produced documented miracles, and was the birthplace of many saints, all incontrovertible evidence that nature had not overpowered man's highest moral attainments. In Italy, Francisco Xavier Clavijero, exiled from Mexico with his Jesuit brothers, sought to show there were far more species in America than Buffon, who misunderstood Indian taxonomies, had calculated. Clavijero and others held up the mounting evidence of advanced cultures created by the Aztec and Inca elite, which was greatly bolstered in the 1780s by the discovery of Maya Palenque's rich art, monumental architecture, and evidence of writing. And Manuel de Salas argued that Europe's domesticated animals in 300 years of colonial breeding did not degenerate but, in fact, improved in size, quality, and productivity due to the beneficial qualities of American nature.

Despite such vigorous, largely rational responses, the idea of an environmentally benighted hemisphere remained exceedingly influential. Some European visitors to America imagined their powers and energies draining from their bodies as they entered the tropical waters that separated the two worlds. Adele Toussaint-Samson, sailing to Brazil in the mid-1850s, described the bodily effect of entering equatorial waters as one of general torpor among crew and passengers:

> all drag themselves about, hardly speaking; . . . a day does not pass that has not its little scandal and its little attack of nerves. . . . This exciting temperature crazes one at such a point that at night I have often thought myself under the power of hashish, so much my mind was floating while waking and sleeping, taking alternately dream for reality, and reality for dream.[3]

She further observed that this sun-induced lassitude spawned uncontrollable sexual impulses and improprieties, a common corollary of determinism's climatic theories. To the men, even the most "dreadful" females suddenly charmed, and she warned husbands never to let their wives travel alone (as did her husband) on an equatorial voyage. On her arrival in Brazil she concluded that all Europeans would fail to thrive there, and that Brazil's mix of Europeans, Africans, and Indians, what she called the Brazilian race, was physically weak, morally corrupt, and universally arrogant, although she was among those who admitted their acute intelligence. The fear of sun, heat, and humidity followed white Europeans to all their tropical colonies. Imperialists wore their pith helmets and so-called cholera belts because they were specially designed to block the harmful rays of the tropical sun that caused not just disease, but racial degeneracy. White females did not leave the house without a

---

[3] Adèle Toussaint-Samson, A *Parisian in Brazil*, ed. June E. Hahner, trans. Emma Toussaint (Wilmington, DE: Scholarly Resources, 2001), 23.

parasol, and British administrators and Brazil's emperors built homes and palaces with somber interior colors in the highest, coolest mountains to which they had access. And despite overwhelming evidence to the contrary, a few continued to believe that the white race would degenerate so quickly as to become sterile and fail to reproduce. Charles Woodruff, a U.S. Army doctor in the Philippines, argued as late as 1905 in his *The Effects of Tropical Light on White Men* that Europeans migrated toward extinction when they settled in the tropics. In India, he alleged, there were no third-generation Europeans.

Latin Americans lived very much under the shadow of this pejorative ideology, convinced they imbibed a debased atmosphere, doubtful of their society's potential to overcome an enemy so intractable as tropical nature. North Americans continued to fight these formidable theories by insisting the U.S. climate was being mischaracterized, that it was, in fact, temperate and benign, despite the presence of the dark Indian race. They also put forward figures like Jefferson and Franklin as homegrown geniuses to prove the climate did not enfeeble the colonial mind. And late in the nineteenth century, Frederick Jackson Turner turned nature to the North Americans' favor, arguing that the North American environment, particularly the invigorating wilderness at the frontier, had in fact shaped Yankee successes, molding a virile citizenry of hardy, can-do individualists. North Americans, in their own minds, had largely overcome determinism's prejudices by century's end.

By contrast, Turner's Brazilian contemporaries articulated a moody, environmental fatalism. In the mid-1890s, Euclides da Cunha served as a war correspondent during the Brazilian army's annihilation of Canudos, a militant, millennial society in Brazil's northeast. The people of Canudos were a textbook example of a racially mixed community with unequal parentage from Portugal, Africa, and indigenous America. But Da Cunha recognized that racially they were little different from the rest of Brazilians. What made them so opposed to modernity and liberal reason was not their race but the nature in which they lived. Da Cunha blamed the region's environment, which was irrepressibly hot, plagued with a spiny, desiccated vegetation, and scourged by drought, for the creation of a backland "race" with its feral, religious fanaticism. Canudos' indomitable citizens defeated three expeditions sent against them; the third of these was a slaughter. The fourth, consisting of national troops and artillery, finally annihilated the community, which would not surrender. The defenders fought like demons, Da Cunha argued, because they had been nurtured by a hellish landscape.

Likewise, Aluízio de Azevedo, a novelist who eloquently denounced racism and racist ideology in nearly all his books, could not come to throw off the pervasive influence of environmental determinism. Unlike the North American frontier, Brazil's nature, he maintained, degraded civil humans. In his most famous work, *The Slum*, he described on one hand the tenacious ambition of a female African slave whose intelligence makes her Portuguese master rich and respected, a pointed challenge to racial determinism. However, the novel's main thread is the retrogression of a Portuguese immigrant couple, Jerónimo and his wife Piedade, who arrive in Brazil with aspirations, property, sobriety, and fidelity, but who under the influence of Rio de Janeiro's sultry, lascivious climate, end up drunken, lazy, riotous, and criminal. Piedade, abandoned by Jerónimo, becomes a prostitute; Jerónimo, to win the exclusive affection of his mulatto mistress, commits murder.

Even the Nazi sense of racial superiority was seemingly defeated by Latin American nature. In the 1930s, the Nazi government sent a German geographer to study German immigrants, not in Brazil's temperate south where most Germans settled, but in tropical Espirito Santo well to the north. He expected to prove that the Aryan race excelled in all climes. He was greatly disappointed. What he found was a squalid settlement made up of a peasantry that other than its light skin and blue eyes was indistinguishable from their racially mixed neighbors. Not surprisingly, the report was suppressed in Germany.

If tropical nature determined the fate of individuals and cultures, as was so often portrayed, Latin America truly had reason to despair. But neither theory, racial or environmental, was backed by anything more than biased, carefully selected evidence by individuals who for the most part had never visited the American tropics. It was fairly obvious that some of the first and greatest civilizations arose in hot, even humid, places inhabited by peoples with dark skin, both in the Old and New Worlds. Some of the most "favorable," temperate climes, such as Northern Europe, had been inhabited by white people who for thousands of years remained barbaric despite frequent contact with civilized tropical peoples. Despite continuing, credible attacks on this worldview, especially by Latin Americans in the early twentieth century, the educated white classes found it difficult to renounce that which justified their high social and economic positions over the assumed racially and environmentally determined under classes. Few of those in power in Latin America wanted to entertain the possibility that nondeterministic cultural, political, and economic factors might explain the region's relatively slow development. It was easier to believe in determinism and fatalism than it was to struggle to change, at great social risk, what, in fact, could be changed. As a result, determinism's popularity and academic credentials were ascendant right into the 1940s. It was not until Nazism promoted the genocide of inferior races, determinism's logical, horrible, conclusion, that environmental determinism was finally discredited and its academic boosters removed from the universities. Latin America's elite finally threw off the chains of environmental determinism, for they, like North Americans, did not like what it said about them and their potential for cultural progress. However, vestiges of racism remain unofficially in place and continue to justify the inequitable features of Latin America's material gains.

TROPICAL DISEASES

That environmental determinism brushed in such large strokes proved imaginary and excessively fatalistic does not mean that the American tropics did not present substantial challenges to culture. Nature decided neither race nor intelligence, nor did it determine the region's ultimate cultural success or failure, but it did profoundly shape the contours of Latin American civilization, just as it did others. The same climate that permitted the harvesting of multiple crops each year and that indeed made it possible to grow such export crops as sugar, coffee, and bananas, also presented culture with diseases, insects, weather extremes, and natural disasters that plagued human bodies, attacked plant tissues, destroyed urban infrastructure, and even influenced geopolitics. It bears repeating that little of this led to inevitabilities. Both nature and culture are too irrepressibly clever to be entirely determined by the other, and altogether too doggedly tenacious to fail to transform one another appreciably. What remains difficult to quantify is whether tropical nature presented greater challenges to human culture than did temperate nature. Recent work on disasters, diseases, and agriculture in temperate climes seems to suggest that the term temperate may be a misnomer. But there is little question that tropical America offered entirely different challenges than those faced by Turner's North American frontiersmen, and the European settlers' lack of tropical experience must of placed them at some disadvantage.

As we have seen, disease conquered the human species in sixteenth-century America. But come independence, it also helped liberate it. The French colony of Saint-Domingue, as Haiti was formerly known, had surpassed Barbados as the most valuable real estate in the world by the late eighteenth century: its 7,000 plantations produced much of the world's sugar and coffee, as well as indigo, cacao, cotton, and tobacco. Saint-Domingue alone accounted for 40 percent of the value of French foreign trade, and France's rivals coveted its productivity.

The French Revolution introduced ideas and made promises too heady to suppress on an island with a half a million slaves, as many slaves as held by the entire United States. The first group to speak of rights, however, were Haiti's free mulattos. Because they owned slaves, they did not speak of liberty, but because they held land, they began to demand fraternity and equality with the colony's white population. Unsatisfied with the whites' unenthusiastic response, the free mulattos took up arms in 1791, and in the chaos of one race war, another erupted of far more serious consequence. The black fear prudently hidden at the back of every slave master's mind, white and mulatto, burst into dreadful reality. Slaves in the north of the colony rose against their masters, killed, often by the cruelest means, everyone who was white, and destroyed everything that reminded them of their bondage. Bands of slaves set fire to their masters' homes, to the churches whose bells had called them to work, to sugar mills, fields of cane, and to groves of coffee. Within a week, 180 sugar plantations and 900 coffee estates were in ashes. The conflagration spread, and soon the former slaves controlled the entire colony. Haiti had effectively become the first independent state in Latin America. The slaves' fight for freedom, however, was far from over.

Slave anger, numbers, and organization explained the revolution's initial success, but disease played a central role in keeping Haiti free. It was the British who first thought to take advantage of the French loss. In 1793, they invaded Haiti, hoping to make it part of their Caribbean island empire. The plan was to take the land, kill all the rebels, and replace them with new slaves imported from Africa. When the news arrived that British troops had captured Port-au-Prince, London's church bells rang at length in celebration. However, within a couple years, 50,000 British soldiers in Haiti had died, most of them to yellow fever, and the few, fortunate survivors fled for home. Haiti survived its first test of freedom.

When Napoleon came to power in France in the next decade, the recapture of Saint-Domingue was an obvious imperial priority, one that would enrich the new French empire and help extend it effectively into Louisiana. In 1802, under the leadership of Charles Victor Emmanuel Leclerc, his crack general and brother-in-law, Napoleon dispatched a massive expeditionary force to the island, the first wave of which comprised some 54 ships and 23,000 disciplined, motivated soldiers. In lightning strikes, French forces quickly occupied much of the colony. But then they too started dying. French soldiers who contracted yellow fever complained they felt as if their brains would burst. Their bodies yellowed as they neared death, the source of the disease's English name, and they expired vomiting waves of black blood, the origin of the disease's Spanish name, *vomito negro* (black vomit). Mortality among the soldiery was more than 80 percent, and the generals died right along with the rank and file, including Leclerc. The French buried their dead at night to hide their declining numbers from the enemy, but the former slaves knew the toll, and even though they often bested the French on the field, they were also willing to watch and wait rather than attack. Haitian general Jean-Jacques Dessalines told his troops to be patient: "They will do well at first, but soon they will fall ill and die like flies."[4] Despite massive reinforcements, disease continued to overwhelm the invaders, and Napoleon began to pull out by late 1803 after a total of 55,000 French dead. Fewer than 4,000 of the expedition's entire force survived the disaster. Napoleon gave up Saint-Domingue, and he sold Louisiana, now a lost cause, to the United States. Haitians officially declared themselves America's second independent state on January 1, 1804.

Just as yellow fever assisted Haiti's slaves, over the previous century and a half it had also helped the Spanish to maintain their colonial possessions against foreign invasion. Yellow fever had become endemic in the circum-Caribbean by the mid-seventeenth century, and did so largely because of the arrival of sugar and white Europeans. It is likely that British slave ships introduced the virus and its mosquito vector, *Aedes aegypti*, which thrives on human blood, but can survive in a pinch, believe it or not, on sugar cane juice. The first major yellow fever outbreak occurred in 1647 killing as many as 30 percent of the population in affected areas. But the killing was discriminate. Yellow fever can infect anyone, but it is most lethal to white adults. Children of any race who contract the virus suffer very little, if at all, and thereby acquire lifetime immunity. And as we have seen, West Africans, who have lived with the virus for centuries, appear to inherit a genetic immunity from their

---

[4]   Quoted in J. R. McNeill, "Ecology, Epidemics, and Empires: Environmental Change and the Geopolitics of Tropical America, 1600–1825," *Environment and History* 5 (1999): 181.

parents. So in the Caribbean, established whites, who often contracted yellow fever as children, and their slaves tended to fare much better during an epidemic than outsiders. And the outsiders at most risk were British and French expeditionary forces, made up almost entirely of white, adult males who had never been exposed to the disease. In 1655, the British captured Jamaica in a single week, but in six months, 47 percent of their soldiers had died, almost none due to battle, and half the remainder were sick. Some admirals had learned that you either conquered a Caribbean possession quickly, as in Jamaica, or yellow fever conquered you first. Over the course of the seventeenth century, the Spanish had strengthened their fortifications such that quick victories were more difficult. During the War of Spanish Succession (1701–1714), the British and French mounted 19 expeditions against the Spanish Caribbean, all of which failed, 18 of them due to the microbes that so promptly latched on to the outsider's susceptible bodies. There were many other such examples in the eighteenth century but neither the French nor British seemed to remember past lessons when they set off disastrously to re-enslave Haiti.

If before and during independence tropical disease favored Americans against their European enemies, there was nothing favorable about its persistent presence thereafter. Yellow fever, malaria, schistosomiasis, hookworm, among many other viral, bacterial, and parasitic infections, harmed tropical civilization by reducing life expectancy and population growth. In temperate regions, these diseases were intermittent, seasonal, or nonexistent. Mosquitoes that carried yellow fever, for example, could not thrive below 24°C. So, while a city like New York might have an occasional summer outbreak with the arrival of an infected ship, cold weather snapped the epidemic. In the warm, humid tropics, although generally more common in the rainy season, epidemics could occur at any time making them more detrimental to human populations and far more difficult to control. Between 1850 and 1901, an astonishing 56,000 persons died of yellow fever in Rio de Janeiro. And during the nineteenth century, little or nothing could be done as science had not yet discovered the causes of most diseases. Even quarantine was largely useless in cases where mosquitoes were the vectors, a link not proven for malaria and yellow fever until 1897 and 1900, respectively, and not widely accepted for another two decades.

Hence, life expectancy in Latin America was considerably lower than it was for North America. We explain today's gap in life expectancy, which has greatly narrowed, by poverty and limited medical services.

In the early nineteenth century, when both regions were equally poor and equally ignorant about the causes and cures of disease, the gap was cavernous. North Americans lived, on average, to age 40, far longer than Brazilians of the same period who only lived to age 27. In other words, North American lives were a third longer than Brazilian lives, which gave women living in temperate regions many more years of potential childbearing. Even among slaves, the differences in life expectancy, north and south, were substantial. Brazil's slaves lived to an average age of 23, whereas in the United States, slaves lived to age 35. Some argued that this was evidence that North Americans treated their slaves better than Brazilians, but tropical disease can alone explain most of the gap. Free people in both societies lived about 15 percent longer than their slaves. And among slaves too, life expectancy made a significant demographic difference. The only place in the Americas where slaves consistently reproduced their population by birth was the United States, and this was largely due to their longer life expectancy. In tropical Latin America, from Havana to Rio de Janeiro, too many slaves died before they reached or exhausted their reproductive years.

A final example of the impact of tropical disease in Latin America is hookworm, just one of many potentially debilitating parasites that have attracted less attention because their effects are usually chronic and unseen rather than catastrophically apparent. José Bento Monteiro Lobato was among those of Latin America's landowning class that accepted wholesale the implications of tropical determinism. In a mean-spirited editorial he penned against the peasantry who lived on and about his own land in Brazil, he characterized the rural laborer as a racial degenerate who destroyed the landscape, including Monteiro Lobato's own property, by fire and ignorance, just like his Indian progenitors. His fellow landowners admired the piece so much Monteiro Lobato turned the attack into a literary career. He created the character Jeca Tatu, literally translated as "backward armadillo," who came to represent the national hillbilly, not just a punching bag and butt of jokes, but a symbol of Brazil's failure, a symbol for whom there were no remedial lessons. In story after story Monteiro Lobato ridiculed, condemned, and damned poor Jeca Tatu. Slack-jawed, squatting on the ground, Jeca stared mesmerized at his wasteful conflagrations, enunciating with characteristic twang "ain't that fire purdy." Monteiro Lobato smirked that the peasant destroyed 50 square kilometers of good land in order to harvest just enough food for him, his wife, and his dog to go hungry. For that is the way his parents did it. And like his Indian parents before him, he was "incapable of evolution, impervious to progress." Monteiro Lobato chided Brazil's romantic novelists who had tried to redeem the Indians from racial determinism by literary idealization. "How beautiful they are in a romance, and how ugly in reality," he pronounced.[5]

In the first decades of the twentieth century, contemporary to Monteiro Lobato's popular attacks, both national and international organizations were struggling to defeat the plagues that caused human disease. In Brazil, the Oswaldo Cruz Institute discovered previously unknown plagues, such as Chagas disease, promoted the eradication of the vectors of known diseases such as malaria, and offered vaccinations against smallpox. Of particular attention were parasitic worms that through microscopic analysis were proven to be an almost universal scourge among Brazil's rural poor. On São Paulo's coffee plantations, infection rates were essentially 100 percent among workers above the age of eight.

Hookworm was among the most prevalent. To detail the parasitic life cycle of a hookworm in its human host is to confront a story most of us would prefer not to hear, nor to believe. The hookworm larva, which resides in the soil, enters the human body by burrowing powerfully into the soles of the feet or between the toes of field workers, leaving an intensely itchy red rash at the point of entry called ground itch. The larva continues tunneling until it enters a blood vessel whose current it rides through the body, passing through the heart, to the parasite's first destination, the outer surface of the lung. It then mines its way to the lung's interior and climbs the windpipe to the back of the throat. If the infestation is heavy, the number of larvae in the windpipe can cause the host to cough them up. The larvae that survive expectoration are swallowed and enter their domain in the small intestine. The unerring migration of birds, at which we marvel, seems a small accomplishment compared to the hookworm's navigational feat. The hookworm attaches itself with claw-like teeth and consumes not the host's food but the blood of the intestinal wall. The males secrete sperm and the females produce thousands of eggs which exit the body on defecation and thus reinfect the soil. The fully formed worm, about 2 centimeters in length, has a lifespan of 14 years, and by repeated infection an individual host can carry several hundred hookworms which together cause anemia by consuming the blood's iron. Japanese immigrants, who brought with them to Brazil the native Asian hookworm (*Ankylostoma*

---

[5] José Bento Monteiro Lobato, "Urupes," in *Obras Completas*, Vol. 1 (São Paulo: Editora Brasiliense, 1968), 275, 279, my translations.

duodenale), hosted, on average, an additional 233 American hookworms (*Necator americanus*) within 8 years of their arrival. The hookworms' common symptoms were fatigue and lassitude, just the symptoms determinists argued were inherent to tropical climates and the dark races.

Monteiro Lobato's racism and determinism, with all its vituperation, did not to his credit run very deep. His literary fame had made him eminent friends, some of them associates of the Oswaldo Cruz Institute, and upon learning of their findings he summarily repented of his racist aggressions. Here in the Brazilian gut, Monteiro Lobato now contended, was the cause of our backwardness. It was neither race, nor sun, nor climate: Brazil's lack of progress could be pinned down to a specific, named, blood sucking worm that sapped the physical and creative energies of the rural classes. In the preface to the fourth edition of his popular, damning collection of stories, published in 1918, he prepared his readers with the warning that Jeca Tatu was not backward because he was racially degenerate – he was backward because he was ill; two thirds of Brazilians carried in their blood and guts the progeny of an insidious enemy which makes them, like Jeca, ugly and inert. And most significantly, he continued, Jeca could be cured. Monteiro Lobato from thence used his literary talents to promote the eradication of Brazil's plagues, turning his censorious pen away from the peasants and onto government officials who resisted public funding for vaccinations, de-wormers, and hygienic education. Then, in his most popular and widely distributed story, he wrote of Jeca's son, Jeca Tatuzinho, who discovers his legion of microbial pillagers, seeks treatment, and goes on to become a successful, respected farmer – from ravaged to riches.

The story played an important role in cultural change. By the early twentieth century, yellow fever could be prevented by mosquito abatement, and hookworm could be prevented and cured. But success against these plagues required a population that was educated about their dangers and who trusted government officials. Thousands openly resisted vaccination to the point of rioting in the streets. Many rural workers refused to give stool samples to medical teams and never learned of their parasitic burden. De-wormers could be administered generally with little harm, but many declined to take them. The state, with the aid of international agencies like the Rockefeller Foundation, built rural, public latrines that could solve the problem of hookworm reinfection, but rural workers would not walk to the latrine and continued to defecate in and about the fields they worked unshod, thus maintaining the cycle of infection from feces to feet. A more complete understanding of how nature actually harmed culture increased humanity's power to fight the good fight, but the fight was rarely easy, nor was it always successful. And even the complete conquest of disease did not determine that poor peasants became successful landholders, as the realist Monteiro Lobato had romantically narrated. Racial, social, and economic injustice, more than environmental determinants, remained the primary obstacles to individual economic success. After serving time in jail for his political ideas during the dictatorship of Getulio Vargas, Monteiro Lobato, in one more novel, turns Jeca Tatu into a hardworking peasant who joins the movement for land reform to smash the final barrier to his social and racial liberation.

Natural Disasters

Another set of natural barriers to cultural advance were Latin America's terrible geologic and weather events. Earthquakes and volcanoes, running from Mexico to Chile and across the arc of the Caribbean islands, have also been epidemic to Latin America's tropics, at least relative to the rest of North America. The consequence has been countless deaths and incalculable demolition. Within a single generation, three earthquakes – Mexico City, 1985, 20,000 dead; Managua, 1972, 6,000 dead; and Lima, 1970, 66,000 dead – killed more persons than all U.S. natural disasters of the last two centuries. The Valparaiso quake of 1960, the most powerful ever recorded at 9.6 on the Richter scale, killed 20,000. And San Salvador, El Salvador since 1524 has experienced 19 earthquakes, 12 of them severe enough to level most, and in one case all, of the city's buildings. Hurricanes have also taken a mortal toll. As recently as 1998, Hurricane Mitch killed 18,000 in Central America. To the dead, of course, we must attach billions of dollars in material destruction to civilization's very fabric, infrastructure that has often taken centuries of labor to put in place. Mitch, which parked itself over Central America for weeks, set Honduras back 50 years, some contend, destroying 50 percent of that year's crops, 70,000 homes, 70 percent of Honduran roads, including 92 bridges, and the nation's water distribution system, which left 4.5 million people without safe drinking water.

Hurricanes have probably been the most deadly events in Latin America's history if for no other reason than their regularity. Every July 15 of the late eighteenth century, an ominous salvo of cannon announced the arrival of the hurricane season to the citizens of French

Guadalupe; and on October 15, another salvo mercifully declared its end. It was season of trepidation. The Great Hurricane of 1780 took more lives than did Mitch when it passed over Martinique, St. Eustatius and Barbados. In fact, 1780 was the most disastrous hurricane year ever recorded. Eight total storms killed an estimated 27,000 people on land and at sea, more than died in all the battles of the contemporary, seven-year, American revolution. Partisans of that revolution, however, did not go unscathed. The British, French, and Spanish all had squadrons in the Caribbean in 1780 to either attack or assist British colonials, and hundreds were lost as the succession of storms overtook each fleet one at a time.

Hurakan, the Maya god, was a fearful deity who controlled winds, rains, waves, tides, and floods. The Taino Indians depicted him as a howling head with flailing, spiraling arms, an image strikingly similar to the hurricane's meteorological icon found on today's weather maps. The Taino believed Hurakan's recurrent angry outbursts fractured the islands on which they lived from the mainland, such were the powers of his storms. Hurakan continued to harass and terrorize the region's new arrivals, and Columbus may have been the first European to experience a tropical storm on his second voyage in 1494. Las Casas claimed hurricanes the world's most powerful storms and, like the natives, looked to heaven to explain them. In 1508, a hurricane destroyed the first settlement at Santo Domingo, forcing its relocation, and the Spanish fleet system, in fact, all commerce, attempted to schedule itself outside of the hurricane season. It was occasionally unsuccessful: the entire fleet, 56 ships, was lost off the Florida Straits in September 1622, and the region is littered with the storm wrecks of treasure ships that entomb silver coins whose dates span the colonial era. Without the hurricane, Spanish commerce could have been more consistent and certainly less hazardous.

A hurricane's physical damage to cities and commercial infrastructure could be catastrophic. In the worst storms, not a single building might be left erect, not even the heavily-built, stone churches. Such was the case on Barbados in 1780, and one survivor proposed that an earthquake accompanied the storm in order to explain the flattened public buildings. Warehouses and other commercial buildings, much of them built waterside, were eviscerated by the storm surge, and ships were dashed from their moorings. Havana's 1844 hurricane destroyed 200 ships in the city's well-sheltered harbor; two years later another Havana storm destroyed 300 more vessels. Ships were displaced up to a half mile inland, and not infrequently they served as emergency housing for the inhabitants who had lost their homes.

Because the late summer and fall hurricane season coincided with the harvest of most crops, the storms were particularly devastating to agriculture. High winds reportedly unearthed the cassava plant, despite its deep, heavy roots, which meant that the more tender crops of coffee, sugar, and tobacco stood little chance. A tropical storm might drive salt spray well inland, blackening leaves and salinizing the soils that could take years to recover. Diego Fernández Herrera was faint at the sight of his Cuban plantation after a late season storm in October of 1846.

> I am on my *cafetal*, San José! I no longer see the forests or the numerous palm trees. Nothing of the banana plants. All the coffee trees have been obliterated. The ripened fruit is enveloped in muck and weeds. . . . An indescribable stupor seizes my faculties at that moment. I stop my horse and brace myself so as not to fall off my saddle.[6]

Over vast areas not a single tree, bush, or crop remained standing. If the landholder's spirit was dashed by the wind, it was the poor and the slaves who suffered in body. Even if they survived the storm's battering, death often came in the calm, sunny days following the disaster for lack of food. Slaves, for as much as three quarters of their diet, relied on bananas and plantains, the most fragile of all crops that were decapitated by even the smallest of hurricanes. Chickens, another significant source of slave food, were blown out to sea. Without food and with very little hope of outside aid, slaves starved. Masters, out of humanity and self-interest, sent for food, but the lack of shipping during the hurricane season put most such relief out of reach. One hurricane of the 1780 season killed and starved 15–20,000 Jamaican slaves by one report, nearly 10 percent of the island's slave population, and an English master described the "misery of beholding hundreds of wretched beings wasting around you, clamoring for food, and imploring assistance which you cannot bestow."[7] Another West Indian hurricane in 1785 brought hunger and death to another 15,000 slaves.

It should be little surprising that such devastation might change the course of social and economic history. The Caribbean's islands, due to restricted geography, had few economic choices when it came to

---

6   Quoted in Louis A. Pérez, Jr., *Winds of Change: Hurricanes and the Transformation of Nineteenth-Century Cuba* (Chapel Hill: University of North Carolina Press, 2001), 83–4.
7   Quoted in Louis A. Pérez, Jr., *Winds of Change*, 124.

agricultural exports, and severe weather events further limited options. Three major hurricanes, in 1842, 1844, and 1846, intersected on or near Havana, bringing repeated destruction to western Cuba. All production plummeted. Cotton exports fell from 907 metric tons in 1840 to only 4 tons in 1850, beekeeping was annihilated and had not recovered even by the 1860s, and food production fell short of domestic needs requiring imports. However, it was coffee that took the greatest casualties, for the winds not only shattered the coffee trees, but also the palms and natural ceiba trees that shaded Cuba's quality coffee groves. On the eve of the 1842 hurricane, coffee's value to the Cuban economy was four times that of sugar. After 1846, as hard as it was to let go, coffee planters bowed to the harsh lessons of three successive hurricanes. Rather than reinvest their damaged capital in the reestablishment of coffee trees that took years to mature and produce their first crop, Cuban planters concentrated their efforts on growing sugar. Sugar was also devastated by strong hurricanes, but it could be replanted and harvested for cash within a year. Sugar had already been growing in importance in Cuba, but thereafter it would define Cuba's economy. Coffee exports fell by more than 90 percent over the period 1840 and 1858, and sugar expanded into the coffee void.

The change was lamentable for a variety of reasons, ecological and cultural. Coffee was ecologically more sustainable than sugar. Planters grew coffee in existing forests, or in planted palm forests, which together controlled erosion and made quite a pleasant landscape, according to many observers. They bemoaned the loss of coffee's varied scenery for the monotony of cane plantings. Coffee also did not make the same kinds of fuel demands on the forests that sugar now caused to recede at exceptional rates. Coffee's replacement by sugar also bode ill for the slaves. Coffee planting was smaller in scale than sugar, the work relatively easy, and the relationship with the master reportedly less harsh. Coffee slaves had more free time, better diets, and better housing than sugar slaves. Slave birthrates on Cuba's coffee estates matched slave mortality. Not so in sugar. Annual slave mortality in the sugar mills was a cataclysmic 18 percent compared to the merely appalling 5 percent of the coffee estates. As many as 50,000 Cuban slaves were transferred from coffee to sugar after the 1840s, and the change in conditions probably played a role in increased instances of slave unrest. The world price for coffee was generally higher than sugar, but as hurricanes imposed significant costs of production, Cuba relented. It was Brazil, without hurricanes, that moved in the other direction, reallocating considerable resources and slaves in order to shift from sugar to the more profitable coffee.

In addition to their social, economic, and demographic impacts, hurricanes have probably had a greater psychological bearing on the Latin American mind than all other natural disasters. They were certainly the most feared. Nearly every Caribbean citizen can tell you their hurricane stories, often recalled from an impressionable age that could envisage in the terror of the moment no explanation other than the world was coming to an end. No other natural disaster seems to have the hurricane's power to make an impression on the human mind, and regional histories and individual lives are chronologically separated into the time before and after particular storms. Earthquakes might mete out death in equal measure, but their arrival was infrequent, entirely unannounced, and their departure was immediate; usually the earth stopped shaking about the time people realized what is happening, barring a few after shocks. Volcanoes inspired warranted dread, but their locations were well known, they did not move about unpredictably, and they came once in centuries. Hurricanes, which churned all the elements – earth, wind, and water – into chaos, visited regularly, gave just enough warning to send people into a panic, and, even when moving quickly, subjected their victims to many hours of shrieking terror.

Consider the experience of millions of hurricane survivors who lived before storm prediction and tracking, before electric lighting, and before many residential dwellings could withstand the winds of even a category two storm. At the appearance of dark clouds, a reverse in the trade winds, and a strong sea odor, signs of an approaching storm, the greatest immediate concerns for residents were to get to higher ground and to find shelter. Often, neither was available on short notice, and if the storm came in the middle of the night, a black, impenetrable darkness that could not be lit by candle or lantern prevented flight in any meaningful direction. Many knew that to stay in your home was foolhardy, for outside flooded areas, most of the dead fell crushed beneath their own walls and roof timbers. Churches and large public buildings might serve as refuge, or where possible, caves, but many residents, especially rural folk, were forced to ride out the storm in flimsy dwellings, or to expose themselves to the direct forces of the wind and flying debris. In category four and five hurricanes, in which wind speeds exceed 200 kilometers per hour, gravity becomes a force of secondary influence and persons unprotected were frequently carried away. One desperate tactic involved locking arms with family, neighbors, and strangers, struggling sometimes for hours to tether one another to the ground while the howling wind cast rain, branches, and roof tiles into blinded faces. Still, after the storms, the dead were found high in distant trees, and even livestock were known to crash through roofs onto huddled families.

Natural phenomena do not become natural disasters until they run into humans or their esteemed property. Some cultures learn to adjust to the inevitable. The Inca, for example, lived in constant preparation for drought and built structures that were virtually earthquake proof. We do not know to what extent the Taino attempted to hurricane-proof their culture, but unlike Europeans who tied themselves to the coasts for commercial reasons, the Taino seemed to have prudently lived above the floodplains that European's so blithely inhabited. The Maya elite built some heavy, stone buildings that withstood the force of wind, but most Indians throughout the region built lightly, and at little cost, and probably expected their housing, which was easily and cheaply rebuilt, to disappear in the storm while they took shelter in rocks and caves. The European attitude of impermanence and the dire poverty of much of the Caribbean population worked against coherent preparation for the storms' very mortal blows. Wealthy planters built masonry homes of multiple stories in the cities which could withstand all but the strongest hurricanes, but their tile roofs often crashed down upon them. The poor built of wattle and daub, or in later years sheet metal, that offered no protection. And housing was often located in low lying areas. Even in the colonial era, much could have been done in the implementation of building codes and zoning to reduce hurricane mortalities drastically. But even today, 60 percent of Caribbean housing takes no benefit from building codes or basic technical inputs.

And disaster can emerge from political choices of a more immediate nature. The single worst disaster in Latin America's history was the total loss in 1902 of the thriving city of St. Pierre on Martinique, called by some the "Paris of the West Indies." Despite constant rumblings and a severe eruption and mudflow, local officials and political hopefuls continued to give official assurances that Mt. Pelée, whose steam loomed ominously over the city, posed no threat, and the governor even invited rural folk to come into town where they would find safety. Their reports had no basis in scientific fact but in political expediency, for they wanted everyone in town for the big election slated for May 11. The governor even set up a checkpoint on the main evacuation route to turn back would-be refugees. But the election never took place. A massive eruption on May 8th disgorged a pyroclastic flow upon the city leveling nearly all its buildings and killing 28,000 citizens in an instant. Only two survived, one of them a local troublemaker who had been sentenced to a week's solitary confinement in the town's dungeon. Even in the deep, jail cell, excavated from solid rock, the volcano's furious heat entered his tiny grated window and burned much of his body. His relative good luck turned good fortune, clinching him a contract with Barnum and Bailey Circus with whom he toured for many years as the "Lone Survivor of St. Pierre." Poor preparations and responses can turn natural phenomena into more severe natural disasters than necessary, but to live in the Caribbean or Mexico, regardless of preparation, will be more precarious than life in, say, Brazil where hurricanes, volcanoes, and significant earthquakes have never or rarely been recorded.

Some have blamed natural disasters in Latin America for a pronounced cultural fatalism, but disasters generally create more survivors than victims. The disaster becomes a shared memory, a bond of unity between those who survive, sometimes repeatedly, the most powerful events anyone can imagine. Destruction, but also truly superhuman acts of altruism, are recounted at gatherings, and a sense of shared experience and common challenge distill upon the community. And despite living in the path of death and destruction, humans resist moving, showing that attachment to place, or at least to property, are still functioning cultural elements. When Hurricane Hattie shattered Belize City in 1961, moving the capital inland to higher ground was an unusual response, without precedent, and without imitators. More common was Fidel Castro's attitude after Hurricane Flora in 1963, stating that "a Revolution is a force more powerful than nature;" and his encouragement that "the hurricane has done its thing; now its time to do ours" parallels the way Cubans have together weathered nearly a half century of economic and political hardships unrelated to meteorology. To be Cuban is to be a survivor, to be unmovable and stoic in the face of acknowledged and accepted hazards. The same can be said of the residents of Mexico City, Lima, and Managua who, despite having suffered some of the most devastating earthquakes ever to hit large urban centers, have rebuilt leaving few to no signs of their catastrophic recent pasts.

PLANT MALADIES

Diseases, like disasters, were seemingly inoperable obstacles to Latin America's cultural progress. Before the twentieth century, very little indeed could be done to combat the tropical maladies that weakened and killed the people on whose backs national greatness was to be built. The only remedy was to import more manpower, a need satisfied by slavery before the mid-nineteenth century, and by migration, foreign and domestic, thereafter. Yet there was another class of diseases that while having no direct bearing on human health beleaguered the promoters of the "export for greatness" model. Just as tropical viruses, bacteria, and parasites afflicted humans and animals, so did they afflict plants. And as plants made up a substantial proportion of Latin America's chosen exports, plant diseases thwarted human aspirations by attacking the nation's botanical citizens, both indigenous and introduced. Two stories about fungi illustrate the seriousness of this challenge. South American Leaf Blight, a native fungus that defoliates the native rubber tree, wrecked the Amazon's preeminently profitable position as rubber supplier to the automobile age. And Panama disease and Sigatoka, two introduced fungi that mutilated banana trees, incited a ruinous imperialism that scourged huge tracts of Central American territory and stole away the political sovereignty of entire nations in order to put bananas on the American breakfast table.

Rubber, which derives from the latex, or sap, of a small number of tropical trees and shrubs, was a natural product of fascinating properties. Indians had turned latex into a variety of goods, including the balls for Mesoamerica's ritual games, waterproof textiles, and containers. Latex was not only waterproof, but elastic, an extremely rare quality in a natural product. It could also be molded into any shape desired, and with just a little imagination, one could dream up hundreds of ways this material could be turned into saleable commodities. But up to the 1830s, latex had very limited applications, amounting to little more than the production of waterproofed fabric and pencil erasers (which the English called rubbers, and hence the English name). Natural latex became brittle in cold and gelatinous in heat, making it alternately useless and messy. Here was a raw material that needed to be enlightened by science, and in 1839, Charles Goodyear, a luckless inventor to that point, discovered the process of vulcanization in a kitchen accident. By heating raw latex in the presence of sulphur, rubber became consistent in texture and resistant to abrasion, yet it remained waterproof and elastic. It was a smashing and timely success for human culture. While Goodyear buoyantly predicted rubber would be made into jewelry, banknotes, ship sails, and musical instruments, at first it was employed in more mundane items such as boots, slickers, rubber bands, basketballs, golf balls, and condoms, the first cheap and reasonably reliable contraceptive. But it was tires, first for bicycles in the 1890s, and then automobiles after 1900, which caused world demand to climb fantastically. In addition to tires and tubes, whose constant failure required replacements, cars needed rubber for gaskets, hoses, and belts, making rubber an irreplaceable commodity for the internal combustion age until the introduction of synthetic rubber in the 1930s. Rubber was also consumed by the electrical industry as insulation.

Vulcanization's impact on the Amazon basin was sweeping. Latin America's sleepiest region became a string of riverine boomtowns as the best latex came from one tree species, *Hevea brasiliensis*, which was common to all of the Amazon's southern tributaries. As exports of rubber doubled every decade from 1850 to 1900, the field of extraction spread rapidly west from its beginnings near the Amazon's mouth, upriver to Peru and Bolivia. At the basin's geographic center, the city of Manaus, until recently at the middle of nowhere, built exquisite mansions for the rubber barons, erected a fabulous opera house that contracted foreign talent, and installed electric lights and streetcars well before most European cities.

The urban ostentations belied the primitive nature of the actual rubber industry. Isolated tappers, some of them enslaved Indians, nearly all of them exploited, wandered the forests tapping the wild rubber trees that they found scattered at random in the region's diverse ecology. Each tree produced only a few ounces of latex every other day, and production could only be expanded by the discovery of more wild trees. World demand continued to soar, and as the basin could not effectively respond with more production, so did the price – which invited competitors. As early as 1875, a British adventurer, Henry Wickham, removed a canoe load of rubber seeds from the lower Amazon and sold the lot to the British government, a feat far less daring than Wickham claimed for himself but that earned him knighthood and pension just the same. Sir Henry's seedlings were started in British greenhouses and then transplanted to tidy plantations in Britain's Malaysian colonies, and after a quarter century of care, they began to produce rubber. By 1913, British plantations matched South America's entire production. In fact, by that date there may have been more Brazilian rubber trees in Southeast Asia than in all Brazil as the French and Dutch had also begun Asian plantations. Only six years later, Asian plantations out-produced the Amazon by a factor of seven. The surge in supply was so great that the price offered for rubber fell below what it cost Amazonians to produce it. The boom had bust, the workers went home, and the Amazon returned to somnolence.

The economic difference between Amazonian and Asian rubber was efficiency. Scattered workers wandering a forest that was continental in size, tapping wild trees where they could find them, could not compete with Asian laborers who had installed a rubber tree monoculture. Asian plantations cultivated thousands of trees, row upon row, which they were able to effectively mind and efficiently tap. Why then did Amazonians not also create cultivated rubber plantations and win back their competitiveness? It was not for lack of trying. There were repeated experiments in plantation rubber along the Amazon's course in the nineteenth century, but they all failed, sometimes for lack of investment or practical expertise, but even when cash and capability were abundantly available, not a single venture got off the ground. A figure no less determined than Henry Ford later poured millions of dollars into Amazonian rubber plantations in the 1940s, as did the Firestone, Goodyear, and Michelin tire companies, all of which had extensive experience with plantation rubber in Asia and Africa. They all failed wretchedly.

The environmental difference between Amazonian and Asian rubber was a native fungus, *Microcyclus ulei*, known commonly as South American Leaf Blight. The airborne fungus attacked the leaves of *Hevea brasiliensis*, killing the tree or reducing its ability to produce latex by strangling photosynthesis and the tree's food supply. The rubber tree's only defense was to scatter itself sparsely among the rainforest's myriad other species. Under wild conditions, the fungus, try as it might, found it difficult to infect more than its current rubber tree host. So singly the trees thrived and yielded their latex to the frequent visits of the tappers. However, when humans attempted to improve on nature by congregating rubber trees into plantations, the fungus had a field day, leaping on the wind from host to host. Like yellow fever, leaf blight throve on dense populations of potential victims. Asian rubber's advantage was that the fungus did not follow the seeds of its host to Eurasia. Seeds and embryos are generally free of the diseases that plague their parents, and in a story that has repeated itself many times to America's favor – coffee and sugar, for example – exotic imports flourished in foreign soils far from the native diseases with which they had evolved. To this day, leaf blight has failed to reach Asian plantations. And despite quantum leaps in botanical science and genetic engineering, leaf blight continues to thwart Brazilian attempts to create natural rubber plantations in the tree's native soil. So far, nature has determined that culture will not succeed in the effective production of natural rubber in the Americas.

It was American willingness to try the newfangled, to pedal themselves about on absurd, two-wheeled toys, which began the 1890s bicycle craze that, in turn, set off the Amazonian rubber boom. Likewise, their contemporary willingness to try a bizarre, yellow fruit of dubious shape launched the banana boom. By the early twentieth century, the banana peel on the sidewalk gag was already an American comedy staple, and the banana was about to pass the apple as America's most widely consumed fruit. Popular at breakfast and in the lunch pails of children and workers, bananas were healthy, convenient, and cheap – even the poorest classes could afford the inevitably bruised or overripe fruit. Through advertising, banana importers convinced women that a banana was the ideal baby food and that respectable ladies could eat one in polite company. The banana's appeal was greatly enhanced by the fact that it was about the only fruit an American could eat fresh any time of the year. The benefit of the tropic's perpetual growing season could now be imported, and banana producers and exporters counted on constant sales and constant profits. By the late 1920s, the average American ate more than 50 bananas each year, and avid importers, such as the often villainized United Fruit Company, maintained massive merchant fleets, larger than most national navies, that supplied 1.4 trillion kilograms annually to America's grocers.

Bananas and plantains, of course, had long provided many Latin Americans the majority of their carbohydrates and vitamins. Hence, bananas had already been grown successfully on small farms and kitchen gardens for four centuries. Initially, the United Fruit Company contracted the bananas produced by Jamaican small farmers, and the relationship remained satisfactory until the second decade of the century. Before this time, just as rubber naturally scattered itself in the Amazon, the peoples of the Caribbean had culturally scattered the banana across many landscapes and amongst their other food crops. In fact, they grew a wide variety of bananas. But American demand changed the regime. Americans and their suppliers wanted only one banana, the Gros Michel, due to its size, sweetness, portability, and talent to slowly ripen after being picked. Soon, thousands of genetically identical banana plants were crowded together by farmers seeking profits instead of subsistence. This formed the critical mass for another fungal infection. Panama disease (*Fusarium oxysporum*) attacked the banana's roots and caused the plant to wilt. When first observed in the early years of the century, nobody could determine the cause of the withered trees, so United Fruit, without any evidential grounds, blamed the cultivation

Figure 4. Banana workers of the United Fruit Company in Costa Rica present first-grade fruit, as yet unaffected by Panama disease, 1912.
Source: Edwin R. Fraser, "Where our Bananas Come From," *The National Geographic Magazine* 23 (July 1912): 722.

practices of Jamaican farmers, which were declared shoddy and unhygienic. It was only at this point that the United Fruit Company, and other American and European importers, began to buy up land on which they could produce bananas on their own account, carefully, hygienically, and under factory-like conditions. But as this entailed a yet more intensive monoculture, crowding more bananas on ever larger plantations, rather than improving, the situation worsened.

In 1915, the fungus was identified. Despite significant investment through the 1920s to learn how to defeat Panama disease, nothing proved effective. At great expense, United Fruit attempted to carefully regulate the soil's moisture over vast expanses of banana fields through the construction of drainage fields. By keeping the soil relatively dry and irrigating sparingly, this seemed to reduce the rate of infection. And if infection took hold, workers flooded the fields in hopes of drowning the oxygen-loving fungus. But all the effort, at best, only delayed the inevitable: banana groves sickened, withered, and died.

United Fruit decided that its best strategy was to dodge the bullet rather than bite it, and for the next four decades, they ran from Panama disease. Once the fungus had taken hold on a plantation, an event that sometimes took place fewer than five years after planting, and almost always in less than 10, United Fruit pulled up stakes and moved all its capital and many of it laborers to new, distant locations. They first moved from the islands of the Caribbean to the eastern shores of Honduras and Costa Rica. By 1927, they were planting on the Pacific coasts of Panama, and, finally, they invaded the disease-free forests of Guatemala. They cleared forests, planted rapidly, and struggled to get as many harvests as possible before disease got a toehold. But every place they fled, the fungus soon followed.

The story has parallels with Brazilian coffee, but with a distinct difference. Coffee planters were also extremely mobile; but they, just like sugar planters before them, were running from soil infertility, not disease. In Brazilian coffee, the constant removal and relocation of the plantation created what has been called the hollow frontier, a rather unusual phenomenon associated with Latin America's race for export profits. Since the beginning, it had been civilization's practice to push onto new frontiers, fell forests, and turn ecologically diverse landscapes into monocultural regimes that housed and supported human beings. In other words, healthy civilizations expanded, absorbing and converting wild landscapes into the landscapes of human settlement. The hollow frontier of export agriculture was quite different. Now, rather than convert wilderness into civilization, civilization devoured wilderness and spit it out. In a matter of decades the frontier went from a state of nature to the status of ruins. This was civilization as blitzkrieg, one in which humans no longer tied themselves to a place called home but wedded themselves with utmost fidelity to profit. The result was a spreading cancer, ravaging everything at its perimeter and leaving a black, dead core characterized by deforestation, erosion, and ghost towns. All that mattered, present and future, was the frontier, for everything inside of it was obliterated, hollow. Nilo Peçanha described the ruins of coffee civilization along the Paraíba River, where Brazil's coffee export boom began.

> In those days, whoever saw the Paraíba Valley's splendid display of a vast ocean of agriculture and today observes the desolation of her denuded lands, the decadence of her cities, and the depreciation of her properties, the skeleton of the plantations whose homes leave the impression of piles of bones, feels a sadness clench their heart.[8]

[8] Quoted in José Augusto Drummond, *Devastação e preservação ambiental no Rio de Janeiro* (Niterói, Brazil: Editora da Universidade Federal Fluminense, 1997), 25, my translation.

Banana planters, however, were a cancer of a different sort, one that metastasized, leapfrogging the immediate frontier for more distant virgin territory. The banana formed a riddled frontier, a patchwork of ruin and destruction surrounded by deliberate natural buffers. But its transformation of the landscape was so sudden and so ephemeral that banana planting left not even the shadow of a ghost town but only deforested tracts littered with sickly banana stumps between which poor farmers tried to eke out a bare subsistence. Bananas, coffee, and sugar, the so-called dessert crops, were not laudable advances toward the frontier as much as they were lamentable retreats from various forms of degradation.

By the 1940s, there was a relatively simple solution to Panama disease. A new variety of banana, the Cavendish (today's most common import), was highly resistant to the fungus and its substitution into United Fruit's plantations would have made the business less costly and more sustainable. But until 1962, while other fruit companies experimented with the Cavendish, United Fruit resisted its adoption out of fear that the same American public that had embraced the voluptuous Gros Michel would reject a new variety that was slightly smaller and more prone to bruising.

As United Fruit dragged its feet through the crisis, nature did not let up, offering up new challenges with remarkable consistency. In the 1920s, a new fungus, sigatoka (*Mycosphaerella musicola*), appeared in Pacific island plantations and crossed the Pacific to Central America's banana plantations in 1934. By the end of 1937, in a conquest astonishing for its rapidity, sigatoka had infected nearly every banana plantation from Costa Rica to Trinidad. Sigatoka attacked the bananas' leaves, turning them black. Later, burrowing nematodes (*Radopholus similes*) followed, destroying roots and toppling trees. Unlike Panama disease, spraying was effective for controlling sigatoka and nematodes, but only if done frequently and in great concentrations. The result expresses one of the ironies of the ongoing battle between nature and culture. In the war against nature, culture will frequently sacrifice its own members, some volunteers, some coerced, in order to achieve victory. To defeat sigatoka, or rather hold it at bay, banana workers sprayed a bright, blue-green solution of copper sulfate on the upper and lower surfaces of the banana's leaf using elaborate pump equipment. The United Fruit Company called their spray men chemists, and lauded them as the scientific front in the battle against nature, but the workers referred to themselves derogatively as parakeets. The sprayed solution stained the workers' skin and entered into their tissues. Spray men not only had blue skins, but blue perspiration, saliva, and lungs. Many workers were incorrectly diagnosed with tuberculosis, but the effect on the lungs was similarly mortal. At one point, a quarter of United Fruit's entire labor force worked as sprayers, and some men saw the irony in sick banana trees that could only be saved by the sacrifice of their own health. Copper sulfate was only one of many toxins employed to control the banana's natural enemies. From the 1960s, banana workers applied dibromo-chloropropane (DBCP), a toxin jointly developed by Dow Chemical and Standard Oil that effectively sterilized nematodes and other pesky soil organisms. Not unpredictably, DBCP sterilized banana workers too. To ensure profits, which required the defeat of nature, culture was not only willing to place its own members in harm's way, but to place at risk human fertility itself, historically the most powerful weapon in the fight for cultural survival. Culture errs when it acts like God because it forgets its humble biological origins. Whatever culture accomplishes outwardly, its individual members will always share flesh, blood, and chromosomes with nature. Hence, the weapons we design to defeat our natural enemies will potentially prove dangerous to us as well.

Exporting nature for national development was not a bad plan for nineteenth-century Latin America under the circumstances, but nature was often disagreeable and occasionally unyielding. Nature, both its perception and its reality, deflects history from the course that culture plots for itself. History, which is culture's autobiography, does not happen in a vacuum, detached from its setting. And Latin America's largely tropical set presented a unique set of opportunities and challenges that have yet to be fully included in the story.

When Brazil lost rubber, not just its monopoly but the ability to even compete as a small player, blame was cast in every direction. Those swayed by determinism impugned the benighted Brazilian race and cursed the enervating Amazonian climate. Nationalists accused British imperialism of stealing their natural wealth, the equivalent of kidnapping one's children. But in the end, a microbe that eluded human control killed rubber as a central component in Brazil's basket of exports. The consequences for Brazil were serious, for the nation continued to rely largely on a single crop, coffee, whose world price increasingly disappointed. Rubber, if Brazil had been able to establish plantations, would have earned the nation a fantastic return. Distant Malaya by the 1920s received greater returns on the sale of rubber (and some tin) to the United States than did Brazil from all its U.S. exports, including coffee.

And when Brazil began to industrialize, especially after 1950 with the introduction of automotive factories, it could have saved billions in the purchase of rubber imports. And what is said for Brazil could be said in smaller measure for every other American nation whose bounds fell within the rubber tree's climatological requirements. The Amazon basin itself might have by now experienced a century of development based on a sustainable agro-export instead of going through, in the last 30 years, an economic expansion of unparalleled destructiveness based on deforestation for ranching and farming.

Nature defeated culture in the Amazon. In Central America, nature cast up formidable obstacles to culture's banana plots, but culture, in this case, kept up a good fight. Without disease-free competitors in other parts of the world, banana growers still found the struggle profitable. But Panama disease caused banana companies, such as United Fruit, to do something that is quite unusual for a multinational: consider the long term. Knowing that on average they could only get eight years out of a banana plantation, American fruit growers began to buy, lease, and commandeer tropical farmland on a fabulous scale. Not only were they forced to abandon fields hastily, they had to establish the new planta-tions at a significant, safe, distance from all others. The best solution was to effectively control huge tracts of widely distributed land to which they could systematically flee from the fungus. The United Fruit Company alone came to control more than 12,000 square kilometers of poten-tial banana lands, an area nearly as large as the state of Connecticut, the holdings of which were scattered over a half dozen nations. United Fruit spread its risks and its political and economic meddling as widely as possible.

By the late 1940s, Guatemalans, most of whom had no land, began to chafe at the sight of United Fruit's huge, uncultivated tracts on their national territory. United Fruit cultivated only 5 percent of their Guatemalan holdings. In 1952, President Jacobo Arbenz demanded that the company sell their unutilized lands back to Guatemala at the property value they had declared on recent tax returns. Guatemalan nationalists justified the act in order to get land to the peasants and to make Guatemala prosperous; unused land produced neither goods for export nor did it provide food, much of which Guatemala had to import. United Fruit complained, resisted, and cried Communism, but when land reform went forward in 1953, Arbenz repatriated some 1,700 square kilometers of vacant United Fruit farmland. Obviously, United Fruit had lost much of its influence in the Guatemalan government, but it maintained powerful friends in the U.S. administration. In 1954, an insurgency, created by the CIA and supported by the U.S. Air Force, bombed Guatemala City, overthrew Arbenz, and replaced him with a dictator who restored to United Fruit all its lands and former privileges.

Just as the Iberian conquest of America was a probable eventuality even without smallpox, economic imperialism in Central America was to be expected even without tropical fungi. But in both cases, the story would have been much different if nature had stayed out of the narrative. Panama disease was an important factor in the creation of banana republics. Without it, banana importers might have remained satisfied with the purchasing of contracted bananas from independent farmers, as was their practice at the beginning of the trade. Until the 1920s, United Fruit owned and controlled rail and shipping lines, but very little land. But with the arrival of Panama disease, grabbing land, more than the company could ever plant, became a mania, for land in quantity was prized as a fungus-free refuge, and the company subverted governments or propped up dictators, whatever best fit the circumstances, to protect their future. Economic imperialism would have occurred without Panama disease, but a fungus helps explain why banana republics, such as Guatemala, suffered more from imperialism's fruits than did others.

CHAPTER FIVE

Human Determination

> Rubião stared at the bay. . . . Anyone who saw him standing at
> the window of his home in Botafogo, his thumbs hitched under
> the belt of his robe, would have supposed he was admiring that
> little piece of calm water; but I tell you he was thinking something
> else entirely: he was comparing the past to the present. What had
> he been but a year ago? A teacher. What was he now! A capital-
> ist. He looks at himself, at his slippers (slippers from Tunis, a gift
> from his new friend Cristiano Palha), he looks at the house, at the
> garden, at the bay, at the hills, and at the sky. Everything, from the
> slippers to the sky, gave him the gathering sensation of property.[1]

Joaquin Maria Machado de Assis, one of our great novelists, grew tired
of showing foreign acquaintances around Rio de Janeiro, his much loved
home city. In fact, he despised the outings. He wanted visitors, foreigners
in particular, to recognize his birthplace as the South American Paris, a
place of culture, refinement, and progress, not a mere human enclave
ensconced in an overpowering, flowered jungle. Invariably, however,
his guests were so enchanted by nature, by the bay, the peaks, and the
forests, they failed to see what man had done. On one occasion, a European guest asked to be shown something old and beautiful, so with some
hope, Machado de Assis accompanied him to the top of Castelo hill
to see the ancient church and former cathedral. The author admitted
that it was not the Acropolis, but certainly worthy of human regard. He
was to be disappointed again. After a cursory pass through the church,

---

[1] Joaquim Maria Machado de Assis, *Quincas Borba* (Rio de Janeiro: Ediouro, s.d.),
15, my translation.

his guest headed straight for the hill's brow overlooking the bay and exclaimed, "What nature you have here!"

Machado de Assis took such comments as insults: "it always seemed to me a manner of treading on man and his works." It was not that he scorned his city's natural beauty, for this formed an essential component of his fiction. But for an accomplished author and playwright, to admire nature to the neglect of culture was to put setting before character, prop before plot. One can hardly blame turn-of-the-century visitors to Rio de Janeiro for admiring nature; even today the city's foremost charms remain her naturally curvaceous beaches and stunning mountain skyline. But Machado de Assis, and many of his contemporaries, wanted people to notice man and the works of his hands: buildings, monuments, roads, and bridges. And they strove to make it happen, to get noticed, or, in the lingo of the day, to build "for the eyes of the English." Machado de Assis believed that a magnificent bridge spanning the water would upstage the bay's beauty, just as the Brooklyn Bridge distracted eyes from New York's East River, the Golden Gate Bridge would come to outshine the natural grandeur of the Golden Gate, and a soaring white statue of Christ would eventually draw attention away from Rio's natural skyline. In Rio too, culture had to build on a scale that dwarfed nature in order to grab human attention and respect.

Human aspirations, no doubt magnified by the shame that Latin Americans felt under the eyes of foreigners, were on the verge of being fulfilled in a measure well beyond what anyone could have imagined. The arrival of the twentieth century was a turning point in human relations with nature, and Latin America participated in this revolution with relish. Regardless of the very real power of the dogmas, diseases, and disasters of the previous chapter, culture's age-old determination was about to get the upper hand on nature's determinisms. Before the twentieth century, culture was routinely bent by the wind, blockaded by mountains, harassed by water, stalked by hunger, and infected with disease. Thereafter, culture began to empower itself. Of course, this empowerment was incremental, and nature still gets in her licks, but the power balance has shifted unmistakably to the human camp, which makes the twentieth century a rather different story from that we have addressed thus far.

An essential change in this shift in power was in the nature of power itself. Before the eighteenth century, humans drew exclusively from a solar energy regime. The sun produced vegetation, some of which humans burned to warm themselves, cook a meal, or produce iron, and some of which humans ate in order to fuel their muscles, or those of their domesticated animals, to do the labor that was required to take advantage of the sun's free contribution to agriculture. For its entire past, culture had relied almost exclusively upon the power of muscles, human and animal, to accomplish its ends. Flexed muscles fueled by food made history happen: war, art, trade, sex, production, demolition, construction, you name it. Even the human brain is an organ powered by calories, but its aspirations and calculations amounted to nothing historically until it coaxed the body to exert itself, to perspire. Iberians also relied upon the sun to make the winds that drove their ships over the globe's oceans and to raise the falling water they harnessed to drive sugar and stamp mills. But muscles remained history's primary mover.

It was the discovery of fossil fuels that stoked culture's inborn determination. Of course, coal and oil are also solar products, ancient reserves of fossilized vegetation. We live under a new regime that no longer limits energy consumption to the sun's everyday offerings but dips deeply into the earth's solar bank account, an account that offers no interest because it is nonrenewable. Cultures empowered by these new, prehistoric fuels have quickened history's pace. History is cultural time, and it was at this point that our cultural clock began to outpace the earth's biological clock. Humans were transformed from simple tool wielders to switch throwers and button pushers, tripping with the slightest muscular effort power that before had been inconceivable. During Mexico City's disastrous seventeenth-century floods, victims beseeched members of the saintly Christian pantheon to wield power mighty to save: "I, wretched Mexico, kneeling I beg, . . . my protector, you will, with divine faith, move mountains, dry up lakes."[2] Such supplications were only fully answered by fossil-fueled technology in the twentieth century, for humans only then acquired the faculty, even facility, to divert rivers, drain seas, divide continents, and move mountains. Possibly even more revolutionary, culture came to conquer soil infertility, which, as we will see, began with Latin American resources. We have all but forgotten the experience of hunger, and if some in Latin America still go hungry, it is not for the inability to produce sufficient food. Hunger today is rarely the fault of nature but of our culture's political, economic, and humanitarian limitations. So, the dawn of the last century is a fitting

[2]   Quoted in Richard Everett Boyer, "Mexico City and the Great Flood: Aspects of Life and Society, 1629–1635," (Ph.D. diss., University of Connecticut, 1973), v.

moment to join Machado de Assis and his protagonist Rubião in comparing the past with the present.

Over the course of the nineteenth century a variety of newly endowed technologies – steam engines, railways, steamships – powered their way into the region. Fueled by fossil plants, they could do the work of thousands of men. One booster of the age calculated that a single steamship, laden with goods and immigrants for America, did as much work in a single crossing of the Atlantic as was exerted in transporting and raising all the stones that comprised the great pyramid at Giza. These new, mobile wonders of the world proved essential to the success of Latin America's export-led development model. Their primary role was to conquer time and space, that is, the geographic distances and topographic obstacles that stood in the way of extending the tentacles of globalization beyond the seaports. Without steamships that sail a straight line from port to port, and could push up mighty rivers regardless of winds, Central American bananas and Amazonian rubber, not to mention chilled Argentine beef, could not have reached markets on other continents. And without railroads that could push over broad plains and through high mountains, such goods as coffee, copper, wheat, and bananas could have never made it to port at all. Without the powerful transport ties that bound sellers to buyers, Latin America had little place in the global economy.

At the time, Machado de Assis and his contemporaries expected nothing but good from culture's enhanced powers, and the benefits were obvious. But a few began to notice the costs of human empowerment. The damage to nature was apparent, but this troubled almost nobody. The surprise was that transforming nature produced unexpected costs and often unwanted results for culture itself, eventualities we half expect today but that then took culture unawares. Sometimes, all the power and effort was wasted, for while nature was transformed just as intended, culture missed its ultimate goal of improving human lives. Technology and power sometimes proved as fickle and unpredictable as nature itself. However, those with the most power took the greatest benefit by nature's transformation, and they insisted that the transformation continue apace despite its costs to those individuals and cultures without access to the new levers and buttons.

Mountains Moved

Barring those urban rivers that have been fully converted to sewage transport, Mexico City's Gran Canal must be the world's largest open sewer. It begins, fittingly some Mexicans say, right behind the House of Representatives and then runs northeast from the city's bowels through alternating residential, industrial, and recreational areas, fed by grow-ing tributaries of sewage formed by the city's fantastic recent expan-sion. Despite its length, girth, and stench, it is difficult to locate this immense urban waste stream. It is not represented on many maps, par-ticularly those produced for tourists, and for much of its early course it is surrounded by high walls. My son and I found it with the help of a dated subway map; one of the stations, now named for the revo-lutionaries Flores Magon, used to carry the portentous name of Gran Canal. But today, all reference, access, and vantage to the canal have been virtually denied, and only after considerable adventure did we get a close look. The canal stinks of musty sweetness, and has, due to the mixing of excrement, urine, rinsed soap, industrial effluent, and dis-solved toilet paper, sewage's characteristic gray color. Rotting pipes set in ranks along the canal's edge send surging charges of foamy liquid crashing onto the water's surface. Citizens adorn the canal's enclosing walls with graffiti and dump their trash into the canal zone in heaps of mattresses, plastic, and paper on which vegetation, particularly cas-tor oil, miraculously thrives. The artery is unloved and dishonored, and people live, play, and work near it only because they have little choice (see Figure 5).

What a contrast to the canal's glorious place in public esteem when it was completed in 1900! The canal was a four-century-old ambition tri-umphantly accomplished, and contemporaries hailed it as nothing less than the savior of Mexico City itself. It was a monument that Machado de Assis would have envied, one of engineering's historical marvels, a mighty man-made river running 47 kilometers across the earth in per-fectly straight lines, and another 10 kilometers through a tunnel bur-rowed beneath the mountains. Man had moved mountains to liberate the valley's waters. Its completion was celebrated by its primary spon-sor, Porfírio Díaz, Mexico's perennial president, with pomp and partying; the guests, dressed in semiformal, Victorian costume appropriate to the occasion, gathered at the point where the canal entered the tunnel. The transition from surface to subsurface consisted of an enormous, inverted pyramid, a sort of antimonument to politicians and engineers, whose hollow inside served as gulping mouth to the waters that drained rapidly from the Valley of Mexico's ancient lakes. While for today's citizens, the monument is unvisited, a massive toilet in constant flush, for Díaz, the

Figure 5. Mexico City's Gran Canal, 2005. Photograph by author.

Gran Canal and tunnel were the crowning accomplishments of his very ambitious government, and virtually everyone, his detractors, and even the usually under-whelmed foreigner, agreed.

No subsequent flood matched the severity of the 1629–1634 disaster, but the dream of draining the valley of Mexico of her troubling lakes never died. Each time the streets filled with water, stopping commerce, destroying edifices, and killing city folk, officials put new plans into effect or worked to improve old ones. But it was all to little avail. Despite massive financial outlays over the centuries since the conquest, and the labor of tens of thousands of men wielding picks and shovels and carrying baskets of rock and soil, flooding continued. It was a task beyond the puny power of human muscles.

By the mid-nineteenth century, there were additional, pressing motives for ridding the valley of its lakes. Until the end of the eighteenth century, visitors described Mexico City, situated in a high, dry valley with moderate temperatures and incomparably pure air, as one of the most healthful, human habitations. The reality was that Mexico was as dirty as any preindustrial city with trash, livestock (and their carcasses), manure (of man and beast), as common parts urban life, which was not much different than rural life. But until the Enlightenment, nobody seemed to notice urban filth, or consider it worthy of remark.

However, a growing sense of cleanliness, human progress, and the strict separation of man from nature persuaded the middle classes to recoil at the squalor they had so recently tolerated.

Humans had also tolerated urban diseases in the face of which they often felt helpless. But again, the Enlightenment challenged civilization to fight back, and the ensuing struggles against filth and disease became the same battle. As was happening in many Western cities in the nineteenth century, Mexico City's urban elite took the city's pollutions to task. By the end of the century, Mexico's middle class do-gooders were so convinced of their superior notions they outlawed the keeping of pigeons, pigs, hens, and even dogs in homes. Nature, and its filth, was to be banished from the city. Officials fined individuals who went about in public without pants, and eventually began to publicly scrub the under classes who were notorious for bathing only once a year on Saint John the Baptist's Day. In 1917, 90,000 city residents were given a bath and haircut at city expense.

But compared to citizens of other world cities who were also cleaning up their streets, Mexico City's urban hygienists faced nearly insurmountable obstacles. Most cities were located on major rivers or were seaports, which provided them with nearly bottomless sinks for their urban waste streams. Filth, trash, and sewage were dumped into the water and the currents and tides diluted and carried them away. It was not pretty, and it was not without negative cultural and ecological consequences, but it worked. Mexico City, by contrast, was at the lowest point of a closed basin. Just like everyone else, the citizens expelled their wastes into the nearest water body, Lake Texcoco, but rather than dissipating and disappearing, the filth accumulated, concentrated, and, during the rainy season, came back to haunt them. The city was the bottom of the sink, and poorly protected by leaky dikes.

Through the nineteenth century Mexico City remained very much a city of water. Since Aztec times, the lakes had shrunk and the number of canals had diminished, but the city still abutted an expansive lake on its northeast, and one could still travel much of the city by boat. Small steamboats plied the major canals. Still at mid-century, many considered the canals the city's greatest aesthetic asset. Fanny Calderon de la Barca, the Scottish wife of a Spanish diplomat, wrote of the Canal de la Viga in 1840:

> It would be difficult to find in any country a more beautiful promenade than the Viga, . . . with its fine shady trees and canal, along which the lazy canoes are constantly gliding, . . . the whole under a blue cloudless

sky, and in that pure clear atmosphere, . . . you would believe that Mexico must be the most flourishing, most enjoyable, and most peaceful place in the world.[3]

But the lake and canals became increasingly identified with disease, as foci of infection. In the heat of summer, the stench was nauseating, and according to some traditions, stink and disease were assumed companions. There was no quibbling over the fact that the city was insalubrious. As the population grew from 200,000 in 1858 to 345,000 in 1900, most of this due to urban migration, the sewage load increased, as did disease mortality. Between 1867 and 1877, the latter year when Porfirio Díaz first took office, 83,000 people died of disease, one third of the city's total running population. In 1879, life expectancy for residents was 27 compared to 47 for Paris. In 1900, infant mortality was catastrophic: 40 percent of Mexico City's babies did not survive their first year.

Of course determinism raised its head, and Mexican scholars argued that the filthy waters, even those just beneath the ground, created miasmas that not only produced disease but also enervated the general population, limiting the Mexicans' physical and intellectual capacities. If Mexico could not overcome nature, it could not be civilized. And lastly, the shame of it all, of living in a cesspool in the eyes of the world, of showing the nation helpless, at nature's mercy: all this helped carry the motion that the Valley of Mexico should be drained of its pestilential lakes once and for all, regardless of cost.

Although it would take more than 40 years to complete the task, the time was finally right for such a motion. Picks and shovels had proven poorly matched for the undertaking. With the basin's high water table and clay sediments, digging a canal presented the same problems that colonial inhabitants of the city faced in digging graves: any excavation soon filled with water making it impossible for the diggers to deepen the hole beyond the reach of their shovels' handles. Such had been the nature of the effort before 1890. President Díaz realized the fastest route to success was to contract with foreigners who had proven themselves as movers of mountains in the building of the Suez Canal, completed in 1869. Capitalism's adventurers, such as England's Weetman Pearson, brought in the big equipment: steam shovels and, more significantly, massive dredges, some of the largest mobile machines built to date. Each was manufactured in England and shipped to Mexico in pieces where it

---

[3] Fanny Calderón de la Barca, *Life in Mexico: The Letters of Fanny Calderón de la Barca*, ed. H. Fisher and M. Fisher (New York: Doubleday, 1966), 174–5.

was assembled on site. The largest dredge, once assembled, was chris-tened the Carmen in honor of Díaz's beautiful, very young wife. It may have been the most unsightly object ever named for a woman. This was no graceful ship, but a hulk of filthy timbers, booms, and belching smokestacks mounted precariously on a creaky barge. At one end of its 40 meter length, the Carmen sported 40 buckets linked one behind the other in a revolving chain driven by the dredge's central steam engine. The buckets bit into the lake's bottom and raised the sediment 30 meters before dumping their contents into a large hopper at the top of the dredge. The hopper, into which water was pumped and mixed with the spoil, discharged itself down one of two flumes that extended out from the dredger's sides in ungainly booms, depositing the material on train cars or barges. The Carmen would join the Lucy, Conchita, Annie, and Cuauhtemoc in the battle to drain the valley of its troublesome lakes. In the wake of their churning buckets they marked a new watercourse across the landscape, straight and trim. It was not as easy as I make it sound, but after a decade of trials, landslides, and other setbacks the canal and its tunnel were completed, connected, and the water began to drain freely and rapidly from the valley. Within months, the ancient lakes diminished or disappeared.

In 1910, the centennial of Mexico's independence, the Gran Canal, which had seen additional improvements and beautifications in the decade after its completion, was the centerpiece of the celebration. For-eign representatives from scores of nations came to pay their respects to Mexico, Díaz, and urban modernity. Most were duly impressed. How-ever, if they looked beyond the canal itself and the celebration's main venues, what they saw was water in the streets and desperate sandbag-ging operations to keep news of the same from reaching the foreign press. Despite claims of victory over the valley's waters, Mexicans had to face two troubling facts after a decade of a functioning canal. Yes, they had successfully drained Lake Texcoco: the valley spread dry before them to the east – most of the time. However, in a heavy rainy season like that of 1910, the lake came back and, just as in times past, its waters flooded the city. The canal simply did not have the capacity or slope to han-dle above average weather events. The only real change was that the water filling the streets was cleaner than in the past as it was largely rain water rather than concentrated sewage. It was not until 1975, after the construction of a deeper and larger network of tunnels, that flooding in the city would finally cease. That the flood waters after 1900 were cleaner did not seem to change the second troubling fact: Mexico City

Figure 6. The Gran Canal, under constant repair, just before it enters the tunnel at Zumpango, 1911.
Source: John Birkinbine, "Our Neighbor, Mexico," *The National Geographic Magazine* 22 (May 1911): 482.

remained, by Mexican calculations, the deadliest city in the world, with mortalities higher than Cairo or Madras. Despite draining the lake and connecting much of the city's sewage to the drainage system, Mexico City's death rate in 1912 stood at the same level it had in 1895. After millions of pesos and incalculable man hours, the two threats that had justified the colossal drainage project in the first place remained unresolved. The lakes were largely gone, but flood and disease refused to go with them. The crushing truth was swiftly disseminated as propaganda by those who sought to prevent Díaz from reelecting himself yet again.

Also, playing into revolutionary hands was the fact that the drainage projects served to further concentrate the best farmland, in this case former lakebeds, into the hands of a wealthy few. This left many lakeshore communities high, dry, and angry, for it snuffed the lives of myriad creatures, many of them important to humans for food. Fish and other edible critters suffocated and baked on the dry lake bed, and migratory water fowl no longer found reason to alight in the valley. Miguel Angel de Quevedo, Mexico's leading conservationist at the time, favored flood control by reforestation rather than the lakes' elimination due in part to the large numbers of poor who relied on the lakes' fish, *animalitos*, and fowl for food. But the poor's patrimony, a lakeside existence, was drained away. The lake's disappearance was so sudden that some said that they retired at night with the lake and woke without it the next morning. Local agriculture suffered too, for many shoreline chinampas that had survived the centuries since the conquest now dried up, replaced by irrigated agriculture in the former lake bed. Many lakeshore communities, such as Chalco and Ayotla, pointed to the draining of the lakes, which stole their livelihoods and destroyed their communities, as their primary justification for supporting the Mexican Revolution, a bloody affair that covered much of the second decade of the century and that was driven largely by peasant land losses incurred since independence.

Nobody seemed concerned about the aesthetic loss. A few thousand square kilometers of water vanished leaving a dead, dry lakebed in its place. The lakes had been the central features of the valley, their broad surfaces reflecting towering volcanic peaks for millennia. Jose de Velasco's romantic paintings of the Valley of Mexico, accomplished during the period in which the Gran Canal was being completed, depict a small city dwarfed by the valley and bordered by an expansive sheet of shining water. Now, the landscape's shimmer was gone. Man, with new powers, had transformed the face of the earth on a terrible scale. The Valley of Mexico's lakes, and the nature and culture associated with them, evolved from a precious source of food and water, to a cesspool, and, now, to a faint memory.

But the most significant, and ironically the least apparent, cultural cost of draining the lakes was subsidence. Promoters had believed that the removal of the valley's water would finally firm up the city's foundations, eliminating the soil's notorious sponginess. But it did the opposite. During the twentieth century, Mexico City sank by as much as 7.5 meters. Just as the valley's water was disappearing from view, a growing population demanded more water than local springs, rivers, and aqueducts could supply, so they began to tap the lake's underground remnant for drinking water. Already by 1900, there were more than 1,000 wells within the city, and their numbers grew rapidly. As citizens drew the water down pale by bucket, the previously saturated lakebed soils began to contract, and the city, and all its buildings and infrastructure, began to sink at an alarming rate, particularly after mechanical pumps were installed to raise water from ever deeper wells in the second quarter of the century. Citizens watched their steel well casings, the tops of which originally sat at the earth's surface, push themselves many meters above the ground. They assumed that the earth itself could not move and hence could not explain what made the well casings rise. In fact, the city's sinking was not discovered until 1925 and not fully understood till much later. The tops of the well casings, standing 5 or more meters tall, showed the level where Mexico City's residents used to live. The casings did not sink with the city because their lower extremities were embedded in stable rock below the lakes' sediment. Buildings sank unevenly with the soil beneath them causing bell towers and apartment blocks to lean precariously out of plumb to the point that many had to be condemned or shored up. That some still stand astonishes, especially after the 1985 earthquake. The Gran Canal itself sank, reducing its slope that had initially shuttled water along at 90 cubic meters per second. Capacity fell to a mere 7 cubic meters per second. Only closely spaced pumping stations kept the canal flowing uphill, protecting the city from drowning in its own sewage. Slowly, almost imperceptibly, that sinking feeling, the awareness that Mexico City was slowly collapsing in on itself, gnawed at the back of the inhabitants' minds. Children, for fun, marked their heights on the protruding well casings in order to match their growth against the valley's sinking. On subsequent visits they found their marks on the casings standing well above their heads. The landscape was sinking faster than Mexico City's children were growing, which was something of a prophetic metaphor. In the coming decades, nature's ecological services, including the provision of clean water and oxygen, have failed to keep pace with Mexico City's growth.

Guano Happened

Rich Peru was Spain's last colonial holdout on the American mainland. Her independence was not complete until Simón Bolívar's forces captured Lima's port from the Spanish in 1826. But while Spain retained a few island colonies, such as Cuba and Puerto Rico, and for years refused to recognize Latin America's fledgling republics, to all appearances, she had given up her American empire and posed little threat to Latin America's independence. But in 1856, Spain suddenly attacked and took possession of Peru's most prized territorial possessions, not her mountains studded with silver but her coastal islands encrusted with bird droppings (yes, bird droppings). Thus began the first Guano War (there was a second) in which this time Peru prevailed. Nations spilled blood over guano, the excrement of seabirds, rather than over silver because guano, still largely unheralded, would play the central role in conquering what had appeared to be nature's unassailable curb on soil fertility.

"Guano ain't no saint," Peruvians liked to say, "but it works mighty miracles." Since Inca times, Peru's coastal farmers continued to rely on guano to maintain the fertility of their soils, and a few outsiders took note of the significant quantities used, but it remained a very local practice. The traveling scientist, Alexander von Humboldt, imported guano samples to Europe in about 1805, but no real interest was taken in the foul-smelling material, despite favorable scientific reports, until sufficient quantities got into the hands of farmers who could test it in their own fields. The results were astounding. Robert Bell of Kerry County Ireland sprinkled the fetid magic dust on his potatoes, wheat, oats, and turnips and saw his yields increase by 30–300 percent; applications to his apple trees and raspberry bushes caused both to flower twice in the year. That kind of news, traveling from one farmer's mouth to another, moved fast and carried weight that no scientific paper could match. Soon, every farmer who could afford it demanded it, and guano's use spread across England, Ireland, Germany, and Eastern Europe by the early 1840s. It soon found its way to Eastern and Southern U.S. farms which had been depleted by years of intensive agriculture and that now found it difficult to compete with farmers of the American West who had recently plowed up yet unexploited prairie soils. New England farmers exulted that guano quadrupled their turnip and rutabaga yields, and Chesapeake planters that it was 25 times more powerful than barnyard manure. Between 1844 and 1851, U.S. farmers imported a total of 66,000 tons, and would have imported four times that if they could have gotten it. Most guano went to Europe; in a single year, 1850, Britain imported 200,000 tons. Little Barbados' sugar planters, in dire need of fertility inputs, imported nearly 7,000 tons each year, and even China commenced importing Peru's wonder dung. The guano boom began in about 1840 and continued to gain momentum into the 1870s.

The search was on for other external sources of soil fertility, and many in fact were found: in addition to the already widely used animal manures, ashes, and dead fish, farmers tried chalk, gypsum, feathers, cotton seed, coal tar, sawdust, seaweed, and charcoal, all with some success. Popular as well were dried blood and crushed bones (both products of growing urban slaughterhouses), and Canadians and Americans scoured and burned their prairies to find the bones of the bison they had recently exterminated in order to make bone meal. But nothing worked miracles like guano. This put Peru in an excellent position, and in an attempt to reap the greatest rewards possible Peru monopolized the extraction and export of bird droppings just as the Iberian crowns previously monopolized mercury and diamonds. The right to export guano was sold to the highest bidders, and sizeable foreign loans, backed by Peruvian guano receipts, financed the venture.

It is hard to imagine today the significance guano had in the mid-nineteenth century. Agriculture was the central economic activity of every nation, and a nation's fertility, which was set by the soil's natural bounds, inevitably shaped national economic success, population growth, and immigration flows. Securing dependable guano imports was almost tantamount to our current obsessions and conflicts over oil. And the Peruvian monopoly was viewed much like OPEC is today, a cartel driven by simple greed that harmed the world economy at large. The United States worried that it was to be left without access to this vital resource and debated the issue at the highest levels. In 1856, Congress declared the Guano Act which gave every American sailor the right to make an American possession of any island or rock covered in guano, as long as it was unclaimed by other nations and had no inhabitants. The discoverer held the exclusive right to exploit the guano on the claimed island and had the promise of protection from the U.S. Navy if he shipped his product exclusively to the United States. More than 60 islands, mostly in the Caribbean and mid-Pacific, were so claimed under the Guano Act, and nine of them remain U.S. attachments.

To Peru's good fortune, and the chagrin of the United States and Europe, Peruvian guano had no match for quantity and quality. The guanos found on all other islands were so inferior as to receive epithets and meager prices. Again, nature shaped the course of history, bestowing her gifts unevenly across earth's geography. Peru's guano piled higher and packed more punch because the Humboldt Current brought cold, nutrient-rich water, and very arid air to the Peru's coasts. The cold waters teemed with marine life, especially anchoveta (*Engraulis ringens*) a variety of sardine, creating an immensely successful fishery. The fish attracted millions of hungry seabirds seeking food to breed and to feed their young while they nested on Peru's islands and coastal promontories. Guano was the byproduct of their dense nesting colonies. Aridity's vital role was in preserving the guano's quality, for the islands had received virtually no recorded rainfall in centuries. Hence, guano did not wash away, nor was its uric acid, which contained the precious nitrogen, dissolved. The result was the most concentrated natural fertilizer ever applied to agriculture. Guano from most other islands was severely leached by rainfall and humidity, and hence its inferiority.

Most commercial guano was produced by three bird species: the white-breasted cormorant (*Phalacrocorax bougainvillii*), the booby (*Sula variegata*), and the pelican (*Pelecanus thagus*). The most important was the white-breasted cormorant, which the Incas named the *guanay*, or the guano bird. The word, guano, derives from the Quechua, *hauno*, for manure. The cormorant nested in dense colonies fashioning their nests of the previous year's guano into mounded circles that prevented their eggs from rolling into the sea (see Figure 7). In the nineteenth century the nests numbered in the hundreds of millions, and visitors marveled at the birds' crowded circumstances both on the ground and in the air. It appeared that the limiting factor in bird numbers was not the lack of food, but the lack of real estate suitable for nesting sites. Under such crowded conditions, their accumulated defecations, over many centuries, piled as high as 45 meters. Even the annual rate of accumulation was remarkable. When Peru closed South Chincha Island in 1906 due to guano's depletion, within four years the birds put down another 22,000 tons of harvestable droppings despite the noted decline in *guanay* populations.

Left with little other choice, thousands of ships, forced to make the dangerous passage below South America's horn, flocked like the birds to the tiny islands, lining up one after the other to be laden with tons of bird droppings (see Figure 8). Highland Indians and imported Chinese, the latter of whom were told in China they were going to mine gold in California, mined piles of dung with pick and shovel and transported the droppings to lading stations by wheel barrow or sack. A fair number were essentially enslaved, captive on the islands they worked, and were sometimes chained to prevent not escape, which was impossible, but suicide. During the lading of the ship, the visiting sailors climbed high in the rigging to put some distance between themselves and a cargo that sent off clouds of choking ammonia. Trimmers, who leveled the guano in the ship's hold, wore improvised breathing masks of fiber and tar, but could only stand the hold about 20 minutes at a time. Crews alternated, but bleeding noses and temporary blindness were common complaints. When guano workers died, they were often buried on these rocky islands in the older guano deposits, which were of inferior quality. However, in

Figure 7. Guanays (white-breasted cormorants) tending their nests which are each fashioned of about 5.5 kilograms of guano.
Source: Robert Cushman Murphy, *Bird Islands of Peru: The Record of a Sojourn on the West Coast* (New York: G. P. Putnam's Sons, 1925), after 58. Courtesy of the Harold B. Lee Library, Brigham Young University, Provo, Utah.

later years, when the depletion of the best deposits forced the work into these poorer layers, excavation disinterred many bodies, most of which were flawlessly preserved by the desiccating feces.

During the boom, Peru exported some 12.7 million metric tons of dried excrement. In the middle of the boom this amounted $30 million per year in national revenue. The money financed the building of the nation, including urban improvements and the purchase of the ships and cannon that soundly defeated the Spanish invasion of 1856. Not until the 1870s did anyone show concern that the resource might fail. Guano was potentially a renewable resource, as the Inca and their predecessors had shown, but the current pace and global scale overwhelmed even the most dedicated avian parents who refused to leave despite human intrusions. Many colonies, however, were abruptly pushed aside, nests and all, by the guano workers, damning any chance at even modest guano replacement. When the first rumors of exhaustion were finally verified, the boom evaporated as quickly as it had appeared.

Figure 8. Awaiting a cargo of guano, ships anchor between Middle and North Chincha Islands, Peru, 1863.
Source: The Illustrated London News, February 21, 1863, p. 200.

But Peruvians did not despair, for they had the next best thing in far greater abundance and transferred their guano workforce, spades, and picks to nitrate fields located on their southern border with Bolivia. Sodium nitrate had been employed since the beginning of the century in small quantities for the manufacture of gun powder, but now its major markets were the world's farms. Nitrates were inferior to guano as fertilizer, but they were abundant, better distributed, and considerably cheaper. It was a decade or more before farmers made the transition: farmers were conservative by nature and balked at a material that was inorganic and almost odorless; they had judged the power of guano by its stench. But they had little choice; farmers were now entirely addicted to heavy doses of nitrogen regardless of the source's origin, price, or bouquet.

This time, nature had blessed Peru and Bolivia, as their borders were then constituted, with the latest fashion in soil fertility. But initially Chileans mined the nitrates, and they did so on Bolivian national territory under favorable leases. When Peru entered the picture, they tried to convince Bolivia that monopolization, a binational cartel, was the best way to secure national profits. While Bolivia mulled their options, they decided in 1879 to raise taxes on Chilean nitrate companies, despite preexisting agreements, which caused Chile to simply invade and expropriate the Bolivian province of Antofogasta, depriving Bolivians of not only their nitrate fields but also their only access to the sea. Peru reluctantly declared war on Chile due to an existing treaty of alliance with Bolivia, and the Chilean navy responded by snatching up Peru's best guano islands, to deprive Peru of both foreign cash and loans, and then captured Peru's nitrate fields as well. The war lasted five years, but it was a fitful affair, hardly worthy of its glorious official name, the War of the Pacific. It was Guano War II, and this time Chileans were the uncontested winners adding nearly 1,000 linear kilometers, all with prime nitrate deposits, to their already elongated country.

Of all agriculture's revolutions – settled agriculture of the tenth millennium B.C., seventeenth-century crop rotation, twentieth-century plant and genetic breeding – the modern fertility inputs revolution, which began with bird droppings, ranks high. Fertilizers, of course, had been used before guano, but they were of limited powers and labor intensive. By these means, before the nineteenth century, world agriculture supported millions of mouths. Only with bird droppings and, later, nitrates and other chemical sources of fertility, could farmers support billions. The burgeoning human population also needed fuel, which consisted of food, and until the nineteenth century, soil fertility was a limiting factor. Crop rotation had made important progress, in many cases doubling agricultural yields, but guano alone more than doubled yields again, and more importantly it permitted farmers to grow what they wanted where they wanted, without rotating crops and without fallowing fields. They got high yields every year, year after year. Guano even permitted farmers to grow crops in soils that previously offered little return. It is difficult for culture to admire guano. We much prefer to exalt human genius and extol technological advance: inventors of seed drills and cotton gins, designers of steel plows and tractors, developers of crops and breeding techniques. If familiar with agricultural history, you can rattle off the names: Jethro Tull, Eli Whitney, John Deere, Luther Burbank. Inventors and their inventions brim our history text books, but their genius made no greater contribution to human agriculture than the lowly *guanay* doing its business. Even the leaps made in plant breeding and genetics, the so-called Green Revolution, were not as revolutionary as bird dung and its fertilizing successors. Bred plants are entirely reliant upon concentrated fertilizers and in fact are bred to take full advantage of synthetic fertility. They are superior, engineered plants only as long as they get superior, artificial nutrition.

The central benefit of guano was more food for more people. It, not technology, played the central role in thwarting Malthusian pessimism. Ironically, however, the first cost of culture's conquest of fertility may have been starvation. Europe's potato blight, which killed and displaced millions of Irish, among other northern Europeans, beginning in 1842, probably did not travel to Europe in guano itself, spread as farmers fertilized their potato fields. But the blight likely traveled in the ships that carried the guano. The intensification of world trade contacts with Peru, the home of the potato and all its endemic pathogens, explains the coincidence of the simultaneous opening of the guano trade and the outbreak of the potato famine in guano's primary destinations. Demographically significant as well, hunger in Ireland and northern Europe kicked off the Great Migration to the New World that finally began to fully re-people the American landscape.

On the whole, guano and globalization were net gains for humans. The more ominous, largely unrecognized cost, however, was the explicit end of agricultural sustainability. Until powerful external sources of fertility such as guano were discovered, farmers had had to learn to maintain soil fertility or see their children, or their children's children, go hungry. Colonists and immigrants might enter new territories and mine virgin soils of their accumulated fertility, and they could keep moving toward the frontier in search of more untapped soils, but eventually frontiers meet and vanish in the collision. Frontier farmers were then forced, like their nonpioneer colleagues, to recycle fertility, to take the wastes produced by farming and reapply them to their fields. Livestock were pastured in the stubble of old crops which they converted to manure. Urban manures, the castoffs of food consumption by both humans and animals, were collected from city streets and cesspits, sold to farmers, and again spread over the fields. Silage, leaves, seaweed, ashes, and fish were collected locally. But their fertility was of limited capacity, and soils gave up their abundance grudgingly and only after much human effort. Guano broke agriculture's fertility barrier.

As farmers imported fertility from distant places, the market for urban manures and wastes declined, and urban hygienists found new modes of disposal. The toilet flushed away human waste, to be forgotten with the turn of a small lever, and animal waste was disposed of along with the nonorganic trash. It was a slow process, tempered in part by the limited nature and cost of such resources as guano and nitrates. Even today, some cultures cannot afford modern fertilizers and maintain the old systems.

The depletion of nitrates themselves threatened to take back the gains of the new agriculture. But it was, this time, a human, both hero and villain, who discovered a synthetic means to produce nitrogen. The German chemist Fritz Haber invented a process in 1908 that captured nitrogen from the air by bonding it to hydrogen stripped from coal. Fossil fuels, thus, give us liquid ammonia, NH_3. The Haber–Bosch process, as it came to be known, was enormously energy intensive, requiring high temperatures and extreme atmospheric pressures, but by the 1920s, it outstripped all other sources of agricultural nitrogen. For his efforts, Haber was awarded the Nobel Prize in chemistry in 1918 despite that his research was largely funded by the German war machine to produce gunpowder, not fertilizer, and that he enthusiastically headed up Germany's notorious chemical warfare department during World War I. He was the first scientist to be made an officer in the German army, the reward for introducing civilization to the possibilities of mass destruction. His wife Clara, also a chemist, was so opposed to his involvement that within days of his return from directing the world's first gas attack at the battle Ypres in April 1915 she shot herself. But synthetic nitrogen has saved more lives than chlorine, phosgene, and mustard gas (all Haber inventions) have killed, and we have Haber to thank for saving modern agriculture. But it was Peru's guano that set us on the path to a modern agriculture that involves massive fertility inputs and has led to similar external inputs of herbicides and pesticides. Now we run the danger of poisoning the very soils that have formed the foundation of all civilizations. Today, the Haber–Bosch process produces 500 million tons of fertilizer each year consuming 1 percent of the world's total energy output, not including the energy expended to transport and apply it to the world's farms. Without synthesized nitrogen it is estimated that 40 percent of the world's 6 billion people, predominantly first-world citizens who are most dependent on it, would starve to death.

Rivers Reversed

And the cultural conquests of nature kept coming. At the same time that humans convincingly demonstrated their capacity to move mighty mountains in such works as the Gran Canal and the Panama Canal, they also began to get the upper hand against tiny microbes. By the 1880s, Louis Pasteur had proven the link between human diseases and specific germs, but for tropical diseases, such as yellow fever and malaria, the question of how these germs were transmitted and contracted remained debated and unresolved until the turn of the century. The theory of mosquitoes as vector was first pronounced in 1854 in America and France, and in 1881 Carlos Juan Finlay of Havana stunningly identified the single mosquito species, out of a possible 800 candidates, that transmitted yellow fever. But it was not until well after Walter Reed's work in 1900, also at Havana, that the medical community became fully convinced of the mosquito's role. Thereafter, mosquito eradication campaigns across Latin America had tremendous demographic impacts. While never fully eliminated, mortality from these terrible tropical plagues declined wherever significant civil campaigns were implemented.

Latin America, with close ties to the northern hemisphere, benefited from and contributed to the progress of the age. Steam shovels, railroads, guano, nitrates, mosquito netting, and vaccinations bettered the quality of human life at an unprecedented pace. Human determination paid substantial dividends, whether exercised abroad or at home, for not only did knowledge and technology transfer rapidly from one culture to the next, but many Latin Americans too were impeccably trained and singularly motivated to advance agriculture, defeat disease, and build civilization.

However, Latin America lacked an essential ingredient of the modern age. Fossil fuels were the root source of culture's empowerment. Coal had powered the industrialization of the northern nations, forging iron and driving steam locomotives, ships, and factories. By the early twentieth century, coal was even synthesizing fertilizer. But most of Latin America's nations had no known coal reserves, and for those few that did, the reserves were small, of poor quality, or inconveniently located. In fact, there was little call for coal. Much of the region would continue to rely on firewood for both residential and industrial fuel needs.

Of greater concern, most of Latin America lacked petroleum. Mexico and Venezuela were, of course, important exceptions. When foreigners began to tap Mexico's oil fields just after 1900, they were often overwhelmed by what they found. Jack London visited Tampico during the Mexican Revolution and was informed by a former acquaintance from the Alaskan gold fields, now prospecting for oil, that Mexico's oil boom made Alaska's gold rush look like a church raffle. At some of the first test drillings it looked more like doomsday. On July 4th, 1908, American oil riggers drilling south of Tampico took a break for a patriotic lunch in honor of the holiday. Mid-meal they heard the tell-tale hiss of natural gas escaping from the well and rushed out to douse all the kitchen and boiler fires. They had found a gusher, and cries of "Eureka" must have been raised, but almost immediately cheers turned to screams of terror. The well began to come apart. The workers, many of them from Texas, were familiar with gushers, but this well jetted so much oil that it dismembered the huge derrick's timbers and scattered them in the direction of the workers. The riggers hoped the oil would ease back, allowing them to valve it off, but then the earth literally caved away, swallowing what remained of the derrick. The well casing itself was ejected from the earth precluding any possibility of capping the flow, and a second blow hole erupted nearby, an event never before witnessed. The earth's crust itself had been shattered by the deep oilfield's pressure. Two fountains of oil shot into the sky, one of them 12–20 meters wide and peaking at more than 300 meters. Around the well a crater formed 350 meters in diameter. Local Indians believed that hell itself had been unleashed and refused to be coerced into containing the flow. The gushing oil ran in a viscid river to the Tamiahua lagoon smearing everything – trees, vegetation, fish, birds, and crocodiles – with sticky, volatile crude. A week after the disaster, the fountains and river of oil took fire, possibly from lightning. The Well of Two Mouths (Dos Bocas), as it came to be known, turned into a veritable volcano, and residents of a town 27 kilometers distant claimed they could read the newspaper at night by its pillar of fire. It burned for two full months and virtually destroyed the forests and fishery upon which the local Huasteca Indians depended. Even after the fire had been extinguished, the oil kept gushing, a complete and total loss of a well that could have produced many millions of barrels of oil over many years. And although the Dos Bocas was the most catastrophic, many other wells also spread oil over the landscape and took fire. But for oil investors, uncontrollable gushers proved Mexico was a good investment.

Despite substantial revenue from leases and royalties, neither Mexico nor Venezuela would take much in the way of direct energy benefits from their oil reserves for decades. Not only was early oil production controlled by foreigners, the oil itself was almost entirely consumed by them. Petroleum was a commodity for the automobile age, a development Latin America would not experience for another half century.

So, with little coal and most of her oil spoken for, Latin America had little choice but to seek alternative sources of power. While continuing to consume firewood and small amounts of coal and oil, in the end, the region embraced hydroelectricity, and in many respects, it was an excellent choice. Electricity was the cutting edge power source and it held advantages that coal's steam and oil's internal combustion could not match. Electricity made cities visibly modern by lighting streets and homes, powering streetcars, and pumping sewage out of sight. While it required a monumental upfront investment, once in place a dam could produce power with little effort, mess, or pollution, at least compared to a coal mine or oil well. The source of the energy, falling water, seemed infinitely renewable, and, most important, electricity was by far the easiest and cheapest form of power to distribute. Threadlike copper wires could transport it instantaneously, with no additional energy inputs, to every citizen within reach of the rapidly expanding grid. Electricity, it was acclaimed, with its distributional advantage, would democratize power itself.

The same Latin American geography that made so many of her rivers unnavigable, dotted with falls and rapids, also made them excellent candidates for hydroelectric dams. Unlike fossil fuels, electricity did not have to be imported. Even where there were no falls and rapids, the volume of many tropical rivers was enough to turn massive turbines without significant head or a substantial reservoir. The region today, with only 8 percent of world population, contains 30 percent of world run off and produces 21 percent of the world's hydroelectric power. Already by 1900, a number of small, private hydropower stations had been established near Latin America's cities, mostly by foreign utility and trolley companies, but here, unlike in petroleum, the power benefits were felt by locals despite the sometimes high, monopolistic prices. Nascent industries such as textiles, automobiles, and chemicals, also took advantage of the new power. With electricity, factories could be built anywhere the wires could go, and were no longer limited to sites near water power or coal mines.

It is not improbable that at some future date the twentieth century will be known as the Age of Dams. They are culture's most massive constructions and transform the face of the land like no other technology by covering it with water. Civilization built dams from the beginning, but only at the beginning of the twentieth century did culture acquire the ability to stop nearly any river, no matter how mighty. While even today many dams are nothing more than carefully piled rubble, the central innovation was concrete reinforced with steel. Cements of many varieties had been used before to bond masonry, plaster walls and floors, and waterproof canals and water storage facilities, but nobody had used concrete structurally since the Romans. By 1900, with reinforced concrete, culture could build structures of unprecedented mass and strength.

And despite their monolithic quality, they could express substantial sophistication. While we think of the Panama Canal, the quintessential natural conquest of the period, as an expression of culture's ability to move mountains, the canal's success was in fact due to the new-found capacity to divert and dam rivers. Not to take away from the epic Culebra Cut through the continental divide, the Panamanian Isthmus was conquered by water control, not mountain removal. The canal is in reality a reservoir, a water bridge whose abutments are two massive concrete dams located at the reservoir's two extremes. The dams serve the purpose of supporting the water bridge, but they also consist of locks with the power to raise and lower massive ships. And the Panama dams produce electricity that powers the hundreds of electric motors controlling the complex locks. All that new technology came together at Panama, and then it spread across the world in thousands of hydrological projects.

Latin America, with few alternatives, joined the damming craze. The dams' promoters promised so much that it was little wonder that both populist and military regimes were willing to expend unprecedented quantities of public money and borrow as much again to build them. In addition to power, the primary justification, dams would stand to service culture's advance and comfort by irrigating parched soils, controlling devastating floods, offering navigation where ships could not previously go, supplying drinking water to thirsty, growing cities, and creating areas for recreation. For nations seeking modernization, large dams were the panacea.

Since the beginning, however, Latin America's dams generally shed the promises of multiple use in favor of exclusive power production. Electricity was the most important product of dams, and its primary consumer was to be industry for the sake of national advancement. Between 1900 and 1940, dozens of large, single-purpose concrete dams were constructed, such as Necaxa northwest of Mexico city and the Billings' system south of São Paulo, the latter named for the American engineer, Asa Billings, who had the audacity to not only stop a river, but to force it to flow backward. His efforts contributed substantially to São Paulo becoming Latin America's largest industrial center. Brazil's south coast presented a unique challenge and opportunity. The coastal range rose abruptly 700 meters out of the sea and received an astonishing 4,500 millimeters of average rainfall that together offered an incredible potential for power generation. The problem was that most of the rainfall flowed inland away from the Atlantic over rather flat terrain. Billings dammed the Pinheiros River such that its reservoir, once full, ran in reverse, spilling back over the coastal mountains down to the city of Cubatão where he located Brazil's largest generating plant. Water flowed down the mountain turning turbines, and power streamed back up to the city on high tension power lines. Electricity processed coffee, built automobiles, produced petrochemicals, and synthesized nitrogen, powering the growth of the greater metropolitan area and eventually turning Cubatão, at the base of the mountains, into Brazil's most heavily industrialized and lethally polluted city.

But it was after the 1940s when dam building in Latin America truly began in earnest, with completions peeking in the 1970s and 1980s. There were, no doubt, substantial gains to civilization as a result, all of them much touted by elected officials. By century's end, South America would have more than 900 large dams over 15 meters high, 500 of them in Brazil. The region has become more dependent on hydroelectric power than any other. Mexico derives 30 percent of its electric power from dams; but Chile relies on falling water for 60 percent of her electricity, Colombia 75 percent, and Brazil 95 percent. By contrast, the United States, which relies mostly on coal for electrical production, gets only 13 percent of its electrical generation from dams.

The benefits were obvious. Electrical consumption since 1970 increased by as much as fourfold per capita in some nations, which made life healthier and more comfortable for millions. Dams also reduced the region's dependence on foreign oil significantly. But only after a century has the region begun to fully realize the costs of large dams. Despite the purported cleanliness and renewability of Latin America's so-called white petroleum, rarely did nations sit down before a project and attempt to accurately weigh its benefits against its costs. And if they did, they only looked out a few decades.

The most destructive consequence of dam building, and one rarely included in the equation, is the obliteration of the landscape beneath the reservoir. In the process, both nature and culture have been drowned. Many of Latin America's reservoirs are monstrous, inundating vast landscapes that were formerly important for agriculture, fisheries, lumber, trade routes, and even urban services. Lake Mead, the largest U.S. reservoir, floods an astonishing 640 square kilometers. Brazil's Sobradinho reservoir on the São Francisco River covers 4,200 square kilometers, and the waters contained behind the Tucuruí and Balbina dams in the Amazon submerge 2,800 and 2,400 square kilometers, respectively. The Amazon's reservoirs have by themselves contributed substantially to the basin's deforestation and habitat loss by simple submersion. If Brazil were to build all the hydroelectric dams pro-posed for the Amazon basin, 75 in all, they would drown an area the size of Montana.

Nearly all dams in Latin America have been built not to meet exist-ing electrical demand but to create it. They have been seen as the engines of national development and have been overbuilt in the expec-tation that more electricity means more growth. Many Latin American dams took years to find customers for all their generating capacity. Reser-voirs are permanent civil constructions that fail to take into account the opportunity cost of flooding areas that on aggregate amount to a modest nation's entire territory. It is striking how nations who can spill blood over a few useless acres, such as the Falkland Islands, can so blithely sac-rifice sometimes extensive, priceless tracts of their own territory on the altar of power.

Sacrificed also are individual livelihoods and entire cultures. Since 1930, more than a half a million people have been displaced by dams in just Mexico and Brazil. Brazil's Sobradinho and Itaipu dams displaced 70,000 and 50,000 people, respectively; in Mexico, the Culiacan and Zimapan dams each inundated the homes of 25,000. Sometimes ris-ing reservoirs overtook communities entirely unawares. In 1956, soon after a Haitian dam closed its gates, local villagers in the valley above the dam awoke to find water swallowing their riverside crops and rising rapidly toward the village. Many reported they had time enough only to gather their children and their goats before being forced to abandon their homes and walk to higher ground. Everything they knew disap-peared before their eyes in an afternoon and was never seen again.

Even in more recent times, victims have either not been notified of their impending losses (all too often engineers fail to correctly estimate the size and reach of reservoirs) or are denied any compensation for the loss of their homes, jobs, farms, and fisheries. Their lifestyles and livelihoods have been drowned for the good of the nation. Even when compensated financially, or granted new lands outside the reservoir's reach, the displaced have been forced to live in new surroundings and with the consequences of the dams' expansive ecological transforma-tions. We moderns, with our extreme mobility and complete lack of attachment to place, truly fail to understand the deeper consequences of flooding someone's home. Criticism of dam construction usually empha-sizes waste, corruption, mismanagement, incompetence, and, above all, the very real fact that the benefits of power production are unjustly dis-tributed away from locals and in the direction of distant urban workers and often foreign corporations. But we miss the greater tragedy because we no longer understand that culture attaches itself to nature, and that if you tweak, transform, flood, or destroy nature, invariably you do the same to the cultures that inhabited it.

During the early phases of construction of the San Juan Tetelcingo dam in Mexico, the indigenous Nahuas who lived beneath the surface of the proposed reservoir stated their grievances as a list of the things they would lose by Mexico's drive for more electrical power consumption. Addressing themselves to President Carlos Salinas de Gortari in 1990, they enumerated the coming losses: their homes, their farms, their churches, their cemeteries, their ruins, their sacred caves and springs, their irrigation systems, and the natural resources on which they relied for food and income. "We would lose so many things we cannot express them all here because we would never finish this document." What they were trying to express but could not quite put into words was that the proposed dam was the prospect of cultural annihilation. They knew instinctively that the dam would be the death of their culture and the drowning of their history. Since the conquest they had survived and adapted as a culture on the valley lands that had remained in their possession, lands that for them, like their Aztec Nahua ancestors, held cultural meaning so strong they as a people could not be disassociated from their lands without cultural dissolution. Mexican history had shown repeatedly that indigenous cultural survival depended primarily on the Indians retaining their lands. Without indigenous nature, indigenous cultures almost inevitably dismember. The struggles over dams then really amounted to a cultural struggle, two different ways of life fighting over nature and its uses. Urban Latin Americans, whose culture is expansive, even imperialistic, are as dependent upon hydroelectric dams to maintain their culture as the Nahuas are dependent on unflooded homelands to maintain theirs. Fortunately, and to the surprise of many, this time democracy in Mexico worked to protect the minority party and the dam was cancelled in 1992.

A more cynical view would argue that the Tetelcingo dam was cancelled due to Mexico's abysmal financial straits at the time. A century of history predicted an outcome unfavorable to the Nahuas. Scores of cultures had been drowned by water and now lived a transformed existence. Tucuruí, a massive dam located on the Tocantins River of the eastern Amazon completed in 1984, exemplifies the disastrous cultural and environmental consequences of large dams. The dam's primary beneficiary is Alcoa, a foreign aluminum producer, which receives two thirds of the plant's generating capacity and employs very few people. The dam's reservoir displaced 35,000 people in 17 towns and villages, both indigenous and nonindigenous, all of whom lived by flood agriculture, fishing, turtles, and river transportation services. All these activities were destroyed or disrupted. Those who lived by fishing saw dozens of species disappear and an overall decline of 60 percent in the catch soon after the dam was completed. The dam made no provision for a fish ladder, so spawning fish could not migrate above it to breed. The downstream side of the dam experienced reduced water flows of clear, blue water that eroded the river banks. Previously, the river had flooded predictably providing riverside farms with new fertile silt every year. One downstream farmer was entirely disoriented by the dam's changes, claiming that without seasonal flooding he did not know when to plant or even whether it was summer or winter. Without a natural flowing river and its consistent seasonal behavior, locals were at a loss as to how to behave and survive. The forests above the dam were entirely flooded due to a failed attempt to clear them for timber before the dam's gates were closed. The result is a highly acidic, poorly oxygenated lake that not only kills certain species of fish but even damages some of the dam's delicate mechanisms. A huge skeletal forest stands naked under water. And although part of the original plan, the dam does not have locks, so the river is less valuable for moving goods into and out of the region than it used to be.

Among the most serious problems was a rise in the incidence of disease in and around the reservoir, which served as an excellent breeding ground for mosquitoes. The incidence of malaria rose, especially among children. Mansonia mosquitoes, potential carriers of filariasis, throve on the new reservoir and teemed in such numbers that they forced the evacuation of some of the newly relocated towns. Farmers complained mosquitoes hampered their work even at midday when they were usually inactive. In one study, researchers recorded 500 mosquito bites per hour per person in the early evening hours. Locals were forced to stay inside their homes, which they filled with unhealthy smoke to find relief.

Of course change, even destruction, can bring new opportunities previously unavailable. The tucunaré (*Cichla temensis*), known as the peacock bass to sport fishing tourists who will pay a price to experience its celebrated resistance to the reel, flourishes in the reservoir, along with a few other species, and locals have found a substantial income chartering fishing trips among the dead trees that still poke out of the lake near the shoreline. The fish also feed local families. And the submerged trees themselves, an estimated 1.5 million high-grade hardwoods, are being harvested by adventurous men who dive to the forest floor with breathing gear and special, underwater chain saws. Once cut, a process of about five minutes, the tree falls up instead of down and is towed to the sawmill where it is turned into flooring for American dining rooms.

Culture changes nature, nature changes culture: it has been an active dialectic since the arrival of the human species. And it is impossible to say if life is better or worse for the people living with large dams. Which is exactly the problem. After spending billions of dollars, their benefits to humans should outweigh their costs in the most obvious manner, but they often do not. A large portion of the debt that hangs around the neck of developing nations derives from these massive power projects. After so much sacrifice and sometimes fiscal ruin, dams should have more to show for all their troubles. The reality is that while most of them provide more power than most cities can initially consume, their single-minded justification, more power, has made such basic dam services, such as providing clean, sustainable water to urban residents, often not even an afterthought. Power companies have been happy to let falling sewage run their turbines.

The most pressing question, even if we assume that some dams have brought measurable benefits, is one of longevity. Other than outright structural failure, which is not improbable in a region of notable seismic activity, how long will dams, the largest, most expensive human constructions in history, service our needs? When constructed, many dam boosters naively assumed these monuments were to be permanent fixtures, as timeless as the pyramids. But time is not a friend to most dams. Sedimentation is a major menace, particularly in rivers that carry heavy loads of silt as do many in Latin America, or in areas where erosional processes are exacerbated by human activities. While governments throw billions at dams they frequently spend little to nothing on protecting the reservoir's upriver watersheds, forests and soils. The Billings reservoir, once centered in the midst of the Atlantic forest, is now fairly surrounded by São Paulo's urban expansion, and its waters are silted, threatened not only by filth but by the loss of depth. The Haitian dam that flooded out peasants in 1956 was closed in 1986 as the reservoir became uselessly filled with sediment. Was the cost, financial and human, worth 20 years of power production and flood control? José Lutzenberger, Brazil's late environmental leader and a biting critic of national development schemes, estimated that Itaipu, the world's largest hydroelectric dam, rising 196 meters, spanning 7.7 kilometers, producing 12,600 MegaWatts, and costing $18 billion, would silt up in a matter of 30 years. Most agree his prognosis was too pessimistic, but with increasing population growth, agricultural development, and deforestation across the Paraná River's extensive watershed, time will tell.

The other concern is climate. Dams only produce electricity if the rains come, and dams were built without the slightest calculation of the risk of climate change, or of the danger of putting nearly all of one's energy eggs in a single basket. In 2001, a severe drought gave Brazil a taste of what could happen. Reservoirs fell so low that the federal government, as of May, began to mandate a 20 percent reduction in electrical usage. Many Brazilians responded admirably, shutting off lights, buying compact fluorescents, disconnecting appliances and air conditioners, and taking the stairs instead of elevators. Residential demand fell by a commendable 22 percent. Still, many were angry at the inconvenience and cold showers: protesters marched in the streets carrying candles that on this occasion suggested the government's poor planning was going to send them back to Stone Age. The government cancelled all nighttime public events, including soccer matches. There were probably fewer public expressions of anger than the potential because every third street light was shut off: people stayed inside for fear the streets were to be taken over by the criminal element. The President's approval rating fell to its lowest level. Economists warned that Argentina's economic crisis was certain to spill over into Brazil, but Brazilians, always calm in a crisis, weathered the lack of weather. Brazil's projected economic growth for the year, however, was set back about 50 percent. Brazilian officials responded quickly to popular pressure by announcing the construction of more than 50 new electrical plants, most of them powered by natural gas imported from Bolivia, to reduce their dependency on the climate by increasing their dependency on an unpredictable foreign supplier. There was even official talk of nuclear facilities.

The problem with power has always been that it goes to one's head, that it becomes an end in itself rather than an instrument. Even for Machado de Assis who sought cultural recognition for Rio de Janeiro, a bridge across the bay had as much symbolic value, evidence of man's conquest of nature, as it had practical utility. And little had changed by the time Brazil's military government, notorious for pharaonic projects, finally bridged Rio de Janeiro's bay in 1974. Officially named for the military president who ordered its construction, when completed the government touted the bridge as the world's longest. But it did not have to be. The bridge spans more than 13 kilometers despite the fact that there were two sites at which the bay could have been spanned in less than 3 kilometers. Pride, bragging rights, and symbolism beat out practicality in the bridge's siting.

Culture's empowerment in the twentieth century has contributed wildly to human success in the face of nature. Humans today are more numerous, wealthier, healthier, and safer than we have ever been. But power has become addictive, and it remains our cultural panacea. The presupposed solution to many of our problems is more – more power, more oil, more dams, more nuclear power plants, more ethanol – and we spend billions in public money to enhance our powers while we invest comparatively nothing in technologies that could maintain and enhance standards of living while reducing our need for power. Our current way of life is maintained by the constant addition of power-hungry, technological props. Kick any one of them away – internal combustion, synthetic nitrogen, concrete dams, paved highways, pesticidal agriculture – and much that we take for granted comes crashing down. Rather than adding more props, or propping up current props, our investments ought to evidence wisdom instead of betray insatiability.

CHAPTER SIX

Asphyxiated Habitats: the Urban Environment

> From dawn to dusk you will see a constant multitude . . . that comes
> and goes along the ten great streets that open on to the square. . . .
> In the space of one paving stone you will see a civil guardsmen, a
> match-seller, a financier, a poor man, and a soldier. Groups of stu-
> dents pass by, servants, generals, ministers, respectable folk, bull-
> fighters, ladies, . . . everywhere high hats, a smile on the lips. . . .
> And it is not the bustle of a busy people; it is the vivacity of cheerful
> persons, a carnival-like joy, a restless idleness, a feverish overflow
> of pleasure that takes hold of you and makes you want to go round
> and round the square without leaving it.[1]

Human activity has ranged across the landscape leaving footprints in
every corner and clime. Some of our tracks are insubstantial and easily effaced by natural forces; others are disfiguring, virtually indelible.
We have trampled the earth, creating pockets of devastation, temporary
and permanent – holes in the forests, holes in the mountains, and now
holes in the atmosphere. But in favored locations, civilization has built
rather than gouged. If deforestation, mine tailings, and ozone depletion
are the negative evidence of culture's historical presence, the city is
culture's positive manifestation, testimony to human creativity in the
midst of so much destruction, evidence of the attempt to achieve constructive permanence among so many other transitory undertakings.
Cities are one of culture's few enduring commitments to the landscape:
monuments, homes, and streets that are intended to outlive their

---

[1] Edmondo de Amicis [describing Madrid's Puerto del Sol square], quoted in Elizabeth Nash, *Madrid: A Cultural and Literary Companion* (New York: Interlink
Books, 2000), 24–5.

builders to be inherited and improved by succeeding generations. And thus the city becomes part of the environment, what some have labeled the built environment.

Increasingly, and particularly in Latin America, civilization's success will stand or fall on the sustainability of its cities. Holes and monuments, of course, are inseparably connected. The city is a multicelled organism that sends out its tentacles – roads and railroads, power lines and pipelines – to strip from its hinterland the food, water, power, and building materials it requires to feed its voracious maw. As different as we are from nonhuman species, much of the time we humans act like animals, driven by primitive instincts to compete, consume, and reproduce. Like cormorants and coral, the human species builds a complex, crowded home from which it sallies forth to gather the resources to feed itself and its progeny. But humans are a sort of super species with an almost unlimited potential for consumption. All creatures can increase their consumptive impact through population growth, but we are the only species that can realize growth per capita, and today we tend to measure human success not by what we have accomplished but by the rate we add thereto. As a result, the principal human habitat of our age, the city, and all its material demands, has expanded at the expense of nearly all nonhuman habitats, particularly during the last century. But rather than see the city as a spreading cancer, a common metaphor for urban growth and consumption, it is more constructive to see the city as the appropriate habitat for modern humanity, a human nest or hive that in its strivings for cultural immortality plants the seed of cultural sustainability.

Foreigners who concern themselves with Latin America's environment have generally either damned the region's cities for their environmental sins or have overlooked them in favor of rainforests, endangered species, and national parks. But to write off or neglect the city, particularly in Latin America, is a mistake. As a region, it is among the most heavily urbanized: 75 percent of its inhabitants live in cities, equaling the urban intensity of the United States and Europe. South America, after Australia, is the second-most urbanized continent at 80 percent. Contrast that with Asia or Africa, each with rates of less than 40 percent. And individual Latin American nations present impressive urban concentrations: Brazil, 83 percent; Chile, 87; Venezuela, 88; Argentina, 90; and Uruguay, 92. Again, by contrast, Spain and Portugal, the Iberian cultural precedents, are respectively only 64 and 48 percent urban. Latin America has more than 60 metropolitan areas with populations in excess of 1 million. The city, particularly the big city, is the overwhelmingly preferred habitat for Latin Americans, despite its notorious tribulations.

Urban Traditions

Fortunately, Latin Americans love the city and aspire to an ever-ascendant urbanity. Unlike North Americans who historically have had a palpable apprehension, even dread of urban agglomerations and urbane morality, preferring with Jefferson the farm, the field, and a bit of distance between one's neighbors, Latin Americans held the city, the townhouse, and the plaza in the highest esteem. To be happily civilized was to have a street address, and the Incas, Aztecs, and Ibero-Americans were in full agreement on this point. North American colonists established farms and let cities take root organically, if they did at all. Iberians, where there was not already an indigenous city in place, platted out their towns before all else, more than a thousand of them just in the colonial period. Already by 1600, 48 percent of those in Spain's American colonies lived in cities, a rate not achieved in industrializing England until the mid-nineteenth century. After a century of British colonization in North America, only 5 percent of British subjects could call themselves city folk. Even for rural Spanish landholders, the townhouse, not the farmhouse, was generally their primary residence, and the high incidence of absentee, rural landlords was not so much for lack of interest in the farm but due to an abiding desire to spend as much time as possible in the city.

The Latin American city was made for people, to meet their needs for economic and social life. Iberian city planners took their cues from a city ideal created by the Romans but scarcely implemented in Europe. A New World offered a rare opportunity: to build new cities, from scratch, on perfect, rational lines. The resulting Ibero-American city revolved around the plaza (which, like the English word "place," originated from the Latin *"platea"* for "broad street") that served as the city's essential public space, the setting on which conquerors could be feted in parades, saints honored in processions, heretics punished at the gallows, and where citizens could mingle with one another in daily, almost ritual strolls as well as at frequent markets, bullfights, and festivals. Accentuated by the religious, civic, and residential edifices that surrounded it on

Figure 9. The street as public space. The feast of the Holy Ghost at the Church of Santa Ana, Rio de Janeiro, circa 1850.
Source: Thomas Ewbank, *Life in Brazil* (New York: Harper & Brothers, 1856), 341. Courtesy of the Harold B. Lee Library, Brigham Young University, Provo, Utah.

all sides, the plaza was the city's stage for the sacred, profane, and mundane (see Figure 9). From the central plaza, topography permitting, the city extended in an orderly fashion along the cardinal points.

In the city dweller's mind, the city was divided into two spheres: the house, which was private in the extreme, even cloistered, to protect the property of men and the virtue of women; and the street, which was usually dirty, sometimes dangerous, but public space, and best understood as an extension of the public plaza rather than as exclusive to transportation. Wheeled vehicles made no appearance in pre-Columbian cities and were of little importance in the colonies until the late eighteenth century, or even later. Indians and slaves carried most loads on their backs. We generally describe Hispanic city planning as the laying out of rectilinear streets, but that probably shows our bias toward the street as transportation. When the king set down the rules of city planning in America, he insisted that a cord and rule be used to set off plazas, streets, and city blocks, but it is quite probable city folk thought of the city more as regular blocks of buildings than as a grid of streets. Quite often, it

is the blocks of buildings in colonial cities that are regular; the streets
dead end, bend, or broaden inexplicably. Western maps, well into the
nineteenth century, represent cities as blocks of buildings, not as grids
of streets; the streets were the empty space left over once the city's carefully delineated blocks were filled with buildings. That negative, unbuilt
space, the plazas and the streets, formed the urban commons that served
multiple uses, none of which were zoned. Streets had no sidewalks, and
plazas were not raised; each was continuous with the other, the plaza just
a broader "street" as the Romans understood it. Today's plazas are usually
landscaped, pedestrian spaces enveloped in a rancorous ring of halting
traffic. In the colonial era carts, carriages, and mostly pedestrians traveled in any direction and paused in any location on the plaza and street;
there were no traffic lanes, sidewalks, or designated parking. And streets,
like plazas, were given names not as an address system to find one's way
around as today but because they were public spaces worthy of a name.
The fact that streets were renamed every few blocks (sometimes every
block) suggests they were thought of more as distinct spaces rather than
linear continuities connecting one part of town with another. The street
was where life took place. Until the arrival of the automobile, the street
was never perceived as an exclusive corridor through which goods and
people shuttled to other locations.

In addition to the urban layout, the king also required a host of other
minutia that would help make the city a functional human habitat.
Foremost, he insisted that cities not be built in areas where the surrounding countryside, the city's hinterland, could not supply sufficient timber,
pasture, farmland, fuel, and fresh water. Successful cities depended on
sufficient natural resources, and to build them elsewhere was to squan-
der rather limited human resources. Cities were not to be built up into
the hills as this would expose residents to the fiercer elements and winds
and make their servicing with goods and water more difficult. Nor were
cities to extend into low, swampy areas that might expose citizens to
fevers and epidemics. The king zoned all offensive occupations, such as
tanning, fishmongering, and butchering, downwind and downriver of
the city center. Even the climate was considered. Streets were to be ori-
ented so as not to be exposed to the strongest winds. In cold climates, the
streets were to be broad to let the sun warm the populace; in hot climes,
narrow to provide shade. And homes and edifices were to be built of a
single style to give the city aesthetic unity. Of course, not all of these
regulations were implemented, and cities across the region show considerable variety, but official visions of the ideal city left an impressive

mark on Latin America's urban design during one history's most active periods of city building.

Despite holding substantial populations, at least relative to North American cities, Latin America's cities did not sprawl beyond human scale until the end of the nineteenth century. Even the region's largest city, Mexico City, could be comfortably traversed on foot. But the scale of the human habitat was about to explode due to the two congruent processes of population and urban growth. In the industrializing north, population growth preceded urbanization, but there is good evidence that population concentration began in some Latin American cities well before the region fully entered its surge of demographic growth after 1940. In Mexico City, prominent citizens were complaining of urban growth in the late eighteenth century, and one suggested building a wall and taking censuses to prevent rural folk from making the choice of an urban lifestyle. By the end of the nineteenth century, the city's growth was noteworthy. From about 200,000 in 1858, Mexico City grew to 345,000 in 1900 and then jumped to 471,000 by 1910, a 28-percent increase in a single decade. The city's footprint increased from a mere 8 square kilometers in 1858 to more than 40 in 1910. But this growth, though notable, was still a gentle prelude to what was to come.

For most of human history, population has hardly grown at all. If, since the opening of settled agriculture about 10000 B.C., the human population had grown at a rather modest 1 percent per year, today the world's population, as painted by one scholar, would be a sphere of human bodies larger than the known universe that would be expanding, barring the laws of relativity, at a rate faster than the speed of light. Such is the power of compounding progeny. The historical failure of humans to attain even modest, sustained growth before the modern era is because death focused most of its powers on human babies and children: until recently, death had its greatest successes among the very young, killing most humans before they had the chance to reproduce. Infant mortality, the number of children who died before their first birthday, was commonly above 35 percent in the preindustrial era. Hence, until the demographic revolutions, periods of sustained population growth that began in the late eighteenth century for Europe and the mid-twentieth century for Latin America, human populations remained comparatively small.

Population's rise in the modern era is the result of death control. In preindustrial Europe, births added about 4 percent to the population each year; but death decreased the population by about 3.5 percent, on average. However, over a period of two centuries, the death rate declined to less than 1 percent annually, and death, while declining overall, increasingly visited the aged instead of the infant. This initial conquest of death was due almost entirely to more food in more varieties, a belated benefit of the Columbian Exchange. Medical advances played little role in thwarting death in early industrializing nations. And populations grew at unprecedented rates because European birth rates remained high for nearly a century after death rates had begun to fall.

Latin America's demographic revolution came much later than Europe's, but it was far more rapid and pronounced. First of all, for reasons not yet understood, birth rates had been higher in Latin America than in Europe, as high as 5 percent per year, near the historical human maximum. But high death rates persisted in Latin America until the twentieth century due to tropical diseases, particularly malaria, yellow fever, and a number of gastrointestinal infections. Here, medicine played a central role. The increasing availability of vaccinations after the 1920s and the discovery of both penicillin and DDT in 1939 sent Latin America's death rates into a tailspin. What took Europe and North America two centuries to accomplish in death control, Latin America experienced in a couple decades. By 1960, death rates had fallen to 1 percent of the population annually, and by 1980 to 0.6 percent. And since birth rates remained high, above 4 percent until the mid-1970s, Latin America's population grew at 3.5 percent or more per year even without a boost from foreign immigration. While the baby-booming United States grew at an average 1.5 percent each year from 1940 to 1970, Latin America grew by more than 3 and 4 percent.

And if national population growth set new records, urban growth rates shattered them. Mexico City, which had only 1.5 million people in 1940, grew by 100 percent in the 1940s, and doubled again in the 1950s; during the 1970s and 1980s, the city increased 50 percent each decade. The contrast to Europe's urbanization is telling. In its 50-year growth spurt (1850–1900) London grew from 2.7 to 6.6 million, about 2.5 times. Mexico City, a century later but in the same length of time (1940–1990) grew from 1.5 to 15 million, a factor of 10. Each on its own schedule, and in current order of metropolitan size, Mexico City, São Paulo, Buenos Aires, Rio de Janeiro, Lima, Bogotá, Santiago, Belo Horizonte, Guadalajara, Porto Alegre, Caracas, Monterrey, Recife, Salvador, Guayaquil, Medellín, Fortaleza, Curitiba, and Santo Domingo, many of them quite small to start, all became immense cities of more than 3 million within an historical blink of the eye.

Why did Latin America's rural peoples migrate to the cities in record numbers? We tend to emphasize the push factors of rising rural populations, insecure land tenure, and the mechanization of agriculture, which were, no doubt, leading causes. It is also probable that erosion and increasing infertility in the countryside forced some rural people to the city. But the city has had its own gravitational pull. First, as we have noted, the city had long been attractive to Latin Americans, and in fact many of those who did migrate came not from farms and ranches but rural towns; these folk were already familiar with the street and the plaza. By contrast, North America's rural folk had very little experience with cities of any size and feared the move more than their southern neighbors. Additionally, as opportunities and employment declined in the countryside, they were on the rise in the city. Many chose to move to the largest national and provincial cities because they offered better opportunities for industrial and service work with steady, nonseasonal wages. Formal unemployment was high, but the city presented a multitude of informal prospects unavailable in the countryside, including peddling and domestic service. Moreover, despite the city's often grim poverty, the majority of those who moved from the country to the city improved their standard of living, gaining access to education, healthcare, clean water, sewers, and electricity. In 1960s Mexico City, urban household income exceeded the national average by 185 percent. When word got back to rural relatives of their city cousins' relative gains, people voted for the city with their feet. City immigrants disparaged those who stayed down on the farm as lacking courage and ambition, expressing pride in their new urban identity by casting aspersions at the peasant culture to which they were born. A move to the city also entailed enhanced freedoms. The landless poor, who had lived under the economic and political thumb of their landlords, now had the chance to vote their own conscience, to own their own self-built house, and to either choose their employer or work for themselves.

Whatever the motives, the consequences of such rapid urban growth were painful. Even if city officials had had the best of intentions, had inherited their colonial kings' rational plans, and had full coffers, the city's explosive growth would have negated the best of policies. If first-world cities like London and New York could not avoid crowded tenements, unemployment, street children, and piles of refuse while their cities grew comparatively modestly, third world cities, which grew more than twice as fast, appeared doomed. People crowded into old tenements, almost to the point of standing room only, and then began to squat on the city's perimeter, the hills above and the swamps below, where the king had prohibited growth in the colonial era. Whereas the city had previously been planned and platted ahead of potential growth by royal officials, now it expanded organically with little or no order. Beginning in the 1930s, Rio de Janeiro's immigrants built their shanties right up the sides of steep mountains or on stilts out over the swamps. In Lima, entire neighborhoods appeared overnight, as was the case with Ciudad de Dios in which thousands of squatters successfully conspired to rush and claim the desert south of the city on Christmas Eve, 1954. And even where surveyors worked ahead of the immigrants, the growth was so fast and in so many directions that urban services often lagged years behind. Growth's pressures were greater than any city, no matter how nimble its planners, could manage. There was too much infrastructure to build, and the cost was overwhelming. Again, to get a sense of the scale of the challenge, metropolitan Mexico City today has more inhabitants than Australia, Greece, Portugal, Sweden, Austria, Chile, Hungary, or Bolivia; and more than any Canadian province or U.S. state except California.

We do not have space here to do justice to all of Latin America's urban environmental crises. Many, like Mexico City, suffer from insufficient and increasingly contaminated water resources. The cost in dams, pumps, and pipelines to bring fresh water to urban residents must be heavily subsidized or the poor could not afford this most basic of human requirements. Due to the immediate health dangers of sewage most cities do provide sewage hookups, but the effluent runs in open ditches, and only a tiny percentage is treated before being pumped into rivers, bays, and oceans which themselves threaten downstream water supplies and fisheries. Cities have had even less success with solid waste. Across the expanse of slums where it is sometimes impossible to send garbage trucks due to narrow or steep lanes, refuse piles in streets and vacant lots where the final solution is to burn it creating an acrid black smoke that hangs over many such neighborhoods. Much of urban housing is wholly inadequate, built of castoff materials hobbled together as primitive shelter. It is, however, surprising how quickly much of this self-help housing transforms itself from cardboard and corrugated panels to masonry walls and tile roofs, evidence of the residents' successful scrabble for urban pay and their willingness to work with their own hands. But much of it remains substandard, woefully unprepared and precariously sited for natural disasters as recent earthquakes, hurricanes, and even thunderstorms have shown.

Automotive Carnage

Water, sewage, solid waste, and housing, as pressing as they are, have troubled cities for ages, but one of Latin America's most urgent environmental problems is of very recent birth. Not 40 years ago, the skies above Mexico City were still generally described as remarkable for their clarity. Today, elementary school teachers in Santiago, São Paulo, and Mexico City have noted the first generation of children who paint their skies as they see them, not in the ordinary hues of transparent blue but in grotty grays and browns. City dwellers in Latin America have long dealt with filth on various levels, but only now are human beings threatened with asphyxiation by filthy oxygen. The automobile is the most recent urban plague, and unfortunately air pollution is not its only contribution to civic misery. The car, as favored transportation, has sideswiped Latin America's venerable urban traditions.

Of course the car's history in Latin America reaches back to the beginning of the twentieth century. Even a century before that people were already complaining of the increasing number of wheeled vehicles in the streets, a rather new development in a region that for centuries had relied on Indian and African backs to move goods and people. In Mexico City, residents grumbled about private carriages driven on public streets as much for ostentation as transportation that increased city noise and imperiled pedestrians. Brazil's emperor, Pedro I, detested the teams of noisy oxcarts traveling about Rio de Janeiro. Ox drovers refused to grease their axles in the belief the whining axle heartened the ox in his work. Pedro passed an ordinance against unlubricated axles and would, when occasion warranted, descend from his own carriage to impose the fine personally.

The automobile itself began, as elsewhere, as a toy for the rich. Automobile clubs formed in various Latin American nations before 1910 creating opportunities for the rich to tour the countryside in boisterous, weekend cavalcades on narrow, rutted highways. Their sons pitted courage and horsepower against one another on race tracks improvised of recently plowed fields. The clubs formed a natural lobby for government-funded road building, and they were joined in particular by foreign auto, tire, and road-building equipment companies. U.S. automakers, such as Ford and General Motors, sponsored all-expense-paid junkets to bring Latin American officials to the United States to see the blessings of the automobile age, and most were duly impressed. Railroad construction and investment had begun to stagnate just before

World War I, and roads were increasingly seen as the future of transport, the least expensive way to open new areas to agriculture and beat the railroads' unpopular monopolies.

By the 1920s, road construction in Brazil had become an obsession as another symbol of modernity, and each year the government increased its financial commitments, the beginning of a massive, ongoing subsidy to the automotive transport sector patterned after that of the United States. In 1915, the Ford Motor Company opened its first assembly plant in São Paulo, and then others in Porto Alegre and Recife in 1925. By 1928, Ford had 700 dealers in Brazil. Ford promoted auto and tractor sales in annual caravans of the latest models that paused to parade in a new town each afternoon and to show promotional films at night. Movies of Henry Ford and his factories, shown at no charge in theaters and on town squares, were the first films ever seen by some town folk. General Motors countered with its Chevrolet Circus that included a much-promoted charity raffle for an Oldsmobile Sport Roadster. Monteiro Lobato, a car lover and ever the champion of modernization, translated Henry Ford's autobiography *My Life and Works* and considered it the most important piece of literature a Brazilian could read to advance the nation's material gains. By 1930, Brazil had about 100,000 cars on its expanding highway network, and the truck increasingly replaced the train as the preferred way to move Latin America's goods.

But the car remained a status symbol and toy of the very rich, a small market indeed. The also tiny urban middleclass could rarely afford the car, so until the last quarter of the twentieth century there were relatively few private vehicles on Latin America's city streets. In fact, the car's real advantage was in the expansive countryside, not in cities; the early auto clubs were made up largely of rural landholders. For most of the twentieth century city dwellers did not need automotive transport. Beginning in the mid-nineteenth century, Latin America's cities followed earlier trends in mass transportation, installing horse-drawn omnibuses, which were enclosed, passenger wagons set on rails. Horses fueled by hay and emitting manure formed the first public transportation, and only then did cities extend much beyond the bounds of a comfortable walk. The rich began their move away from their traditionally prized location at city center to build suburban mansions on the new, broad avenues. Beginning in the 1890s, electric streetcars, also running on rails, would come to replace horse-drawn public transportation and assisted the city's further expansion. The streetcar was very popular with citizens: it was modern, comfortable, fast, and produced neither horse manure nor exhaust. More than lighting, the need for movement brought electricity to the cities, and the streetcar dominated urban transport in Latin America for more than half a century, its clanging bell and clacking track becoming an accepted part of the public street and plaza.

However, just as Latin America followed first-world demographic and urban trends, it has also closely followed its transportation fashions, for good and ill. In the United States, the private automobile and the public bus had almost completely replaced streetcars by the 1930s turning the city streets into the car's exclusive domain. Lacking mufflers and emission-control devices, early vehicles cast horrendous noise and spewed noisome exhaust in the faces of pedestrian shoppers now banished by fear, if not law, to narrow sidewalks. Car ownership tripled in the United States in the 1920s, and in succeeding decades urban super highways designed to move more private cars more quickly divided or obliterated city neighborhoods. Latin America, largely due to lower per capita income, lagged behind the first world in motorization, but here too, by the 1970s, urban streetcars were phased out in favor of buses, and then private cars. A number of factors have been raised to explain this universal transformation including dirty dealing by the automotive industry, accused of buying public transport so they could destroy it. Whatever the motives, the city converted its streets, its public spaces, into roads, that is, open highways. The conversion of streets to roads was universal: in most cases not a single street evaded vehicular traffic except the narrowest and steepest of alleys. This conversion cost considerable money, and increasing fractions of public outlay subsidized cars and buses while neglecting other forms of transport. Streetcar lines had had to build and maintain their tracks and electrical infrastructure, often on unpaved, unimproved streets. With the public funding of road paving, lane demarcation, signalization, and parking, car owners had a free infrastructure over which to roam, and streetcars could not compete fairly for the space. The road subsidy (combined with the already powerful incentives of status and freedom associated with the private car) explains why the car invaded and conquered the urban commons.

The consequences have completely transformed the city as human habitat. While some benefits do come as a result of car ownership, in Latin America they accrue almost entirely to the wealthy and impose a multitude of costs on everyone, rich and poor alike. The most obvious and pressing is air pollution, and in cities like Mexico City, Caracas, and Santiago, asphyxiation is not a great exaggeration. Oxygen is the human organism's most immediate need, more critical to life than food, water, or shelter, and on bad days breathing can be difficult in some cities, especially for children and the elderly. For years Latin Americans had blamed industry and greedy capitalists for the air they breathed, but automobiles and trucks now produce 60–80 percent of urban air pollution, a fact that has become more apparent as urban industry has declined, relocated, or turned to natural gas. Citizens complain of sore throats and burning eyes, and drug stores do a steady business in surgical face masks. In a single day of walking about the big Latin American city one's mucous membranes blacken, and, if its hot and humid, one contracts a black case of ring around the collar as the pollution that settles on your skin dribbles down your perspiring neck.

Most Latin American cities pollute no more than U.S. cities, and often much less. In the United States there are 780 cars per 1,000 inhabitants; most Latin American nations have fewer than 150, although many of the vehicles are older models, and only recently have leaded fuels been banned and catalytic converters required. However, many cities are plagued by winter inversions and mountain valley locations. So, while Mexico City, Santiago, and Caracas produce far less pollution per capita than most U.S. cities, they are forced to live in their own filth, much like Los Angeles and Salt Lake City, because on many days of the year the filthy air around them, compressed under a temperature inversion or pinned behind high mountains, does not ventilate and blow away with the predominant winds. The air is visible, almost palpable. Some of the residents of Santiago, a city named for Saint James, refer to the city as Santiasco, literally Saint Nausea, or loosely translated as Smogtiago. On one particularly bad air day in Mexico City, suffocating birds dropped from the sky mid-flight onto the main square, veritable canaries in a coal mine. An estimated 4,000 persons, most of them elderly, die of respiratory conditions related to Mexico City's air pollution each year, more people than die annually in car accidents. Mário Molina, the Mexican chemist awarded the Nobel Prize for his discovery that common refrigerants, chlorofluorocarbons, eroded the earth's protective ozone layer, possibly the biggest environmental save of the twentieth century, has reminded Mexico City's residents that a mere 10 percent reduction in air pollution would reduce human deaths in the city by more than 1,000 per year. The number of children admitted to hospitals and clinics during severe air pollution events increases substantially. And while most child deaths remain the direct result of car accidents, for adults, air pollution may be the most mortal factor of urban life as it has been shown to contribute substantially to heart disease and lung cancer.

There is no simple solution to air pollution. One Mexican official argued that the air problem, compared to the city's water difficulties, was minor, for it could be fixed in a day by simply banning all vehicles from the roads. But to turn off the city's internal combustion engines would bring the city to a veritable halt as quickly as would cutting off its water. All cities are dependent upon transportation systems: to earn, to eat, and to live, people must get to work and to market, and goods must get from farms and factories to markets and homes. Due to the way we have built the human habitat over the last century, a habitat that answers to the needs of car owners, most of that must happen on rubber tires.

The solutions proffered to clear the filthy air are legion. Mexico City officials have been particularly imaginative. It was proposed that a huge hole be drilled in the city's ring of mountains to let the polluted, inverted air drain from the Valley of Mexico not unlike the Gran Canal did for polluted water. Another useless proposal considered placing gigantic fans at the valley's canyon exits to ventilate the city. In Santiago a massive air filter was installed, a sort of tremendous bong that passes polluted air through a water filter to put nary a dent in the problem. The best-known program is Mexico City's "Hoy no Circula" (Today, this Car Stays Put) instituted in 1989. In an effort to reduce pollution by reducing the number of commuting cars, the city banned each car from the road one workday per week. If your license plate ended in 0 or 1, you could not drive Monday; 2 or 3, Tuesday, and so on. The ban is strictly enforced with substantial fines, and compliance is quite high. The result, ironically, has been more cars and more pollution. Many families and businesses that owned one car refused to live without it even for one day and solved the problem by buying a second car, usually an older, more polluting model. Within six months after the program began, the city's gasoline consumption rose substantially rather than fell. The used car market before the ban exported some 75,000 cars each year to Mexico's lesser cities. After the ban, the flow of used vehicles reversed, and the city imported 85,000 cars annually. The second car was initially purchased to drive on the one day the family's primary car was excluded from the roads, but once in hand, both cars were often driven four days a week creating far more congestion and pollution than had there been no ban.

Movement is critical, but the central question is at what cost. Consider another difference between traditional streets and auto roads. Streets carried tiny public price tags. They appeared by the happenstance of the construction of city blocks which defined their space, were usually unpaved – a reality that persisted into the early twentieth century for even U.S. cities – and required, or at least received, very little maintenance. Roads, on the other hand, required grading, paving, repaving, sidewalks, signalization, complicating drainage systems, and parking. The cost of converting streets to roads, and as Latin America's cities have expanded in the last quarter century, of building enormous networks of new roads, has been tremendous. Today, Mexico City has some 14,000 kilometers of roads, not including urban highways, most of them built in the last 30 years. Multiply that by an average construction cost of $1 million per kilometer, and by average annual maintenance of $22,000 per kilometer, barring corruption, and you only begin to calculate the subsidy to the private car. We hear complaints about subsidies to public metros, trains, and buses, or even private airlines, but these are minuscule in comparison to the car's ongoing subsidy. And in Latin America, the auto subsidy benefits a very small part of the population as still fewer than 20 percent own cars.

Billions are spent to increase the average speed a car can travel in the city by a few kilometers per hour, by adding new highways or broadening old ones, destroying the very neighborhoods these new roads are supposed to service. Money spent on highways leaves the citizenry with an undersized, under-funded, dirty, and sometimes dangerous, public transportation option. The urban poor frequently must live on the outskirts of the city, many spending a quarter to a third of their income just to get to work. Some residents of Rio de Janeiro spend all their income on the commute. The law requires employers to offset this cost to their employees by offering them bus vouchers, but employers, to save money, tend to hire people who live close to work, or even better, who own a car. The poor, then, remain immobile and unemployable, and some just do not bother to apply for work to which they cannot afford to commute. Money unwisely spent on cars and roads cannot be spent on public transport, nor can it be spent on myriad other urban problems that are notoriously under-funded, including sewage treatment, education, water purification and distribution, law enforcement, and healthcare. By some strange logic, the car takes priority over nearly everything else we expect a civilization to provide.

The car makes astonishing demands on the landscape, and some Latin American cities, especially young cities like Brasília, approach the developed world in the proportion of their surface dedicated entirely to the automobile. Many U.S. cities devote one third of their landscape to the car in roads, freeways, interchanges, parking lots, garages, driveways, drive-ins, drive-throughs, gas stations, and other services required by the car. Central Los Angeles, possibly the worst case, has purposed two thirds of its land surface to the car. We are all too happy to allocate in perpetuity 20 square meters of ground to park a modest car, even though the space, paved at great cost and to the exclusion of all other uses, will sit empty and unused more than half the time. Thousands of shopping mall, parking spaces remain empty even on the Friday after Thanksgiving, the busiest shopping day of the year. Latin Americans also have so far failed to consider the cultural and economic opportunities lost in permanently paving substantial percentages of the places they call home.

Beyond the poor use of space, car culture is wasteful of time and energy. Ten percent of Mexico City residents, most of them poor, spend more than five hours in traffic each workday. Congestion has not yet reached the levels of a Bangkok or Jakarta where auto commuters are known to bring along portable toilets to keep them comfortable during unpredictably long commutes, but at current motorization rates, it may only be a matter of time. The very rich in Mexico City and São Paulo have begun to give up on the car altogether for reasons of both congestion and safety, turning to the helicopter, one of the fastest growing transport services. São Paulo has more than 300 heliports, more than New York City or Tokyo, and 70 percent of these are located atop high rise apartments and office buildings offering door to door service and better parking odds than the street. And in an age of increasing energy costs, the car is truly a dead end. Barring the helicopter, the car is the most energy intensive means to move goods and people around a city, two or more tons of machinery that generally haul one person and tiny payloads. But the failure to create effective public transport makes car and minibus services primary people movers in most large Latin American cities. Many entrepreneurial citizens turn to the car for a living. Street vendors pack their tiny cars with merchandise and follow the shifting public markets. Mexico City has more legally registered cabbies per capita than Madrid, Paris, or New York City. There are another 18,000 illicit cabs. Cabbies of all stripes roam empty most of the day trying to capture that one that will pay their gas and put food on the table.

Catch a cab in Lima and the driver may ask you to pay up front so he can add the liter to his tank necessary to get you to your destination. Half a million people in Mexico City rely on cab fares for income. Hence, the city is choked with cars that are not moving people but simply hoping to move people for a fee. And as the city sprawls, a trend driven by the car subsidy and already noted in many cities, there will be exponential increases in time lost and energy wasted.

The heaviest casualties of the motorized city have little to do with economics or efficiencies. Community and livability are what suffer most. Latin Americans are city lovers not primarily for the architecture, the cuisine, the entertainment, or even the traditional street, per se. Latin Americans crave community; they love people. With rare exceptions, the street is no longer a lively place where people gather, mingle, shop, and play. The street is gone, universally converted to roads, and there is little to love in a city where fast moving machines driven by clutch-dropping motorists fill the narrow urban highways with noise, stench, and erratic danger. As has happened in the developed world, many urban centers are already in decline as places people want to live or work. The car chases people out of the city as much as it carries them to the leafy suburbs.

CURITIBA'S PRESENT

In 1950, Curitiba, the state capital of Paraná, Brazil, was a quiet, provincial town of 180,000. Few of the streets were paved, and a handful of streetcar lines effectively moved bureaucrats and faculty to the state capitol and the state university, the two institutions that comprised most of the city's economic activity. Outside of town, however, the state was booming. The depletion of soil fertility in São Paulo's coffee plantations had pushed the coffee frontier south into Paraná by the 1930s, and by mid-century the state produced 60 percent of Brazil's coffee in addition to being Brazil's largest producer of mate tea and pine lumber. However, within decades, severe frosts in coffee and deforestation in the pines reversed the state's rural dominance. Farmers turned to soybeans, which required fewer workers than coffee, and peasants, as elsewhere, flowed toward the cities. From 1960 to 1980, the state's urbanization rate rose from 37 percent to more than 75 percent, and most of the migrants converged on Curitiba. During that period, Curitiba was Brazil's fastest growing large city, doubling in population both decades. Today, its metropolitan population exceeds 3.2 million.

With people came traffic, and the downtown in the late 1960s was already being described as choked with cars and buses whose noise and exhaust invaded shops, offices, and apartments. Just getting around the city had become unwieldy, and while bicycles had previously been in common use, traffic and its dangers also banished bicyclists from the streets. Initially, Curitiba intended to follow the example of other cities in solving their transportation problems by broadening streets, which would have required tearing down historic edifices, and constructing paved, multilane, urban highways with greater vehicular capacity. But Curitiba made an abrupt U-turn, head-on into history's prevailing traffic flow.

The eccentricities of a military government that appointed "elected" officials brought Jaime Lerner and his architectural colleagues into the mayor's office, the same set of urban planners whose radical proposals had recently won the competition to design Curitiba's future growth. In a rare opportunity, those who wielded the pencil and sketchpad found that the scepter had been dropped in their lap. Lerner was only 33 at his mayoral appointment. He had grown up playing on Curitiba's streets and working in his Polish father's dry goods store where he had come to know intimately the cross section of its people, from peasants to politicians. He had earned degrees in engineering and architecture and had traveled a bit in Europe, but was otherwise without experience that might qualify one to run a large, growing city. Nevertheless, for the next three decades, Lerner dedicated his notoriously boundless energy into making his city a place where people would like to live rather than drive.

Lerner's first move was his most revolutionary, exhibiting both daring and political naivety. In 1971, Curitiba's main street, 15 de Novembro, had been slated for widening and a broad overpass. What to traffic engineers was a solution to the city's gridlock was to Lerner and his colleagues the destruction of the city's cultural and economic heart. Over a Friday night, on the mayor's unpublicized executive order, city workers and volunteers began ripping up Main Street's very pavement, an act of such militant extremism it may be one day considered a turning point in man's global relationship with the car. In three days they transformed a short length of the city's most trafficked avenue into a pedestrian mall replete with trees, lampposts, benches, and flowers. Members of the local auto club declared the invasion a sneak attack on the automobile's legitimate territory. They countered swiftly, arriving in their motorized divisions to reestablish their claim, but when they found children painting long sheets of paper laid strategically in their former lanes, they desisted.

Shopkeepers along the street were in an uproar, fearing the loss of customers who could not drive to their storefront door, but Lerner assured them that if they did not like the change in six month's time, the new street would be returned to its former status as a highway. In no time, businesses beyond the pedestrian mall noted that the new public space in fact drew customers to the carless storefronts, and they demanded it be extended to their shop windows. Within a few years, Curitiba had Americas' largest commercial urban space set aside entirely for pedestrians. One short road had been converted back to a street.

In the decades since it was reclaimed from cars for people, the Street of Flowers, as it is now popularly known, has been an unchallenged success and widely copied. Here, one can hear the murmur of voices and the patter of footsteps instead of the revving of engines. Here, people walk slowly, their shoulders relaxed, their eyes roving at will over the shops, restaurants, and fellow walkers rather than locking on to the nearest fast moving object. Here, parents hold a toddler's hand out of affection rather than fear. The street again becomes a place to be rather than only a means to get somewhere else.

The Lerner Group, as they came to be called, realized the central importance of urban transportation, but instead of subsidizing the car and letting its promoters determine the future shape of the city, they implemented rational plans for both growth and movement that were intimately linked. First, Curitiba resisted the temptation to build multi-lane freeways. Few such concrete monstrosities disfigure the city's face, cutting across or cutting off one neighborhood from another; nor do they prevent the flow of local traffic as they do in nearly all other cities. Second, the city resisted the temptation to channel people underground in subways, in part due to their exorbitant cost. And third, to prevent chaotic sprawl, the bane of other fast growing cities that makes the creation of transport infrastructure so expensive and inefficient, city planners projected the city's growth along corridors that extended in five orderly lines radiating from the city's center. This has helped concentrate the city's growth and expansion along lines that are easily serviced with transport as well as water, electricity, and sewage.

Along these corridors runs one of the most innovative and least expensive public transportation systems in the world. In another example of putting the public before the private car owner, the city dedicated two lanes exclusively to buses along the city's main corridors, a system that over two decades evolved into the busway, also known as bus rapid transit or the metro bus. It is essentially an above ground subway.

Extremely long buses carrying up to 300 passengers whisk along exclusive bus lanes with prioritized signalization. The buses' large, multiple doors match those of large glass tubes that form platforms where passengers who have already paid their fare board quickly and get on their way. In heavy traffic, such buses can move considerably faster than cars. And, in addition to price (subways cost more than $90 million per kilometer compared to busways which cost only $200,000) the busway holds a variety of other advantages over subterranean transport. Busways allow people to travel through the city instead of skulk beneath it, enjoying as they go daylight and views out the windows. Subways tend to be disorienting, and because they are perceived as more dangerous than buses, some citizens of the middle class and above refuse to ride them. The busways are interconnected with the rest of the city's color-coded bus system, and riders can travel just about anywhere within the system for a single, modest fare. Curitibans have responded enthusiastically to the city's approach to public transportation that makes all commuters first-class citizens. Curitiba has the highest per capita car ownership in Brazil, excepting Brasilia which was built solely for the car, and yet 75 percent of its citizens use public transportation. Since 1974, despite continued rapid population growth, traffic in central Curitiba has declined 30 percent, an unprecedented reverse.

Bicycles, which had been important before the car came to dominate the city, have made a comeback as well. Today, the city has 150 kilometers of bike paths that link the downtown with distant neighborhoods and neighborhoods with nearby parks. The city's Kick Start program permitted workers to use their employer's commuting allowances to purchase bikes offered by the city. And although it is illegal and posted, most bicycle commuters, rather than use the bike paths, stake their claim to the dedicated bus lanes, weaving right or left to avoid the occasional passing bus. As an avid bike commuter who has faced the dangers of the streets of Uberaba, Brazil, New York City, and the suburban United States, I found riding Curitiba's bus lanes with the locals on their way to work an extraordinary experience: the pavement is yours, uncontested, and the commute is almost communal as bikers ride in confident packs rather than fearful single files. The near-empty bus lanes are also used by emergency vehicles which must give Curitiba one of the fastest emergency response rates of any large city.

Consider the benefits of such a system. Compared to Brazilian cities of similar size, Curitiba uses 30 percent less fuel, according to a national study. On average, citizens spend less than 10 percent of their income

on transportation. In the United States, where incomes are much higher
and the price of both cars and gasoline are lower than in Brazil, Americans still spend more than 18 percent of their considerable income
on transport, and the poorest Americans spend 40 percent. So many
Curitibans can afford a car because they can frequently leave it and its
expenses garaged at home and use public transportation. Not only does
the city get around more cheaply than other cities but it also does so
more quickly and with far less pollution. The world has taken notice:
Curitiba's busway system has been adopted in Mexico City, Bogotá,
Quito, São Paulo, Nagoya, Ottawa, Pittsburgh, and elsewhere.

Curitiba has also set aside space where people and nature can commingle without endangering one another. A large number of small rivers
flow across the cityscape, and for years their periodic flooding caused
considerable damage. At first, the city canalized the rivers in deep, concrete culverts, some of them hidden underground, as is common practice worldwide, for this was the only way to protect housing built in the
natural floodplain. But it was decided that it would be wiser to design
with nature. The city banned further building in the floodplains and
designated river right of ways as city parks and the remaining forests
as absorbers of excess rainfall. This alone substantially expanded open
space for public recreation. Today, Curitiba has more green space per
citizen than most first-world cities, and when the rivers flood they at
most silt over a jogging path or overturn a picnic table but impose few
real costs on the city's infrastructure and housing. Curitiba's open rivers,
while not always clean, add to the city's beauty and give cause to citizens
to want to improve them. Once canalized or en-sewered, the problem
of filthy water and its causes are forgotten. The city also prizes trees and
has placed severe restrictions on cutting. The result is a leafy city with
abundant shade and vegetation to take off urbanization's rough edges.

Another environmental advantage Curitiba and most other large
Latin American cities have over North American urbanism is density. Mexico City covers about the same amount of ground as Portland,
Oregon, although it has 10 times the population. Bogotá, another city
that is downplaying the automobile, would cover 20 times its current
land area if it had the density of Atlanta. Living more densely is not
only more efficient in energy use, transportation and urban services but
also preserves space both within and without the city for recreation and
nonhuman habitats.

The international press and Curitiba's own propaganda mill have
given the city global visibility. It is often referred to as the ecological

capital of Brazil and has been ranked as one of the three most livable cities in the world, certainly an exaggeration. Yet, while there is little to see there of historical or cultural interest, and guidebooks either ignore it or briefly explain how to get in and out of the city quickly, for urban planners, environmentalists, and other idealists, it has become something of a place of pilgrimage. What one finds there brings hope, but its future is in doubt. Curitiba is still a growing city, and it has been more difficult to deal with the edges than with the center. Suburban developments, many of them gated communities, are starting to appear with their golf courses, garages, and big box stores, very much along the model of the United States. Sprawl has begun in part because Curitiba remains a driver's paradise. In addition to a fabulous public transport system which keeps many people off the road, planners have focused as much attention and intelligence on moving the car efficiently, dedicating broad, one way streets that parallel, at a distance of one block on either side, the development corridors' busways. But with the constant rise in car ownership and the growing tendency of the wealthy to live at a distance from the city, one wonders how long Curitiba's streets can remain uncongested and the air unpolluted. One of the primary reasons people leave cars at home in Curitiba is not because of congested traffic, but because parking, although one of the most ubiquitous downtown businesses, is limited and expensive. When the city expands, when malls and businesses, now concentrated downtown, begin to appear in the suburbs surrounded by parking lots, the major disincentive to drive in Curitiba will have disappeared, and many more may take to the roads.

Much that is spoken and praised of Curitiba's ecological reputation is mythical. Myths are generally lies about the past. But in Curitiba's case, the myths are half-truths about the present that have pretensions of becoming true in the future. There is the distinct possibility and palpable hope of self-fulfillment. Curitibans are both proud of their reality and believe strongly in the myths. Almost 100 percent of citizens surveyed are happy with their city. It is a genuinely livable place by big, Latin American city standards, and many of the companies that have set up business here since the 1970s, that have helped raise incomes in the city 65 percent higher than the rest of Brazil, came in part because the city was an attractive place to live. Good places make good homes. What is most appealing about Curitiba, compared to many cities, is that people have a sense of place and of community. They can sing their village, and the city officially brands itself not the ecological capital of the world, but the "Capital Social," a place, a habitat, for people.

DEMOGRAPHIC FUTURES

Just as Latin America's demographic revolution arrived later and got on faster than it did in the developed world, the same can be said for the region's demographic transition, that is, its move to lower birthrates, and hence, slower population growth. In the United States, the total fertility rate, the average number of children born to each woman, was seven in 1800. That number made a gradual decline, but not until after the baby boom ended in the mid-1960s did total fertility fall consistently below three children. Mexican women were still having seven children on average in 1970. Today they have fewer than 2.5. Again, what took the developed nations a century and a half to accomplish, in this case in fertility reduction, Latin America did in a single generation.

Many factors assisted in the region's rapid decline in birth rates. Some were due to technological and medical breakthroughs. Progesterone, euphemistically known as *la píldora* (the pill), was synthesized for the very first time in Mexico City by Luis Miramontes in 1951, for which he was awarded the Nobel Prize. Syntex, the Mexican company holding the patents, became one of the world's primary producers of the pill and Mexico's fifth largest exporter by the late 1950s. The pill enabled women, especially in nations like Mexico where the pro-natal Catholic Church was weak, to medicate themselves against pregnancy, and it entered wide use in Mexico by the late 1960s. Where the influence of the Catholic Church was stronger, or where contraceptives were difficult to find or expensive, women looked to other solutions to their fertility. Many turned to abortion which was usually illegal and often medically dangerous. Others found a solution in female sterilization by tubal ligation, euphemistically known across the region as *la operación* (the operation). Female sterilization was favored by Latin American governments concerned about political unrest, by the U.S. government alarmed by the temptations of communism to the poor and growing masses, and by a range of international groups and agencies who were working to thwart the population explosion for reasons of poverty eradication, gender equality, or environmental protection. All contributed funds for sterilization, making the operation cheap, or even free, and many groups emphasized sterilization because they believed other forms of birth control too complicated for lower class women to follow, permitting women few alternatives to surgery. The poor and indigenous were most commonly targeted, and sometimes efforts were coercive. Medical personnel provided little information about the procedure's possible side effects, not to mention its permanence. However, while too many women have been sterilized without their consent, possibly the most intimate violation of a woman's human rights, the majority who underwent the operation did so voluntarily, even if poorly informed. Women elected *la operación* at the delivery of their last intended child, and sterilization rates skyrocketed. By 1968, an incredible one third of all Puerto Rican women of childbearing age had been surgically sterilized. In Brazil, female sterilization has been the most common form of birth control since the 1980s, and by 1996, 40 percent of all Brazilian women who were married or partnered had been surgically sterilized. Doctors helped create these numbers by performing unnecessary cesarean sections for which the public health system paid them more than a normal delivery and which conveniently opened the woman for tubal ligation. In some towns of Brazil's northeast, where politicians have campaigned on indigenous sterilization platforms and even offered the procedure free to women as a campaign promise, rates are the highest. In São Luis, 76 percent of all women in their fertile years have been sterilized.

The choice to reduce the one's fertility, to have fewer children, has many motives that I will not take time to delineate here. But many of the disincentives to large families are associated with urbanization. The city profoundly changes reproductive behavior, and there is a high correlation between high urban concentrations and low fertility rates. Nationally, Brazil's total fertility rate is 2.3, slightly above the long-term replacement rate of 2.1. At long-term replacement, a nation will, in the long run, experience population stability; barring immigration and emigration, census numbers will change little from decade to decade. However, many of Brazil's cities are already well below long-term replacement. Salvador, one of the nation's poorest large cities, has a fertility rate of only 1.8, as does Belo Horizonte. In fact, many of Latin America's biggest cities have fertility rates that are below replacement and have seen declines in overall population as migration patterns have shifted away from the biggest to more modest-sized cities. Rapid urbanization has caused national fertility rates in Latin America to drop drastically. Most nations are nearing long-term replacement; some, such as Brazil, Argentina, Costa Rica, and Uruguay, are essentially there; and a few, such as Cuba, Barbados, and Chile, are already well below it.

Still, since Latin American populations are generally very young, the region will continue to experience high to modest growth for much of the next 50 years, but if current trends play out, the end is in sight. From one perspective, declines in population growth rates bode well for the region. Cities and economies will be given a chance to catch up, to provide jobs, housing, urban services, and healthcare to their citizens. On the other hand, Latin America, as a whole, remains underpopulated compared to most developed nations.

Slower population growth may or may not contribute to national development and taming poverty, but it would seem reasonable to suggest that smaller populations would stand to benefit nature, or reduce culture's impact. Yet, while the city inhibits family fertility, it breeds household consumption. As humans move from the country to the city, the species is bombarded by broadcast media, billboards, and, more significantly, the consumption patterns of other humans who conspicuously display to the newcomers what they lack. Wants and needs expand more rapidly than urban fertility contracts. Even if the region were to double over the next 50 years, which now seems unlikely, that alone would have less environmental consequence than if a stable, or even declining, population were to successfully eradicate poverty and achieve first-world levels of consumption. Nearly every urbanized Latin American wants a larger, more comfortable home, more appliances, and a car, or a second car if they already have one. It is no surprise they aspire to the same wealth as the developed world. But currently, Latin Americans, per capita, consume 85 percent less oil than Americans, 85 percent less electricity, and 80 percent fewer cars. For two centuries, most of Latin America's natural capital has been exported to the first world, with significant environmental costs. The growing market for goods, however, is at home. If poverty is solved, even if population growth is checked, Latin America's environmental problems are likely to get much worse rather than better. Rather than a mere 4 million cars in Mexico City, which already pollute at dangerous levels, there will be 20 million, if first-world motorization continues to be held up as the model. And so far, it is the model. Only China's auto sector is projected to grow faster than Latin America's.

The expansive, apparently unlimited desire for material things is a cultural trait inherent to pre-Columbian and postmodern societies. Goods are intoxicating and once imbibed difficult to renounce. The city's consuming influence now reaches to every corner of Latin America, infinitely multiplying wants and needs, and few are immune. In Tingo Maria, an emerging center of coca production in Peru, newly rich drug lords purchased luxury sedans to wow their neighbors although their vehicles were largely undrivable on the rough local roads. The Kayapó of the Brazilian Amazon, after selling timber rights for handsome prices, have imported automobiles to their road-less villages, just to park them for their neighbor's admiration. And one anthropologist who has worked her whole life to save the Lacandon Indians and their forest habitat on the border of Mexico and Guatemala has observed that the Indians have lost touch with nature as consumer goods distract them from subsistence. The new Lacandon god, she observes, is the automobile.

At the end of the nineteenth century, Latin America's major cities attempted to modernize, to make the city a showplace, the center of culture, just at Machado de Assis had dreamed. And no construction was as important as the opera house or theater, which was often the largest, and certainly most ornate centerpiece of the modernizing city, be it at Mexico City or Manaus. The final evidence that Latin Americans had achieved high culture was the hiring of headlining European stars to sing in the tropical theater. Many of them came, from Enrico Caruso to Sarah Bernhardt, and the tradition has continued to the present. In 1997, Placido Domingo took the stage at the Santiago opera to resounding applause, but after only two songs he desisted and exited the stage complaining of throat irritation due to the severe smog. Is Domingo too a canary in a coal mine, a signal that our abusive relationship with the natural world will result in the destruction of the high culture we claim to have created? We have created cities, modern human habitats, in which people cannot breathe, sing, or even move, without difficulty.

Cities will remain central to understanding environmental change and degradation in Latin America. Done poorly, the city mocks and mars the landscape, degrades much that is within and without its bounds, chokes its residents on their own filth, and can enthuse social anarchy and criminality. If planned, built, and administered well, cities can be places of beauty, safety, and community, an adornment that can compliment, even combine with nature, and increase the odds of civilization's sustainability. Currently, cities are a source of environmental despair and worry across the region, but to turn our backs on them will only make things worse. The city is Latin America's biggest environmental problem and its only solution. There are no other viable human habitats: Latin Americans cannot return to the farms they abandoned so recently, nor can they sustainably follow the model of energy-intensive suburban sprawl established in North America. For the foreseeable future, the dense city is key to culture's success at creating a sustainable home in the Neotropics.

CHAPTER SEVEN

Developing Environmentalism

This land belongs to the Costa Ricans: many have already died, some are still living, but most are yet to be born.[1]

When Yuri Gagarin successfully entered earth's orbit in 1961, humans, for the first time, caught a god's eye view of the planet they live on. The perspective was novel, but for the next two decades the views were limited to a few cramped astronauts peering through thick portholes, or to satellite cameras spying on Cold War enemies. But that all changed with the launch in 1981 of the space shuttle. Now, scores of humans spent weeks in orbit gazing through picture windows on the world below them. Eyes and handheld cameras were attracted to phenomena that spy and weather satellites had overlooked. Among the more captivating features were human marks on the earth's face, and the most apparent of these was the destruction of the world's largest tropical forest. At night, shuttle crews exposed to film thousands of fires in Rondônia in Brazil's Western Amazon. By day, they measured a pall of smoke that spread over 3 million square kilometers. They also documented the unusual patterns of forest removal that followed the expanding highway networks punched into the forests by states eager to develop their jungle frontiers. In Rondônia, peasant and rancher clearings looked like zippers, roads whose borders were checked with rectangular clearings that extended from narrow frontages. Over two decades, shuttle photographs recorded the haphazard spread of these clearings back from the roads until they began to join the bald plots extending

---

[1] Costa Rican saying, quoted in Sterling Evans, *The Green Republic: A Conservation History of Costa Rica* (Austin: University of Texas Press, 1999), ix, my translation.

from other roads, leaving, at best, thousands of patchy forest remnants. In the Bolivian Amazon, deforestation sometimes took the form of asterisks, acute triangles of denudation radiating from the point at which roads intersected or towns formed. And in the southern Amazon the pattern was more familiar: heavily financed soybean farmers, in orderly fashion, hacked out massive polygonal tracts. What was being documented, of course, was an old story, history re-repeating itself; humans had deforested, although in dissimilar patterns, in nearly every historical period. But now the scale was without historical precedent, and we all became spectators of the destruction, forced to watch the carnage in real time, and in total. The view from the shuttle enabled us to see not only the rapid rate of the forest's destruction, but also the potential scale of the disaster, for below us spread a forest roughly the size of the contiguous United States that was burning at the margins as well as its heart.

Latin American nature has generated an unusually large share of first-world environmental anxiety. In fact, citizens of developed nations often appear more concerned about the ecological condition of the Amazon than they are about their own landscapes. Of course, environmental degradations, including deforestation, are global phenomenon, and history and orbital photographs have shown that culture tramples the world rather equally; so why so much consternation about the distress of one region among so many others? There is little qualitative or quantitative difference, for example, between rainforest destruction in the Amazon and that in Indonesia, Malaysia, or West Africa. Part of the explanation resides in the geographic proximity and cultural linkages that the most environmentally progressive nations have to Latin America: the region forms North America's backyard and remains the most European of Europe's former empires. Some of the anxiety comes out of a practical concern for human survival: the Amazon as the earth's lung (an idea now discredited), the burning forest's contribution to greenhouse gases and global warming, or the hope that among Amazonia's millions of plant species might be found the cures for cancer and other currently untreatable diseases. But most important may be that America's Neotropical nature is still strongly imbued with the symbolic association of paradise, pristine and unsullied. The Amazon, which has long epitomized the Pristine Myth, is regarded as Genesis's last page, the earth's final remnant from the time before humans entered the scene. Reports of its destruction suggest the final holocaust of paradise, snuffed, ironically, just as we claim to have come to our ecological senses.

Amazonia's incremental disappearance, it is believed, robs us of the chance for ecological redemption from centuries of sins against our supposed Edenic origins.

The myth of a remnant terrestrial paradise shapes our perceptions of the Neotropics almost as much as it did that of Columbus. The myth, hence, is quite old, and hardly news. So, the real story is not the surviving myth of a tropical paradise but the sudden popular concern about its future. During the last third of the twentieth century, environmentalism, the idea that humans have profoundly degraded nature, that such activity can in turn harm human well-being, and that something ought to be done about it, has become a popular movement that despite its flaws and fissures is quite radical and broadly based. There have long been lone prophets of environmental doom as well as official, if fitful, efforts to check human depredations on nature's resources, but now the concern has become popular: school teachers, politicians, and rock stars are all doomsayers. By 1990, as many as 75 percent of North Americans accepted the label environmentalist in some form. Of course, many of them believe environmentalism is little more than recycling trash at home and saving rainforests abroad, but that they care at all is nigh unto mutiny against their parents who believed human progress accepted no natural bounds and that nature's utility had neither ethical nor material limits. As with recent converts to any faith, new ideas are embraced without seeing the incompatibility of the old, so we live in a time in which the old ideology of developmentalism coexists awkwardly with the new idea of environmentalism, a compromise expressed in the term "sustainable development." Whether or not we can have both is a burning question, particularly for Latin Americans whose yearning for material equality has paralleled their own growing unease about the state of their homes' ecological foundations.

Conservationism and Wilderness

Environmentalism, very broadly defined as human concern for nature, has had many historical expressions. But to deserve significant historical mention, the concern must be embraced by more than a single individual. Dozens of personalities, going well back to the ancient period, qualify as environmentalists, but most of them were lonesome souls crying unheard in a disappearing wilderness. For example, there were environmentally conscious observers among the Greeks and Romans who noted with worry the deterioration of forests and soils, but neither Greece nor

Rome made an effort to reduce their environmental impacts. To qualify as environmentalism, worried observers must convince their cultures to act, to achieve some shred of a social program that may involve laws, policies, restrictions, or disincentives that reduce human impacts on nature or reorient human practice toward greater sustainability.

Most early forms of environmentalism can be labeled as conservationist, a strand of environmentalism with a rather long history that dominated environmental thinking well into the twentieth century. Conservationism is entirely human centered, for its primary concern is not to prevent nature's decline per se, but to utilize nature wisely for the sake of civilization's rise. By the careful stewardship of nature, conservationist societies have hoped to enhance their competitiveness against cultural rivals and to increase their chances of long-term prosperity. Unlike monumental architecture, writing, or economic and political specialization, environmentalism is not universal trait we associate with civilization. However, it is more common than we have generally allowed. For some time we have believed that the first qualifiers for environmentalism were the conservationist movements in the United States and Europe after the mid-nineteenth century, but this is to largely pat ourselves on the back for the rediscovery and elaboration of what quite a number of cultures had previously implemented. It is nigh impossible to say who was first, and one can quibble over the essential qualifications, but if not universal, conservationist policies are not unusual before the nineteenth century, particularly those implemented in the interest of forests. Islamic Egypt, as early as the eleventh century, made remarkable efforts to reforest areas that the ancients had left denuded; Germanic states had fairly sophisticated forest policies by the fourteenth century; the Venetians, who relied heavily on local forests for timbers to build ships and for piles to support their homes soggy foundations, implemented strict forestry laws by the end of the fifteenth century; in Portugal, the pines of Leiria were reforested in the early fourteenth century, guarded by mounted forest rangers who managed local firewood collection and expelled trespassers for timber theft and even for carrying firearms, flint, or tobacco in the forest out of fear of fire. Regarding game, medieval European kings maintained game preserves for their own pleasure hunting, and more general laws regarding hunting and fishing; for example, seasonal restrictions on taking game and prohibitions on the use of fishing nets, were not uncommon. And outside the West, at least by the end of the seventeenth century, Western India, China, and Japan had relatively successful soil, forest, and water conservation policies, some of which were to influence European colonial practice in the eighteenth and nineteenth centuries.

As we noted, although not as well documented, the evidence is suggestive that both the Incas and Aztecs in the fifteenth century had some conservationist policies relating to forests or wildlife. Iberian colonists brought their environmental concerns with them, but with the decline of the Indian populations and the regeneration of nature, few felt compelled to protect that which was perceived as abundant to excess. However, the Iberian crowns, to protect their assets, did eventually set aside forest reserves in the interest of mining and shipbuilding. In Brazil, in 1655, the crown identified about a dozen *madeiras de lei* (timbers under the law), the best trees for building ships, that were to be protected from axe and fire whether found on public or private property. And by the early eighteenth century, the Portuguese king, upon learning that mangrove deforestation by planters and tanners destroyed local fisheries, an important source of food, preserved mangrove forests in perpetuity in the interest of local fishery conservation, apparently one of first environmental steps to take ecology, the interconnectedness of nature, into consideration.

Interconnections are what distinguished the rise of what might be termed scientific conservation in the late eighteenth century, first observed in the Americas in Britain's Eastern Caribbean colonies. As we noted, climate was a major concern among Europeans for racial and developmental reasons, and by the late eighteenth century long-held assumptions regarding the role of forests in climate control had been entirely rethought. Prior, most Europeans believed the tropical forest a negative influence on culture's progress; not only did forests harbor man-eating beasts (not to mention cannibalistic Indians) and encumber the land on which they wanted to grow crops, but forests, they believed, made the landscape unhealthy, promoted disease, and increased dampness and humidity. Deforestation was defended as a social good as much as an economic necessity. However, the experience in Barbados and other tropical colonial islands where deforestation ran its course in just a few decades seemed to suggest the opposite. Not only did removing the forests impose substantial economic costs, requiring the import of timber and firewood, but it also dried up local springs, reduced perennial stream flows, initiated erosion, increased average temperatures, and, many claimed, reduced rainfall itself. These ideas found their most compelling telling in the works of Alexander von Humboldt and George Perkins Marsh, but their origins are to be found earlier among Europe's colonial officials in America and Asia who personally and officially had to face the consequences of rapid deforestation on tiny tropical islands. Alexander Anderson, superintendent of the botanical garden on British St. Vincent from 1785, argued for the human benefits of forest protections:

> A proper proportion of woodland always tends to keep a country cool. How necessary then for man and beast within the tropics. Nor is there any reasonable doubt that trees have a very considerable effect in attracting rain, upon the certainty of which no crop depends so much as that of sugar cane. From the same cause they promote the circulation of the atmosphere and consequently health of the inhabitants.[2]

He suggested there would be little colonial success without trees, and the rash actions of former planters on Barbados and its imitators elsewhere caused colonial officials to reconsider their approach to tropical nature. The so-called desiccationist theory, that trees attracted rain and improved the climate, to which must be added theories regarding the role of vegetation in purifying the air humans breathed, gave colonial powers incentives to set aside forest reserves on as yet forested islands such as Tobago and St. Vincent. On Tobago, the British reserved notable tracts of forest in every district in order to ameliorate the climate, maintain rainfall, and reduce disease, and these designated stands remained largely untouched for the following two centuries. Science has proven most of the forest benefits claimed by the eighteenth-century theorists, although the role forests play in attracting and increasing rainfall has not been fully settled.

The desiccationists' theories spread almost instantaneously into the Iberian colonies, and small groups of vocal critics, best documented so far in Brazil, argued against the destruction of trees for reasons of the forest's economic, social, and medicinal utility. Independence brought political chaos for most Latin American republics, so the vocal conservationists had few stable governments to hear their warnings, and in fact most of the old conservationist policies inherited from the colonies by the new states were overturned, voided, or forgotten. Some states, such as Mexico, worked hard to put as much public and Indian land into the hands of private men who promised to quickly turn natural resources

---

[2]   Quoted in Richard H. Grove, *Green Imperialism: Colonial Expansion, Tropical Island Edens and the Origins of Environmentalism, 1600–1860* (New York: Cambridge University Press, 1995), 301.

into national wealth, regardless of the cost to forests, waters, and soils. But even here, Mexico set aside a significant forest reserve, Desierto de Leones, in 1856, and Benito Juarez decreed Mexico's first national forest law in 1861, suggesting that conservationism, while it suffered, did not entirely die with independence.

Independent Brazil, which remained under the sovereignty of a branch of the Portuguese royal family, saw more continuity with its colonial past than did Spanish America. For example, brazilwood remained a monopoly, and other specific timbers remained protected to almost the end of the century, at least on paper. Also, Brazil's relative political stability made it possible for her desiccation theorists, most of them born in Brazil but educated in Europe, to convince the emperor of the necessity of some action, and Rio de Janeiro, the emperor's residence, got the most attention. Till just after 1800, the forests of the Tijuca Mountains immediately above the city were in pretty fair shape, thick enough to conceal sizable runaway slave communities, one of them with more than 200 residents. A smattering of foreign tourists gloried in this urban jungle as they hiked to the forest's most prominent peak, Corcovado, to overlook nature's marvelous city. But coffee, which grew best at higher altitudes, began to invade the city's forested mountains and rather quickly denuded the urban watershed which reduced the city's water supply as well as denied slaves a place to hide. And after 1808, the royal family and a crowd of Portuguese officialdom who had fled Napoleon's invasion of Portugal, themselves found sanctuary in the Tijuca Mountains where they built homes to escape the city's oppressive heat. The presence of so many royal hangers-on christened the mountain suburb Imperial Tijuca. This early suburbanization mixed with coffee cultivation denuded much of the area.

With the city still entirely dependent for water on the Tijuca Mountains, out of which originated a handful of streams, by the 1840s, citizens had faced repeated water shortages. The doctrines of desiccation held that reforestation would solve the water crisis although it had never really been tried and proven. Brazil's emperor, Pedro II, after 1844, expropriated critical areas of the mountain watershed and began to replant the trees, at first on a limited scale. But in 1861, the emperor appointed Manuel Gomes Archer as the administrator of a conservation area designated the Tijuca Forest. It is not accurate to call the reserve a national park, for it served no other purpose, at this point, than as a protected watershed, but it was a significant milestone in Latin America's environmental history, and over the next century it would evolve into a full-fledged park. Archer, a local landholder who was entirely self-taught in forestry, took to his task quickly. Granted a crew of six African slaves, by name, Constantino, Eleutério, Leopoldo, Manuel, Maria, and Mateus, probably all owned by the royal family, Archer began planting tree seedlings of quite a large variety, focusing initially on the Tijuca Forest's most eroded slopes. At first the slaves dug and gathered seedlings from extant forests for replanting, but Archer developed a successful nursery to turn out the most desirable seedlings more quickly, for this was a forest that was to be shaped by human concepts of beauty and utility. Archer was not opposed to cutting down native trees to encourage the growth of his carefully selected seedlings, and he planted nonnative species along with useful native trees. By the time Archer resigned his post in 1874, his small crew had planted some 72,000 seedlings in the Tijuca Forest, the foundation for much of the cover that still graces today's park. In a very narrow way, Archer was the predecessor of Gifford Pinchot who was central to founding the much larger, far better staffed U. S. Forest Service some years later. Neither Archer nor his Brazilian successors had Pinchot's influence, and their work had been largely forgotten in Brazil until recently, but the Tijuca Forest, as modest as it was, is still the largest replanted tropical forest in the Americas, and probably America's first significant reforestation effort since the Incas.

Research continues to turn up yet more cogent examples of resource conservation in Latin America. From about 1906, Peru began to take guano conservation seriously, hiring foreign fish and bird experts as consultants in a national effort to turn the guano industry from its destructive dead end toward sustained yield. Legislation protected the birds' nesting sites and regulated guano's extraction. A sizable staff of researchers and bird guards were placed under government pay. Within a short time, Peru's annual guano yields quadrupled. Increases in guano's supply were accompanied by a drastic reduction in demand, for Peru, in the interest of creating a sustainable and competitive national agriculture, banned guano's export abroad, denying world trade the power to exhaust a critical resource. But as was typical of conservation efforts everywhere, guano officials protected that nature which brought direct benefits to humans but mercilessly destroyed the nature which threatened human well-being and profits. The same guards posted to protect guano-producing birds from human predation were also deputized to kill any pest or varmint that threatened the same. As a result, gulls and condors, which consumed eggs and hatchlings, and peregrine falcons, which

Figure 10. Two condors sacrificed to protect the eggs of guano-producing birds on San Gallan Island, Peru, 1920s.
Source: Robert Cushman Murphy, *Bird Islands of Peru: The Record of a Sojourn on the West Coast* (New York: G. P. Putnam's Sons, 1925), after 154. Courtesy of the Harold B. Lee Library, Brigham Young University, Provo, Utah.

attacked adults, were pursued mercilessly (see Figure 10). In 1917, in just two months, 5,000 gulls were killed in Peru's southern islands in order to protect the cormorant eggs that would produce the next year's guano.

Elsewhere, conservation laws were passed to protect birds of a different feather. In Venezuela, the already booming trade in the egret's elegant, breeding plumage arrived about 1900. Bird feathers, long esteemed by America's indigenous peoples, finally became a commodity of general western consumption, and within a decade some 10 million Venezuelan birds fell victims to feminine fashion. Per ounce, egret plumes were five times more valuable than gold, and foreign ventures that supplied locals with shotguns gave the human tribe a powerful advantage over their quarry. Hunters, who only wanted the handful of breeding feathers each bird produced, brought the birds within reach of plucking in a flurry of gunfire. Private landholders whose property enclosed breeding grounds learned quickly that since birds always returned to the same rookeries, they could sustain production by protecting their lands against hunters and take their profits in feathers that naturally fell to the ground toward the end of the breeding season. After a series of legislative restrictions on hunting, Venezuela passed a comprehensive law in 1917 that limited feather collection to the breeding season and banned guns entirely. This remained difficult to enforce, but conservation law (and culture's fickle sense of fashion) helped preserve the egret for future generations.

Future research will certainly turn up more examples of early conservation, proving that Latin America, if not as consistent as North America, pursued similar goals by rather similar means, and these efforts were not entirely derivative of activities in northern nations but in a number of cases anticipated them. Policy changes fell far shy of the conservationists' ambitious plans to prevent the destruction and limit the waste of natural resources, but they were not entirely without influence.

One important branch of conservation in which Latin American efforts neither preceded nor paralleled that of North America was wilderness preservation. The United States was rather singular in its early worship of wilderness, its romantic and spiritual connections to wild places that resulted in the establishment of the world's first national parks, places to ease the mind and sanctify the spirit. While conservationists everywhere focused on nature's material utility, American wilderness advocates also promoted nature's spiritual and recreational benefits. The approach was still entirely human-centered, favoring beautiful places and a few charismatic creatures, while ignoring, even systematically eradicating, nature's less sublime manifestations, but it was, nevertheless, a striking development. Latin America, by contrast, had few romantic inclinations toward nature: there are, as yet, no figures comparable to Henry David Thoreau, John Muir, and Aldo Leopold, and landscape painting, other than a brief flowering in Dutch Brazil in the seventeenth century, is virtually nonexistent outside the few foreigners, such as Frederic Church, who found inspiration in Andean and Mexican mountains. Jose de Velasco's paintings of the Valley of Mexico are a rare exception, but even his works generally place culture center canvas in the form of cities, railroads, or ruins.

The late appearance of wilderness appreciation in Latin America needs further investigation. It may be that industrialization's visible costs are a precondition for objectifying nature's beauty and striving to save what is left of it from the machine. In Latin America's case, the industrial machine and urbanization did not arrive in force until more than a century after it did in parts of North America, and hence the long delay in wilderness conservation. Moreover, some have argued that North Americans latched onto American nature, even worshipped it, as a surrogate past in the service of cultural nationalism. Crenellated mountains and painted canyons were the historical objects Americans put forward to compete with Europe's esteemed castles and canvases. Latin America, with its legacy of ancient ruins, baroque churches, and viceregal palaces, did not suffer from the same sense of historical inadequacy and did not need to turn to a compensatory nature.

And part of the explanation may lie in Latin America's lagging historical consciousness. By the end of the nineteenth century, the historical profession in North America was well developed, and numerous historians had taken stock of the unique American past in the context of the rapidly changing times. By the early twentieth century, North Americans were aware of not only the closing of the frontier but also of the disappearance, or near disappearance, of beaver, bison, and passenger pigeons. Many of Latin America's nations, by contrast, which had potentially lost more native animals, had as yet little in the way of a written past, human or natural, and an even smaller literate public to inform. Human beings do not live very long, and without a developed historical consciousness remain as ignorant of nature's past as they do their own. Even today, many Brazilians living in the range of the former Atlantic Forest have never heard of it, unaware that the farms and cities in which they now reside displaced one of their nation's unique ecological treasures. But historical awareness is growing, and if the Amazon's forests should suffer the same fate, Brazilians have become well enough acquainted with the Amazon's recent past that they will feel the loss deeply. If environmental history has an important role to play, it is to remind us of what once was, what has been lost, and whether or not it was worth the price. And as the field of environmental history in Latin America is still in its infancy, we should not completely cede that thinkers and actors of the caliber of Thoreau, Muir, and Leopold will never be unearthed. Environmental heroes, like all heroes, are created as much as they are born, and members of North America's environmental pantheon have had far greater impact on later generations than on their own. Prospectively, Latin America has yet to exhume her environmental prophets, individuals who were ignored by their contemporaries and buried without eulogy or epitaph.

The Limits of Popular Environmentalism

Most historians credit the publication of Rachel Carson's *Silent Spring* in 1962 as the beginning of modern, popular environmentalism, that is, when the concern for nature democratized. Carson's title prefigured a future in which spring mornings would be forever bereft of bird song due to the indiscriminate use of synthetic pesticides. Granted, many people liked songbirds, and some might in fact miss them by their absence, but that claim alone was not about to start the revolution that followed. If the entire avian tribe were to disappear tomorrow, much of humanity would fail to notice, and within a generation many more would forget that the earth, particularly at dawn, had once been filled with nature's singing. And virtually nobody was troubled by the death and disappearance of the insects at whom the pesticides were targeted. Concern for birds and beauty may have been primary motives for Carson, a marine biologist and birdwatcher, but that is not what made *Silent Spring* popular and controversial. Employing stark figures and persuasive evidence, Carson reminded humans that we are in the end members of nature's ecology, and that what harmed bugs and birds could potentially harm us. She raised the specter of a silent, unseen threat that went by the name chemical, a term she made a dirty word for future generations, and linked it to human cancer. Modern environmentalism was born of the fear of progress itself.

This was a revolutionary development in human perceptions of nature. Before the rise of conservationism, westerners viewed nature as an enemy to be conquered, destroyed, and displaced by civilization. Under conservationism, nature was transformed from an enemy to a slave whose obedient labor and sustained production of lumber, water, and food protected society's aspirations to perpetual progress. Those who adhered to the wilderness ideal, which gained popular support in the United States due to auto tourism, saw nature as an amenity and a facility, a playing field in the service of the spirit's lifting and the body's recreation. However, with the birth of modern environmentalism in the 1960s, our perception of nature changed radically. Nature is no longer simply an object to be conquered by civilization, coerced by conservationists, and consumed by campers. We increasingly see nature as a victim, significantly, a fellow victim, of human overconfidence and excess. Human survival is now inextricably linked in our minds to nature's well-being. So, the new environmentalism called for protecting humans not from nature's threats, nor from her stinginess, but from nature's demise.

It was only when humans considered they too might be an endangered species that culture and nature found they had common ground, that ecology mattered. As a result of this revolutionary change in perception, citizens began to add to the perceived threat of synthetic chemicals such concerns as radioactive fallout, air and water pollution, rapid population growth, species extinction, and atmospheric and climatic change.

Not only did Carson's book transform popular opinion but like few works before or since it reoriented science and permanently fixed new state policies whose intent was to protect humans from their own misguided immoderation. Local governments in the United States began to regulate chemicals and their uses, and the federal government banned those perceived most dangerous, such as DDT. By the late 1960s, the concern ranged well beyond pesticide pollution and the federal government passed unprecedented laws empowering the state to protect both human and nonhuman habitats against even the hallowed rights of private property and profit: the Clean Air Act of 1970 and the Clean Water Act of 1972 set stiff standards for purity for two of humanity's most basic resource needs; the Endangered Species Act of 1973 prohibited any action that harmed species so listed, and, remarkably, their habitats; and the Energy Policy and Conservation Act of 1975 attempted to reduce national energy consumption.

The impact of Rachel Carson and other environmentalist pioneers on Latin America has not been fully investigated, but her work was published almost immediately in Spanish and Portuguese. Many have suggested that poor countries are not ready for modern environmentalism, and that even today Latin America fails to qualify as a full member of the environmental movement. However, Latin America is not so different from its northern neighbors in either the breadth or depth of its environmental sensibilities. There has been a noted lag in time and substantial difference in approach, but much of the disparity in attitude and action between North and South is explained by poverty and weak democratic systems rather than environmental immaturity. And many of those who condemn Latin America's environmental underdevelopment work from the overconfident assumption that the North is more ecologically progressive than in fact it is.

It is difficult to adequately summarize the past and promise of environmentalism in Latin America's nearly 30 republics, their attitudes, laws, and accomplishments. For example, the two small nations of Costa Rica and Haiti, while geographically and climatologically close, form two ends of a wide spectrum in ecological damage and environmental outlook. Costa Rica is the darling of biodiversity conservation; Haiti is a disaster almost beyond redemption. There is little question that Latin American environmentalism has been greatly influenced by the movement in the United States and Europe, but in many visible signs it has already accomplished many of the same goals. Of course, Latin Americans have more to be concerned about, more work to do, and fewer resources with which to do it. By the 1980s, most lived in large cities notorious for the kinds of environmental problems we observed in the last chapter. While North Americans after Rachel Carson began to clean up the pollutions of affluence, such as chemicals and industrial effluent, Latin America had to deal with these as well as the pollutions of poverty, such as untreated sewage and solid waste. Residents of Mexico City, Santiago, Lima, and Rio de Janeiro faced lethal, ecological squalor on frightening scale. Farmers across the region worked degraded lands and witnessed declining returns but did not have the cash to buy synthetic fertility. Likewise, farm workers had an intimate working, breathing relationship with the dangerous chemicals that Carson introduced to North Americans only in name, or in inscrutable abbreviations (DDT; BHC; 2, 4-D).

At the United Nations Conference on the Human Environment held in Stockholm in 1972, many Latin American attendees were surprised by the new perspective on nature expressed by the more developed nations regarding pollution, species diversity, and wilderness protection. One Brazilian official argued that if anything, Brazil wanted more pollution, for this was an excellent indicator of the progress of national development. As one writer put it, developing nations were too busy trying to bake an economic pie large enough feed everyone to worry about the vile mess they were making in the kitchen. Delegates from poor nations accused the first world, which had laid waste to their national landscapes in making themselves rich, of attempting to deny them the same cultural right and privilege. Despite the attitudinal gap that had formed between first and third-world environmental perspectives, federal environmental legislation in Latin America's republics came rather rapidly. In fact, Mexico passed the Law for the Prevention and Control of Pollution in 1971, contemporary with the U. S. air and water acts. In response to Stockholm, dozens of Latin American states created agencies patterned after the U. S. Environmental Protection Agency more out of international pressure and the old fear of not looking modern than as a result of domestic, popular demands. Possibly the most radical statement, on paper, was article 19 of the 1980 Chilean Constitution which guaranteed citizens "the right to live in an environment free of contamination." In Chile, pollution was unconstitutional.

In North America, the environmental movement came from the people first and the state responded; in Latin America, it started with the state. And environmental policies descended from both the upper right and upper left. In the Dominican Republic they were handed down by the conservative, anti-communist, and anti-democratic Joaquín Balaguer who served as president for six terms, dominating national politics for more than 30 years. On the one hand, Balaguer had been a willing collaborator of his murderous predecessor, Rafael Trujillo, and himself not above using intimidation and violence against his many opponents. On the other, he was an intellectual trained at the University of Paris and a prolific author whose poems, biographies, literary criticism, and novels rolled off his desk from the early 1920s to nearly his death in 2002. The origins and motives of Balaguer's environmental policies and policing remain a mystery, but from almost the moment he took power until the day he relinquished it, his imprint on the natural landscape is incontestable. Trujillo before him had recklessly logged the Dominican Republic's forests to enrich himself, and during the political turmoil of the early 1960s that followed Trujillo's assassination deforestation by loggers and squatters accelerated, following the ruinous pattern set by neighboring Haiti. But when Balaguer took power in 1966, he banned all logging and sent the army after squatters and loggers who infringed on the national forests. Dozens were shot on sight. Not even the elite friendly to Balaguer's political ambitions were given the slightest license, and Balaguer famously set fire to heavily capitalized sawmills and bulldozed luxury homes built illegally in the forests. He substantially expanded the national park system and set aside some of the first marine reserves, including two sanctuaries for humpback whales. He provided blanket protections to shorelines, river margins, and many wetlands. In the interest of protecting wild animal populations and biodiversity he banned hunting of any kind for 10 years after signing on to the Rio convention in 1992. He pressured industries to reduce pollution, opposed the construction of some dams, and let a number of roads fall into such disrepair that human access to frontier areas became nearly impossible. Even in his last years, increasingly marginalized and nearly blind, he used his political wiles to lock in protections to his system of national nature reserves. Balaguer's literary works have yet to be examined for their environmental sensibilities, and hence any attempt to explain the origins and motives of his environmental policies remains speculation, but his record stands, as extraordinary as it is incongruous.

In Nicaragua, it was the left-wing Sandinista revolutionaries that implemented a wide range of environmental initiatives after they came to power in 1979. As did Trujillo in the Dominican Republic, the Somoza dynasty in Nicaragua raped nature for financial and political gains, and eagerly sold the same opportunity to foreign companies. Logging ventures, such as the Nicaraguan Long Leaf Pine Company, entirely U. S. owned, deforested massive tracts including nearly all the pines in Nicaragua's northeast by 1961. In the 1970s, 30 percent of Nicaragua's forests disappeared, and nearly all the commercial timber along the Pacific coast. Despite Somoza having signed the Convention on International Trade in Endangered Species (CITES) in 1973, Nicaragua was Central America's worst offender, exporting tropical birds, turtle meat, and big cat pelts to consumers worldwide. Somoza himself established Tortugas S. A., a factory that harvested and butchered the endangered green sea turtle; the industry exported some 40 tons of turtle meat each year in the early 1970s. Nicaragua was also among the most polluted nations due to heavy pesticide use. Most rivers and aquifers were contaminated, and Nicaraguans suffered the highest number of pesticide poisonings of any nation per capita, 400 of which resulted in death each year. After Haiti, degraded Nicaragua was the poorest nation in Latin America.

Initially, most Sandinista leaders were not environmentally inclined, but they were easily convinced of the connection between nature's degradation and the suffering the nation's poor. Father Ernesto Cardenal, the radical priest who joined the fight despite the pope's opposition and who was made Minister of Culture to the new revolutionary government, wrote, in verse, "not only humans desired liberation. The entire ecology cried for it. The revolution is also for lakes, rivers, trees and animals."[3] Within a month of taking power the Sandinistas established the Nicaraguan Institute of Natural Resources and the Environment (IRENA) which within a year had a staff of 400. The Sandinistas nationalized Nicaragua's mineral, forest, and marine resources, effectively cutting off national resources to foreign companies. IRENA banned the import of eight of agriculture's most dangerous pesticides and prohibited the export of the nation's most endangered species,

[3]   Quoted in Daniel Faber, *Environment Under Fire: Imperialism and the Ecological Crisis in Central America* (New York: Monthly Review Press, 1992), 150.

including 26 mammals, 19 birds, and 4 reptiles. Aided by a vigorous national education campaign, Nicaragua became the best enforcer of CITES in the region. IRENA established conservation initiatives to save sea turtles and their habitats, and through consistent effort replanted some 27 square kilometers of forests by 1985. Without foreign loggers, firewood collection remained the largest threat to forests, so the Sandinistas sought alternative sources of energy including hydropower dams, a large geothermal plant, and the introduction of solar cookers and improved woodstoves. With the help of Cuba and Sweden, Nicaragua built biomass facilities that burned agricultural waste, such as sugar bagasse and cotton stalks, to produce electricity.

Many of the Sandinista's successes were overturned by the troubles of the Contra War and by their own abiding interest in material development. The Contras made it a point to burn forests and attack environmental facilities as these were symbols of the revolution's success. The Sandinistas, in order to maintain political support, distributed large tracts of unused national land to peasants who converted forests into farms. They also continued to bolster a number of now nationalized industries that were notorious polluters as to abandon them would have slowed national development. To the end of the Sandinista's reign, despite significant educational campaigns, environmentalism remained largely an elite ideology. When ousted by an election in 1990, many, but not all, of the Sandinista environmental reforms fell from national priority.

In each nation in its own time, the environmental movement trickled down both from the state and from the north. As elsewhere (Love Canal, United States; Bhopal, India; Minimata, Japan), highly publicized, environmental disasters, both small and catastrophic, catalyzed the formation of a broader environmental consciousness. In Brazil, the city of Cubatão was the 10-fold fulfillment of Rachel Carson's prophecy regarding the dangers of synthetic substances. Brazil's model industrial city, Cubatão was born in the 1950s of cheap electricity at the base of the coastal mountains supporting the Billings Reservoir on the São Paulo plateau. Other than cheap, abundant electricity, there was nothing auspicious about its swampy location wedged between sprawling mangrove swamps and towering rain-forested mountains. With massive government subsidies and a rush of state-owned and multinational corporations eager to produce petrochemicals such as gasoline, plastics, pesticides, and fertilizers, little Cubatão's more than 100 factories accounted for 16 percent of Brazil's entire industrial production by the early 1980s.

Per square meter of ground, Cubatão made the largest contribution to Brazil's so-called economic miracle that exhibited some of the highest rates of national growth of the twentieth century. In search of work, tens of thousands of Brazilian's migrated to the city, far more than it could fully employ, so the majority settled in slums planted around belching smokestacks, tanks of lethal chemicals, and a labyrinthine network of pipelines precariously elevated above the swampy ground.

Comparable industrial cities may have polluted as badly as Cubatão, but the city's topography and climate made it an utter environmental disaster. By the early 1980s, liquid, petrochemical effluents concentrated in the coastal swamps making the former mangrove forests that had previously teemed with fish and bird life virtually lifeless. The waters were spotted in soapy foam and smothered in a greasy, noxious film. And nature was not only silent, as Carson had envisaged – it was deformed. What few fish remained, fisherman reported, had cancerous lesions and even apparent mutations. Atmospheric effluents discharged from thousands of smokestacks were also concentrated, pinned by the prevailing winds and occasional inversions against the mountains. In addition to sulfur dioxide, a range of far more dangerous chemicals precipitated onto the steep Atlantic Forest in the highest concentrations ever recorded, according to Brazil's own state agencies. The slopes above Cubatão received enormous quantities of toxic rain that first killed much of the vegetation that had stabilized the mountains' soils, and then washed down massive mudslides right into Cubatão's industrial and residential zones.

As in North America, the loss of fish, birds, and forests might be lamented, but it did not spark outrage nor a credible challenge to Brazil's now internationally renowned model of development at all costs. Here too, the fear of human biological survival sparked the popular environmental movement, for in Cubatão, humans lived in the same toxic air and water as did the birds, fish, and forests. It began with reports, to this day not well documented, of congenital birth defects of an unusually high number and of bizarre character, including anencephaly, birth without a brain. Puppies, kittens, and human infants were born without limbs. Better documented is the city's infant mortality which was higher than any other Brazilian city. By the early 1980s, as many as one third of Cubatão's citizens complained of respiratory problems, and on the worst of days locals, particularly school children, fled to hospitals and clinics that had begun the practice of offering free oxygen. The mayor, appointed by the military government, officiated ineffectively from afar, for he refused to live in his own city's filth. The city's bleak reality brought out Brazil's morbid sense of humor, and in the lyrics to one popular song a groom, who takes his betrothed on an apparent cut-rate honeymoon to Cubatão, sings with ardor, "Come my love, take off your gas mask and kiss me."

Human mutations and an industrial tragedy made Cubatão's problems more than a laughing matter. The chronic became catastrophic in February 1984 when a pipeline carrying gasoline from the state-owned Petrobras oil company leaked into the swamps beneath Villa Socó, one of the lowland slums. The smell must have been notable, but residents had lived with a chemical stench so long nobody sensed anything out of the ordinary. Something as simple as a cigarette butt probably ignited the gasoline; the pipeline exploded and obliterated much of the neighborhood. Estimates of the dead, from 200 to 700, based loosely on how many children did not return to school, were so imprecise as to suggest human life did not matter to the industrial juggernaut. The following year, heavy rains caused massive slides on the denuded mountains above the city, one of which dislodged and ruptured a pressurized ammonia pipeline, used for making synthetic, nitrogen fertilizer, forcing the evacuation of 6,000 people and the hospitalization of 65. Another major slide came within 800 meters of Brazil's only nuclear power plant.

Environmental disasters and rumors of disaster have broadened environmentalism's appeal in Latin America, as elsewhere. To those millions who must breath in the presence of autos and industry, who must work with pesticides, who tap rubber trees in forests being converted to cattle ranches, who must live without clean water or sewage hookups, or who must simply eat under the burden of degraded soils, disappearing wildlife, and diminishing fisheries, environmentalism's allegations against greed and waste hold an almost automatic appeal. So, what began as laws on paper handed down by a legislative elite following international trends have become popular tools to improving one's quality of life and one's access to material resources. Before Cubatão, Brazil already had a large body of environmental laws and official agencies, but these were largely toothless. After the 1984–1985 disasters, with national support and international attention, a rising local movement began to tame Cubatão's industries and clean up the city. Today, while it has been spoiled forever as a serious honeymoon destination, life in Cubatão has become bearable, and a strong environmental consciousness among its citizens continues to struggle to make further progress, to put human sustainability at least on par with economic development.

Across Latin America, environmentalism is today present in nearly all forms of media and makes up a significant part of public and private education. Nearly every newspaper features daily articles on environmental issues, disasters, and efforts to save species, and the region's major television networks carry more programming with nature as subject than do the major private networks of North America. In the late 1980s, the Amazon burned almost nightly on Brazilian TV, and elsewhere the plights of loggerhead turtles, humpback whales, howler monkeys, and quetzals entered living rooms just as they did the classroom all across the region. And as environmentalism disseminated to the masses, politics took notice. By the late 1980s, and often earlier, environmental rhetoric became an increasingly common component of political platforms. Both local and presidential candidates appealed to the growing environmental sensibility, and a few green parties were formed on the model of the Germans. A handful of legislators were elected under the green party banner, although most green candidates had their platforms and persons co-opted by mainstream parties, testimony to their popular appeal. Nongovernmental organizations (NGOs) with environmental agendas began to appear by the dozens. Many early NGOs were simply affiliates of larger international organizations, and these groups, such as the Sierra Club, World Wildlife Fund, and many others continue to play significant organizational and financial roles. But there were numerous exceptions. Chile's first homegrown, environmental NGO was formed in 1968, and Brazil's in 1971. By the 1990s, Brazil had as many as 2,000 private environmental organizations, Chile officially had 80, and Mexico had more than 1,000. Even in locations where international groups played almost no role, locals organized on their own. All of the Dominican Republic's environmental NGOs, ostensibly supported by Balaguer's nationalism, for example, are homegrown. Many of these groups are quite active, although their memberships are comparatively small and, hence, their funding limited.

Wilderness conservation has also become increasingly important and popular. A few national parks had been established in the early twentieth century but they had hardly entered the national consciousness. Today, however, there are hundreds, and many nations have national parks, reserves, and sanctuaries that far exceed in relative acreage those of developed nations. Costa Rica has set aside one quarter of its national territory in national parks, most of them to preserve biodiversity; most U. S. national parks, particularly the popular destinations, were set aside for their monumental beauty and for human recreation, not initially for nature's sake. And as we saw among the citizens of Curitiba, environmentalism is an essential component of the Costa Rican's national identity, a point of pride and increasingly a point of principle. Elsewhere, Ecuador protects one third of its national territory, including the Galapagos National Park founded in 1959; Mexico protects 8 percent of its land; Chile, 19 percent. Another distinct difference between many Latin American parks and those of North America is the allowance in some instances for multiple uses, including agriculture and extractive activities, in an effort to recognize that most natural areas have been and will continue to be inhabited by Indians and peasants. In addition to setting boundaries, official and private efforts to save particular species, such as green sea turtles, golden lion tamarins, pink dolphins, blue whales, and white-lipped peccaries, as well as their habitats, are popular and well publicized.

Surveys done in the early 1990s suggested that environmental concern among Latin Americans was higher than it was in the United States. When asked to what they gave the greater priority, economic growth or environmental protection, 64 percent of Chileans and Uruguayans, and 71 percent of Mexicans and Brazilians, chose nature. Of course, sentiment varies depending on educational and socioeconomic levels, as well as on geographic location. There is some truth to the adage that an individual's concern for the rainforest increases the further one lives from it; and that it diminishes to essentially zero for those who live within it. And critics point out that commitment to environmentalism is rather shallow, that it is conveniently forgotten when it conflicts with individual self-interest. One foreign observer likened the impact of the international environmental movement in Latin American to that of American popular music: recorded elsewhere, it washes over the region in lulling tunes that are widely enjoyed but whose lyrics are superficially understood. But many of the criticisms that are leveled at Latin American environmentalism, its superficiality, shallow commitment, inconsistent application, and narrow anthropocentrism can, with equal justice, be leveled at popular environmentalism in the United States and Europe.

There are substantial differences between environmentalism in Latin America and the developed world, many of them related to the region's historically nondemocratic political systems. Citizens have acted under the often correct assumption that their voices carry little or no weight in political and policy debate, and have thus remained quiet. In many nations, until recently, individuals had no right to sue for environmental damages, an empowering avenue entirely shut off. In working democracies, the weak are empowered by law or assembly to ensure the powerful do not unfairly transfer the environmental costs of doing business. Much of Latin America still struggles for ecological justice in societies that are defined by socioeconomic injustice. Latin America's environmental activists continue to be jailed, and a few are still being murdered. However, in the last two decades, even members of the politically weakest groups have felt empowered to organize around issues of environmental justice, often their first entry into political activism, and many such groups have been surprisingly successful.

Another substantial obstacle to environmentalism is poverty. Hunger is a common motive for peasants to invade local forests, including national parks. Even internationally renowned national parks such as Brazil's Iguaçu Falls are susceptible to hunting, squatting, and tree felling by poor peasants. Many protected forests, while still intact, are essentially emptied of wildlife by the hungry and poor seeking food or trading illegally in exotic birds and pets. The United States, with abundant economic opportunities, has not had to deal with such pressures on any scale in their national parks for almost century, although it did initially. On a national level, poverty and debt also hamper green initiatives. Purchasing land for national parks, treating sewage, adopting cleaner technologies, and enforcing environmental laws with police or park rangers, costs a great deal of money, and while cash strapped governments have been happy to borrow money to promote economic growth, many leave the administration and enforcement of environmental laws under-funded, making them worth little more than the paper they were written upon. Debt for nature swaps, in which international NGOs buy a nation's foreign debt at a discount and forgive it in exchange for environmental initiatives, have helped finance a few programs, but much legislation remains unfunded. Government environmental agencies, of which there are almost numberless institutes, centers, and committees, are usually headed by political appointees and are notorious for being understaffed. Without money and strong mandates, they can accomplish little of substance, so the more idealistic among them resort to mere educational and promotional campaigns most often associated with NGOs. One critic described the region's state environmental agencies as football players who, rather than striving to put the ball in the goal, stand about on the field cheering on their fans.

In developed nations, where functioning democracies guarantee all a more or less equal opportunity to produce and consume, environmentalism tends to emphasize wilderness protection, nature recreation, aesthetics, and quality of life. In Latin America, the struggle for nature has spontaneously attached itself to the struggle for economic and social justice. Many fights are as much about access to natural resources – clean water, fertile land, forest resources – as they are about saving them. The Amazon's rubber tappers want to save the rain forest, but their primary motive is to protect their economic livelihood. Central American fishermen want to protect their coastal mangroves and prevent shrimp farming but mostly so they can continue to feed their families. In developed nations, people oppose dams for aesthetic reasons; in Latin America, people oppose dams to defend the landscapes they rely upon for physical and cultural sustenance. For rich nations, environmentalism is driven in part by the fact that modernization and development have alienated us from nature. For the poor, environmentalism is motivate by the knowledge, now nearly lost in developed nations, that people are entirely dependent on nature for livelihoods and cultural survival. The first is driven by dreamy myths; the second by stark reality.

In the end, however, popular environmentalism, of the rich or the poor, remains human centered, nature's merits judged almost entirely upon human value systems. Democracy does tend to reduce pollution, equalize consumption, and enhance quality of life for humans. But in democracies, only humans have a vote; nature's denizens have neither voice nor competent representation, although some humans attempt to speak on nature's behalf. We live in an age of the most progressive and popular environmental attitudes in all recorded history, but in environmentalism, as with every other set of human ideals, we encounter hypocrisy. While collectively we can agree to save the earth, individually we consume the earth at an astounding rate. We speak well of nature but express our true attitudes toward plants, animals, land, and landscapes by how we use our discretionary spending. In democratic politics, the voter is always right. In the human economy, the consumer is always right. And democracy, the expression of the will of the majority, continues to place material prosperity for humans among its foremost goals. As a result, not only do we put culture before nature, we continue to favor culture's material development over culture's long-term sustainability.

The inadequacies of the popular environmental movement everywhere are made apparent in the example of Mexico's monarch butterfly reserves. Monarch butterflies, by most human accounting, are beautiful creatures, a common and welcome presence in the experience of most North Americans. They are a species, most concur, worthy of human protection. From March to September, they migrate northward across the eastern United States and Canada seeking flowers for food and milkweed on which to lay their eggs. With a lifespan of only about a month the monarch breeds frenetically, and new generations succeed one another as they migrate north. But come September, they suddenly lose their interest in sex and commence a 5,000 kilometer, single-generation journey to their Mexican wintering grounds, remote sanctuaries only their great grandparents knew. We still do not understand how they find a home they have never visited, located in the mountains west and north of Mexico City, but when they come they are like fire in the sky, attracting the admiration of humans since before the Aztecs with their annual flocking and arrival. The monarchs winter in the cool mountains, sheltered from the cold by towering oyamel firs from which they cling together in globular clusters, massing to as many at 1.6 million insects per hectare. Many do not survive the long winter, but come the warming sun of spring, the breeding instinct returns, the males expend themselves in a sexual frenzy, and the impregnated females depart for the north to restart the cycle.

Although a few Mexicans living in the Sierra Madre Oriental had long known of the monarch's winter presence, only in 1975 was it discovered that it was to these tiny mountain sanctuaries that nearly all monarchs congregated from the entire North American continent. Fred Urquhart, a Canadian entomologist, had searched for the monarch's wintering grounds since 1940 with the help of thousands of volunteers who carefully tagged monarch wings and tracked their migrations. Kenneth Brugger, an American working as a textile consultant in Mexico City, upon reading one of Urquhart's ads in a local paper seeking more volunteers, responded that he had once driven through a cloud of monarch butterflies while on a road trip in the nearby mountains. At Urquhart's request, Brugger returned repeatedly over the next two years; finally, on January 2, 1975, Brugger, who was colorblind, and his Mexican wife Catalina walked well into a grove of firs before realizing the trees were entirely covered in butterflies. Symbolically, an American and a Mexican at the request of a Canadian, stood in the lepidopterist's Holy Grail, the first to identify the home of probably the most familiar insect in North America. On Urquhart's first visit to the wintering grounds, the culmination of 35 years work, he collected a butterfly that had been tagged by one of his volunteers in Minnesota, confirming conclusively the ecological connection of three nations.

Further ramblings identified an additional 14 monarch sanctuaries, and the individuals involved began a long campaign to publicize the need to protect the monarchs' wintering sites which were threatened by expanding logging operations. Without the oyamel firs, the species was doomed. The monarch's admirers described the sanctuaries to the Mexican public as the eighth wonder of the world, cathedrals whose blazing stained glass dazzled the eyes of those who might enter to worship. For the most part, such rhetoric fell flat; popular environmentalism had not yet made its presence felt among more than a few. But those few took to the fight with exemplary zeal. Gina Ogarrio, influenced by Urquhart's 1976 National Geographic article on the sanctuaries, not only helped search for more sites, but organized Pro Monarca A. C. in 1980, which through constant pressure and press releases delivered their message to upper tiers of government. In 1986, President de la Madrid declared five of the monarch's winter homes as biosphere reserves, maintaining their status as common peasant land but regulating logging under a strict permit system.

The legislative victory in Mexico City, however, was an immediate disaster for the monarch wintering ground at Chivati-Huacal. Peasant holders were outraged by the state's trespass on their forests which they had won by blood in the Mexican Revolution, bewildered that the government would place the interest of "worms," as some locals referred to the butterflies, ahead of their own. The peasants of Chivati-Huacal responded by cutting nearly all their forests. When the butterflies returned the following winter, they flew about in confusion for some days before heading off to parts unknown. The peasants had acted in protest of the state's infringement on their communal rights, believing that by chasing off the butterflies they would retain full control of their lands. While most logging in the reserves has not been as politically motivated, it continues for reasons of profit and poverty. Locals can earn as much as $150 per tree, and since the area is cold due to the altitude, families need to collect fuel for winter heating in addition to cooking. Peasants living near the Rosario reserve, where tourism is permitted, welcome the income from more than 50,000 annual visitors, most of them Mexicans, by selling food, lodging and transportation. They work to protect their forests, have attempted replanting, and a few families have gone without winter fuel to help preserve their new source of income. But the income from tourism is seasonal and does not fully compensate losses in logging, so the devastation continues, especially in sanctuaries where tourism has not developed. Since they were established, two of the five reserves have been completely deforested, and in 1999 the largest remaining intact forest in the area was a mere 5,800 hectares compared to 27,100 hectares in 1971. And maybe the greatest threat to the better protected but touristy Rosario reserve is its popularity which has encouraged the state to improve roads, build parking lots, and campgrounds. No one knows if the butterflies will tolerate ever higher rates of visitation.

Of course Mexican peasants and loggers, many of whom act illegally, shoulder much of the blame for the monarch's documented decline, but their activities, spurred by poverty, are only part of a much bigger assault on the butterfly. Consider some wealthier parties to the monarch's demise. Foreign logging firms came to central Mexico's forests at the behest of Porfírio Díaz in the late nineteenth century and certainly destroyed butterfly sanctuaries long before they were recognized as such. Without peasant and Indian lands that were at least in part protected, the monarch might have quietly disappeared a century ago without us ever knowing why. Moreover, as the monarch is a transnational species, the activities of individuals in the United States and Canada cannot be ignored. The monarch cannot survive without milkweed, and in the long expansion of North American agriculture farmers have plowed under natural vegetation and applied herbicides to keep milkweed and other weeds from returning. Genetic engineers have introduced a more recent threat. Breeders of corn seed, to more successfully market their product to Midwestern farmers, have engineered corn that produces an insecticide lethal to corn's age-old insect pests. It is also lethal to monarch caterpillars who are close genetic relatives. Monarch caterpillars exposed to the genetically modified corn's pollen die at rates of 44 percent, and those that survive are half the normal weight. And suburban North Americans, who have made unprecedented demands for new homes in new developments in the last couple decades, pushing sprawl at astonishing rates, have rapidly converted wild fields of milkweed into monocultural lawn-scapes. To these they also liberally apply herbicides that kill the wildflowers on which the monarch feeds as well as the milkweed on which its caterpillar depends, not to mention the increasing use of pesticides that kill insects directly and indiscriminately. In Mexico, there are laws against peasant settlement in the butterfly reserves. In the north, monarch habitat has virtually no legal protections from genetic engineers and suburban sprawl. And while a single peasant collecting firewood in the reserves can do more harm to the monarch than a thousand suburban warriors, there are in fact tens of thousands of suburbanites for every peasant living about the reserves. Historically, agriculture and natural resource extraction, still the subsistence of Mexican peasants, have been culture's primary impacts on nature. In developed nations, however, human settlement is replacing agriculture and resource extraction as the leading cause of habitat loss; the sprawl of suburban homes and second homes, and the roads and strip malls that service them, are now the primary threats to the richest nations' remaining biodiversity.

Millions of simple consumer choices by educated Americans and Canadians who consider themselves friendly to butterflies and most other wildlife have obliterated habitat on a tremendous scale. Counting stations in New Jersey, Virginia, and Minnesota recorded the smallest number ever of monarchs in 2004. In the end, humans of all environmental and national stripes will continue to reduce monarch numbers and, if nothing changes, bring about their extinction. Environmentalism, including saving species as beloved and beautiful as butterflies, is often more popular than it is operative. Biodiversity is a desirable commodity, but few are willing to purchase it at the price. And if odds on the monarch's survival are long, what chance have other species and habitats that humans consider ugly or useless? We, like Inca and Aztec priests before us, sacrifice nature daily on the altar of civilization. While our approach to animal sacrifice is generally less direct, through the destruction of habitats rather than the severing of jugulars, modern sacrificial rites serve much the same purposes as those of the ancient Americans. We continue to immolate nature to assure human security and prosperity. The scale of the sacrificial holocaust, however, has changed.

INVASIONS OF PARADISE

For much of Latin America's history, the world economy has treated the region as a basket of natural resources that have been packaged and shipped to satisfy the consumption of richer foreign nations. Nature, in myth and reality, means many things to culture, but before all else it equates to a commodity, an article of exchange that brings profit to the seller and pleasure to the buyer. Whether it be sugar, coffee, bananas, feathers, mahogany, or mangos, much of the business of Latin America has been to profit by the export of unique tropical commodities for the delectation of consumers in temperate latitudes.

Tourism, one of Latin America's most recent economic booms, follows this pattern. It is unique, however, in one obvious respect: rather than shipping exotic nature in containers to far away consumers, tropical nations import the consumer so she may purchase nature's beauty in fashionably packaged tours. Surely, tourists to Latin America also seek out colorful cultures, living and dead, but what most tourists go to experience today is not an alien culture but an alluring nature. After all, as cultures have become increasingly homogenized, as tourists seek the same services and acquire similar souvenirs in locations across the world, nature, despite its own transformations, remains a primary novelty of visiting new places. But just as tourism has for some time turned disappearing cultures into saleable commodities for foreign consumption, purveyors of nature tourism have begun to deceptively package a damaged nature.

The nature in utmost demand today is the beach. For the northern consumer, the tropical beach – white crescents of soft sand, calm, aquamarine waters, and the diffused shade of palm trees – represents the superlative landscape, nature's most convivial production. My first encounter with a tropical beach at age nine is among my most memorable, corporeal sensations. Having grown up in a quarter of North America where the beaches are rocky, cold, and bleak, even Waikiki's heavily developed strand was an experience bordering on the supernatural. To walk barefoot in sand on unfenced public spaces, caressed, even at night, by balmy, perfumed breezes, and to bathe in crystal blue waters, is an experience for which those from the chilly, dark north will gladly pay. In a 2004 survey, 74 percent of Americans named the beach as their top vacation destination. Not all of them can afford the tropical variety, but for those who can, Latin America's coral sands and turquoise waters are highly rated products. The result has been that beach tourism now accounts for a major, if not the major, source of income for Latin American nations so blessed with desirable beach fronts. Even for an economy as large and diverse as Mexico's, tourism is its third largest earner of foreign exchange, behind oil and remittances from emigrants in the United States. But as in the former examples of nature's commoditization, be it sugar or bananas, the resources that combine to create and sustain the saleable commodity, in this case the living beaches of our fantasies, are despoiled by their foreign consumption.

Tourism by the elite and adventurous has been around for centuries, but beach going is a relatively new phenomenon. Northern tourists had wintered in the Caribbean since the mid-nineteenth century, each nationality carving up its own favored destination: the English in Barbados, the French in Martinique, and the Dutch in Curaçao. And from the early twentieth century, an increasing contingent of Americans had their first tropical experience on the decks of the very ships that supplied them with tropical fruit. United Fruit and other proprietors of the banana fleets gained additional income by persuading customers to travel the tropics, safe from dangers of foreign cultures, in well-appointed cabins, making stops in designated ports of diversion such as Havana and Kingston. But the beach was not yet a reason for leaving home. The sands remained vacant. The region's attraction was the climate, which was increasingly perceived to be healthful, at least outside those ports still plagued by yellow fever. For others, particularly during the years of Prohibition, the attraction was a permissiveness that embraced gambling and alcohol. The beach itself, it appears, was not discovered until just before World War II. Some credit the discovery to movie stars whose lives were already deliberately publicized, and who began to buy vacation homes in the Caribbean and to sport tans in the tabloids. So the beach, what had before been considered a wasteland, a marine desert frequented only by wind and fishermen, became a destination whose visitation and consumption not only offered restful beauty but could also afford one status. Even at age nine, I was aware that a tan and the right t-shirt counted for some kind of bragging rights on the public school playground. The cultural reevaluation of the beach from barren wilderness to proverbial paradise has not yet been fully explained. Part of the appeal, I think, is that the ocean beach is the last modern commons. Many nations deem the beach public property, free to all, and the beach remains one of the few places one can walk untrammeled by private walls and public highways. Standing on the beach, I am free to roam at will in three directions, up the beach, out to sea, and down the beach, the limits to my movements imposed by nature, not by culture. Most of the rest of nature is fenced off. In the end, however, we may have to attribute the rest of the beach's appeal to advertising's remarkable ability to create in us wants and fantasies that were previously dormant or even nonexistent.

In the 1950s, Hollywood and its entourage descended by plane and ship on Acapulco: Elizabeth Taylor married there, Frank Sinatra sang there, John F. Kennedy vacationed there, and middle class America soon followed. Setting a pattern that has since been followed with little variation, national and foreign investors constructed hotels, nightclubs, restaurants and resorts, and real estate agents began marketing winter homes. From a tiny port, Acapulco burgeoned rapidly, and almost entirely, as a result of foreign tourism. There was not a single good road into this paradise of green mountains and white beaches, so it was easier to get to Acapulco from Los Angeles than it was from Mexico City. But this city of vacationing, temporary migrants, like many third-world cities, grew too fast too: there was insufficient water, garbage began to pile up, and there was little treatment of sewage which found its way into Acapulco's waters. Miguel Aleman, who as Mexico's president personally speculated in Acapulco's boom by buying stretches of empty beach front, would later, as national commissioner of tourism, help build the infrastructure that made the city tolerable for continued recreation, but already by the mid-1960s, people were asking if Acapulco had passed its prime. Those who remembered Acapulco before the boom began to cast their eyes for similarly pristine stretches of coastline, and increasingly, Acapulco's hoteliers had to pitch their somewhat sullied attractions to middle class Mexicans who, with a new highway to Mexico City and less competition from rich Americans, finally found it reasonable to vacation on their world famous, well trod, beach. Today, more than 80 percent of Acapulco's visitors are Mexicans, a location largely abandoned by foreign visitors.

So, due to both Acapulco's perceived decline and the growing numbers who wanted the experience of the tropical beach, resorts for cold Americans began to appear all up and down the Pacific coast: Cabo San Lucas, Puerto Vallarta, and Mazatlan by cruise ship; Zihuatenejo and Huatulco by air; and Ensenada and Puerto Peñasco by recreational vehicle. In essence, each development urbanized the beachfront; Mexican tourist workers arrived and settled well off the beach, and new hotels and resorts pushed the city coastwise in search of fresher, less crowded shores. The pattern is in some ways similar to what we have seen in extractive agriculture. As in sugar and coffee where planters abandoned lands they had stripped of fertility for virgin lands on the frontier, beach tourism tends to expand laterally, in progressive sprawl or by leapfrogging, in search of that pristine commodity that increasingly discriminating guests demand. It leaves behind a damaged, less productive set of goods of ever diminishing value. Few such resorts have been entirely abandoned, including Acapulco, but the rates hotels and other services charge decline with nature's sullying. Nature, when commoditized, must be depreciated by accountants like all capital goods; the used beach must be discounted for sale. Urbanization brings to the beach the same problems it introduces to other developing cities: water pollution, air pollution, noise, crime, overcrowding, unemployment, and cultural homogenization. Reports of fecal material in the water, as has been reported repeatedly at Acapulco and recently at Zihuatenejo, have the potential to devastate beach tourism. This provides incentives for locals to clean up their water, but often the big money prefers to simply move on to virgin beaches rather than work to clean up its own mess and a city's stigmatized image. And messes are only half the problem. One of the qualities that tourists attach to beautiful nature is solitude, and even the most stunning beach, if excessively burdened with oil-slathered bodies, loses much of its appeal. An experienced beach tourist loathes nothing more than crowds of her own species.

The process of despoliation is repeating itself at Cancún, currently Mexico's most popular destination and now the epitome of mass beach tourism. People come to drink, dance, and play, something people can do in just about any location, but they choose Cancún because here nature dazzles. The water is the most celestial blue, and just off the beach, sometimes less than a few hundred yards, is the world's second largest reef inhabited by colorful fish, sea turtles, and delicate corals, the marine equivalent of rainforests in their living density and diversity. It was here that Jacques Cousteau's underwater films introduced the world to coral reefs in a series of popular television programs in the 1960s. But after 30 years of visitation, more than 4 million visitors each year currently, Cancún's natural attractions are showing some wear and tear.

Cancún, in its pristine state, was a bit too wild for tourists, so when this-time President Luis Echeverria bought up land in the early 1970s in anticipation of development, mangroves, where birds nested and fish spawned, were torn up, mosquitoes were eradicated, and swamps were drained. Hotels began to spring up along Cancún's 26-kilometer barrier island, and tens of thousands of hotel rooms, with tens of thousands of toilets, began to flush their sewage, more than they could treat, into the increasingly polluted lagoon behind the now coveted beachfront. Development continued apace until Cancún's strip, with its massive resorts of quirky architecture, was frequently compared to that of Las Vegas. Seeping sewage and beach erosion, much of it due to sand mining for the construction of concrete hotels, pools, and roads, poisoned and choked the coral reefs that have thrived in large measure due to the lack of surface rivers and hence erosion in the Yucatan. The region's rivers run crystal clear underground, another popular diving attraction, but even these have become polluted by the hundreds of hotels and vacation homes that dig cisterns in which they deposit their sewage. The porous limestone and the beautiful white sands, both the former bodies of ancient coral of which the entire peninsula consists, cannot prevent contaminants from passing to the sea. Likewise, the cruise ship behemoths that pass over these waters in apparent, perfect silence also make substantial negative contributions, damaging corals with anchors and marring beach sands with oily bilge. Cruising is one of the largest and fastest growing sectors of the tourism industry, cause for concern in sensitive marine environments like the Caribbean. When an oil tanker spills its ruinous, black contents into the oceans, it is generally accidental. A cruise ship, a veritable sewage tanker, dumps its vile contents of human excrement into the oceans legally and intentionally. Floating cities of indoor plumbing, the cruise ship's passengers can produce 25,000 gallons of human sewage per day, in addition to 143,000 gallons of gray water (waste water from nontoilet sources) which is laced with everything from bath soap to photo processing chemicals, anything dumped down the sink. Little of this material is treated on board ship; none of it is returned to port for safe disposal. All is dumped directly into the oceans, the only restriction, which itself is difficult to enforce, is that sewage and waste water be dumped a mere 5 kilometers distant from shore, well within site of bathers.

Deforestation, declining water quality, and urban sprawl have darkened Cancún's future, much as they did Acapulco's. American tourists name cleanliness as their first criteria in judging a beach, more important than scenery or weather. And they name alcohol consumption as their number one activity at the beach. Tourists will continue to come as long as the beaches are white and the waters blue, but more of them are content to sit at the swim-up bar and enjoy the ocean views from the safety of a chlorinated pool that mimics the natural color of sea water on white sand. Walking one of north Cancún's calm, public beaches on a Sunday afternoon, I admired the glorious, cerulean strait between the mainland and the flat Isla Mujeres, the latter evident only by the hotel towers jutting from behind the horizon, but in the blue water immediately before me floated some unmistakable human waste. Its source may have been a hotel, cruise ship, or, most likely, a bather unwilling or unable to find a public restroom, but it's the kind of news that moves queasy foreign tourists down the beach rather quickly. Cancún's guests, in a recent survey, revealed that only 20 percent intended to return. Those that do will head south into the Riviera Maya, or yet further into Belize where the story is repeating itself but is still in its earlier pages of quiet beaches and living reefs. The question remains whether tourism with nature as the primary attraction will ever be able accommodate large numbers of people without despoiling what they have come to see. One scholar has observed that mass tourism is like oil exploration: you can extract oil carefully or chaotically, but when it is gone, everyone packs.

Some have placed hope in ecotourism, a form of visitation in which guests come to see nature in its most remote beauty and where tourist dollars are supposed to finance preservation efforts. But for the most part, ecotourism has been a financial failure and a natural disaster. Most eco-tourists want to see wildlife, but the tropical forest rarely yields unob-structed views, and the forests of the Yucatan have been depleted of game and fowl by centuries of indigenous hunting. Even when it meets visitor expectations, ecotourism tends to move people into the remain-ing undisturbed tracts where they really should not be if we want to preserve nature, for if they show real enthusiasm for a place, hoteliers and real estate agents are to follow. Worse yet, the term ecotourism has become itself a marketing device for activities as varied as swim-ming with dolphins to racing through mangrove swamps on jet skis. The reality is that most visitors care less about nature than they do their experience in nature. If nature is degraded, they lament, but as temporary, often one-time visitors, they do not demand change. Such is the depth of popular environmentalism abroad. It is locals, who depend on tourism, that must demand change, and more and more voices are being heard. There are technologies that could solve some, though not all, of tourism's environmental woes. The no-flush toilet, if installed in every hotel, vacation home, and cruise ship, would solve the very serious sewage problem instantly. But tourism's purveyors rightly fear tourists would reject such unplumbed devices for no better reason than their novelty. So tourist developers, rather than change, conserve, and improve, move on to spoil new areas, like sugar and coffee planters before them, as long as there are new areas to spoil.

The tropical eco-theme park is the latest phase of nature tourism. Just as cultural tourism has commoditized cultural expressions – indigenous dances and rituals, for example – for scheduled sale to travelers seeking a lost, preindustrial reality, the purveyors of nature tourism, in the face of a disappearing nature, have turned to recreating a virtual nature that serves as proxy for the real thing. As many of the millions of tourists who come each year are first-time visitors, ignorant of both the culture and nature they came to see, they generally do not know the difference between the real thing and the proxy. Such displays, however, are neither nature nor even museums to nature, but more akin to shopping malls in which each boutique sells a unique nature experience that, to all appearances, seems to satisfy the customers. Xcaret, located south of Cancún near Playa del Carmen, is an exceptional example of this type where nature is concentrated and packaged for the visitors' efficient consumption. For the price of a ticket to a Disney resort, visitors gain entrance to a private park that offers the petting of sea turtles and manatees, the observation of captive butterflies and moated jaguars, snorkeling in underground rivers, and relaxation on "improved" beaches. For additional fees, waders can "swim" with dolphins, currently the most popular attraction, nonswimmers in diving helmets can walk the bottom of an artificial bay to feed planted fish, diners can eat local seafood in one of nine restaurants, and couples can contract a marriage. On the grounds, a stunning saltwater aquarium condenses the wildlife seen in a week's worth of snorkeling behind thick panes of Plexiglas.

Xcaret's visitors are educated about the resort's efforts to save the local fauna, from sheltering breeding turtles to rescuing the eggs of abandoned macaw nests. But the resort says rather little as to why such efforts of preservation are necessary. The park's publicity director explains the presence of so many captive-bred macaws, the park's colorful welcoming committee, by declaring that macaws are bad mothers who desert their young at the slightest sound or disturbance. The park also claims the turtles on the local beaches would have disappeared were park staff not there to protect them from predators. If anything, the park's concentrated abundance gives the impression that all is well with nature. Visitors, most of them whisked to the park from swank hotels and posh cruise ships, do not see the damaged reefs; they do not see the limestone chasms quarried to build tourist facilities, now converted to landfills of plastic margarita glasses and dead, rental car batteries; they will not see the leaching cesspits just beneath the public restrooms; and they will not understand that it is tourists and the very resorts in which they luxuriate that have driven mother turtles from the beaches and frightened macaw mothers from their nests, not to mention the hundreds of other displaced creatures Xcaret has shown no interest in saving or caging. A virtual nature obscures nature's tattered reality. It is little surprising then that for many visitors the cunning replication is more appealing and more pleasurable than the degraded reality. Guests leave the park not only with the impression that all is well with nature in the Yucatan, but that the money they have spent will further subsidize nature's enhancement. For the price of admission, the myth of tropical America as an unsullied Eden is persuasively substantiated.

Is it possible that we are clever enough to sustain our existence despite an increasingly degraded nature? Already, we have substantially substituted nature's services with technology and art. Maybe we can sustainably synthesize oxygen and food; maybe we can recreate nature, physically or digitally, to satisfy the human spirit; maybe we could live perpetually in biospheres on the moon, chock full of life-sustaining gadgets and filled with the virtual images, chirping, and scents of terrestrial nature, more abundant and less threatening than the real thing. Examples like Xcaret prove that we are clever enough to fool some of the people with nature's counterfeits some of the time. But as an authentic nature slowly slips through our hands, as reefs and forests disappear, our touted powers, which may in fact allow us to live like astronauts who have severed their umbilical cords to mother earth, are not powerful enough to resurrect what is being lost. What is extinct is nonrecoverable. And virtual substitutes, whether Cousteau's dated reef documentaries or Xcaret's painstakingly arranged menageries, nature recorded and potted for rental and admission, will come to inspire in our children more regrets than delights.

In the timeless tension that exists between us and the rest of nature, some today still strive, as did Columbus and others, for that mythical Eden in which both man and beast were innocents. Greater harmony, the end of enmity, with the rest of nature is one of contemporary culture's most admirable aspirations, however short we fall, and however unattainable it may ultimately be. We can certainly do much better, and ever-growing numbers in Latin America, as elsewhere, have expressed a willingness to make cultural sacrifices to that end, to achieve a better balance. The plausible American Eden is a landscape on which livable cities, sustainable gardens, and intact wilds peaceably coexist and, in some extraordinary cases, beneficially commingle.

Cuba's Latest Revolution

People should not have to depend on the vagaries of prices in the world economy, long distance transportation, and superpower "goodwill" for their next meal.[1]

I have become increasingly aware of how much my day-to-day environment, even as I sit here and write, is already synthetic. The Iberian colonists, who we noted wore shoes and slept in elevated beds to separate themselves from earth's nature, would have approved of there being very little in the way of dirty soil, raw wood, or living vegetation within my immediate reach. Most of what surrounds me is manmade and petrochemical – from the plastic desk, chair, and computer on which I work, the nylon carpet on which I walk, and the latex paint on which I gaze, to the lenses on my nose, aspirin in my drawer, and the residual scent of the shampoo in my hair. Oil makes up the bulk of my material culture, the better part of my consumer choices, and it has improved my standard of living in countless ways.

Petrochemicals are also what keep me well fed. While what I eat is often highly processed, increasingly synthetic, and unnaturally flavored by petrochemical magic, oil plays its most significant role further up the line of production. Oil empowers today's farmer, astride a platoon of machines, to do the work of hundreds of his occupational ancestors. Oil fuels the production of synthetic fertility so the farmer can plant the same crop in the same field, year after year, with unprecedented returns.

[1] Fernando Funes, et al., eds., *Sustainable Agriculture and Resistance: Transforming Food Production in Cuba*, with an introduction by Peter Rosset (Oakland, CA: Food First Books, 2002), xix.

Oil, from which nearly all pesticides and herbicides are derived, permits the farmer to dispatch, with relative ease, those formidable armies of insects and weeds that threaten my next meal. And it is oil that moves my groceries thousands of kilometers: I eat apples grown in New Zealand, melons irrigated in Mexico, and grapes harvested in Chile. I have to. My home county, formerly the domain of small farmers and irrigators who were self-sufficient in food, grows nothing anymore but alfalfa hay and some tasty but token peaches. Without oil, much that sustains me and entertains me vanishes.

This is surely the petrochemical age, and oil explains many of the last century's astonishing cultural gains. Yet, it has also been the power of fossil fuel that has encouraged culture to swagger about in nature doing irreparable damage to soils, waters, fisheries, forests, and the atmosphere. For some time now we have lived and dined like kings on oil's tab and at nature's expense. So, what happens when the oil peters out? How about if it were suddenly shut off, an event with some precedents? For North Korea it has meant the collapse of a nation's agriculture, the hushed starvation of hundreds of thousands, particularly children, and a dependence on foreign food aid. North Korea was entirely dependent upon the Soviet bloc for its oil, fertilizers, and pesticides, as well as for much of its food. When the Soviet political order collapsed, North Koreans lost access to modernity's essential resource and slid backward a century. After nearly two decades, North Korea's leaders continue to live in denial of their demise. Traffic cops, stiff in impeccable uniform, still put in their shifts at Pyongyang's major intersections, dutifully directing traffic on multi-laned streets that for years have been virtually empty of cars or commerce.

North Korea was not the only resource casualty of the Soviet demise. Insular Cuba also lost its petrochemical lifeline. During a long friendship in which Russia exchanged Siberian oil – and its fertile and lethal derivatives – on generous terms for Cuban sugar, Cuba developed one of the most mechanized and chemical-intensive agricultural systems, more akin to California in the quantities of fertilizers, pesticides, and herbicides, applied to fields than to its immediate neighbors in Latin America. So, when the inputs abruptly ceased in 1989, Cubans entered their self-styled Special Period. Imports of oil fell by 50 percent, which shut down transport and disrupted electrical production. Imports of fertilizers and pesticides declined 80 percent, a loss that halved sugar exports nationally and decreased forage and milk production in Havana province by 80 percent. Without electricity farmers could not irrigate; and without diesel fuel, truckers were forced to leave harvests rotting in fields far from their urban markets. But even if Cuba could have delivered her harvests, her people risked starvation. Before 1989, Cuba imported nearly 60 percent of its food, and its citizens consumed an average of 2,800 calories per day. By 1993, average caloric intake had fallen to 1,800. Cubans were eating a third fewer calories and 40 percent less protein than they had been accustomed, and it was expressed plainly in the Cuban physique. The number of persons who were obese or overweight, 33 percent before 1989, fell by almost half. The Special Period diet, which imposed a regime of reduced calories and increased exercise (due to empty gas tanks), made the weight fly off. It also caused malnourishment and anemia in some children and pregnant mothers.

Anywhere else, such a tragedy would have been met with massive food aid, as continues to occur even in isolationist, nuclear-bent North Korea. But in Cuba, little aid was forthcoming. The United States, rather than seeing these developments as a possible humanitarian crisis that would require the relaxation of its decades old trade embargo against Cuba, in fact tightened the restrictions, preventing any U.S. company or its foreign subsidiaries from trading with Cuba even in food; this further reduced Cuba's food imports, and some U.S. elected officials hoped out loud that hunger would bring Cuba to its knees. Cuba was pretty much on her own. At first, Fidel Castro could only ask Cubans to tighten their belts and work to ensure that what food was available got to those most in need, namely children under seven and pregnant mothers. Significantly, while people suffered, and some went hungry, nobody died. Cubans, unlike North Koreans, faced their predicament realistically and began to strategize a long-term solution. Highly educated, technically competent, and politically cohesive, they set out to prove once again that they could weather the worst by sacrifice and determination, just as they had faced climatological and geopolitical disasters in the past. Cuba's response to the national food crisis is the largest experiment in organic agriculture ever attempted.

Without fuel, tires, and parts to run their tractors, many farmers have reverted to the use of oxen to prepare their fields. Aged peasants and dwindling blacksmiths provided the expertise, and the advantages over mechanized traction, despite the increase in human labor, became immediately clear. Oxen did not compact the soils as did tractors, and they could be used year round, even during the mucky, rainy season, a period when tractors had to be garaged. In some areas this permitted a third crop each year, and the oxen's manure, of course, could be used as fertilizer. Without pesticides, Cubans ramped up experiments that had preceded the Soviet collapse in biological pest control. In just one example, from extracts derived from the neem tree, of East Indian origin but now widely planted in Cuban plantations, Cuban scientists produced a variety of pesticides that kill targeted insects without harming many good ones. Neem extract not only kills the right bugs, it repels them, suppresses their appetite, and regulates their reproduction. It is harmless to humans and other mammals. Hundreds of units have been established across the island to produce neem extracts in addition to those dedicated to the breeding of predatory insects, such as lion ants, that have been launched with success in the protection of plantains and sweet potatoes from their respective weevil pests. And farmers have also found that the lack of broad-spectrum pesticides, which kill nearly everything, have helped return a certain natural balance. Previously, when aphids attacked fields of cabbage, they were doused with chemicals. Now, farmers patiently wait: within two days' time parasitic wasps, who used to be nuked along with everything else, take care of the aphids in short order.

The lack of fertilizers, however, has been Cuba's greatest agricultural challenge. After decades of heavy industrial farming that has eroded the soil's natural fertility, fertility inputs have been desperately sought in order to sustain crop yields. In addition to small but growing supplies of manure from oxen, pigs, and chickens, Cubans have recycled crop vegetation, gathered the sludge left over from sugar processing, and embraced vermiculture, that is the use of earthworms to enhance the quality of composted material, all of which they have applied to their fields. Cubans are also mass-producing a number of microorganisms that when applied to the soil help fix nitrogen and other nutrients. Cuban agronomists admit they still fall well short of sustainable fertility, and this may be due to the fact that Havana, for example, still dumps 5 cubic meters of human sewage into the ocean every second, a resource they so far have been unwilling to reclaim. But every discovery gets them a little closer. For example, farmers have developed dozens of rotational and intercropping systems that rationally manage the soil's fertility fluctuations as well as thwart a variety of pests.

The most visible revolution in Cuban agriculture is the marked geographic shift of farming away from the countryside to the city. Havana was in the worst situation, located far from the nation's agricultural production centers. Hungry people in the city with hungry children have become the soldiers on the battle's front lines. Scrounging seeds and cuttings from wherever they could find them, families began to plant food in every available piece of bare ground. Gardens invaded the city's former abandoned lots as well as the patios, balconies, and rooftops of homes and apartments. The state picked up on the trend and began assisting cooperatives in establishing farms on abandoned baseball fields and even parking lots. Where the soil was good, intensive gardens were created. Where there was only pavement, organoponics, rows of raised beds filled with imported soil and organic matter, were formed. Factories and public schools, which had long provided lunch to workers and pupils in Havana, also reclaimed their unused spaces for food production. These institutional gardens provide fresh produce to the tables of more than 300 cafeterias. But it was the family gardens that produced more than half of the city's locally grown food, specializing in vegetables, spices, eggs, pigs, ducks, and rabbits. More than 100,000 family farmers produced 23,000 tons of food by 1999, nearly all of which was sold or bartered in free, local markets. The incentives of hunger and profit turned the city into a garden, and by the late 1990s, not only were Cubans no longer going hungry, they were eating better food and a greater variety of it than they had in 30 years. It was pesticide free, it was local, it was fresh, and it produced more food per square meter of ground than did industrial agriculture. An intensive, urban agriculture removes the pressures that elsewhere continue to push people into wilderness and rainforests in search of food and livelihood, and it also reduces fuel consumption and greenhouse gas emissions substantially. In the United States, agriculture devours 20 percent of national oil consumption, more than private automobiles. Cubans are still not self-sufficient in food production and rely on imports, especially of rice. Theirs is a large population on a small patrimony – population density is three times that of the United States. But given current trends in increasing yields, it may only be a matter of time before food imports will be a luxury rather than a necessity. Without question, Cuba's national food security, and probably her agriculture in general, are better off today than they were in 1989.

It is hard to know if Cuba's move toward sustainable agriculture will last. One threat is Castro's recent reining in of some of the free market reforms that abetted the quick rise of entrepreneurial, organic agriculture. The other threat is that Castro will die and the blockade will end, which would certainly be of great economic benefit to Cuba as a whole, but which might cause unsustainable practice to pick up where it left off. Some fear urban farms and gardens would disappear after the crisis as did victory gardens in America after World War II. But many Cubans protest the changes are here to stay. Once a person who has lived on processed meats and canned vegetables has consistently eaten fresh pork and produce, they will not easily go back. And some argue that even were oil and its derivatives to be available again, most farmers and consumers are so committed to sustainable, organic food and the security it provides that the market for petrochemicals for agriculture would be limited. Many Cubans see the recent changes in sustainable food production as *El Bloqueio*'s silver lining.

And now Cubans, even urbanites, know something most of the modern world has forgotten. We like to fancy that our distant ancestors, without the powers of oil, fertilizers, and pesticides, often did not know where their next meal would come from. That too is a lie born of modern hubris. Even in the distant past, most Americans were well fed, barring catastrophes, and as most of them were directly involved in agriculture, they knew exactly where to find their next meal. Today, by stark contrast, few of us know the origin of our last meal. We no longer know what ought to be the most basic of human knowledge: the origin of our food, how it is produced, or at what environmental cost. The power of oil has separated us from the elemental roots of our biological existence and in doing so blinds us to its accumulating damages and obscures its threatened future. We hold to the faith that food in great quantity and variety will continue to show up in our supermarkets and restaurants as if by magic, like manna from heaven, but it is as blind a faith as there ever was. In the latter-day battles with nature, nearly all humans in developed nations are at the front lines, hundreds and often thousands of kilometers from the home fronts that produce their rations. Most of the food I eat has traveled at least half a continent to arrive on my plate. We are entirely dependent on long supply lines that themselves depend on cheap oil, long-distance transportation infrastructure, stable governments, stable climates, and the absence of major natural and epidemiological disasters, none of which we can guarantee. It may be fine to rely on a globalized economy for big screen televisions, auto parts, and migrant and outsourced labor, but modern civilization's greatest blunder may be to rely upon it for our next meal. Even Mexico, despite its being the birthplace of the Green Revolution's hybridized crops and the petrochemical regime that comes with it, is more dependent on food imports today than it was before modern agriculture arrived. Mexico has fewer crop varieties, poorer soils, and a dimmer agricultural future as a result. Cuba, out of circumstances beyond its control, has become a potential model for the future of agriculture. If they are successful, proving that a nation can sustainably feed a dense population with low-input, local, organic agriculture, it will be the long Cuban Revolution's greatest legacy.

SUGGESTED FURTHER READING

GENERAL

Brailovsky, Antonio Elio, and Dina Foguelman. *Memoria verde: Historia ecológica de la Argentina*. Buenos Aires: Editorial Sudamericana, 1991.

Castro Herrera, Guillermo. *Los trabajos de ajuste y combate: naturaleza y sociedad en la historia de América Latina*. Bogotá: Ediciones Casa de las Américas, 1994.

Dean, Warren. *With Broadax and Firebrand: The Destruction of the Brazilian Atlantic Forest*. Berkeley: University of California Press, 1995.

Evans, Sterling. *The Green Republic: A Conservation History of Costa Rica*. Austin: University of Texas Press, 1999.

Fernández-Armesto, Felipe. *Civilizations: Culture, Ambition, and the Transformation of Nature*. New York: Free Press, 2001.

García Martínez, Bernardo, and Alba González Jácome, eds. *Estudios sobre historia y ambiente en América I: Argentina, Bolivia, México, Paraguay*. Mexico City: El Colegio de México, Centro de Estudios Históricos, 1999.

García Martínez, Bernardo, and María del Rosario Prieto, eds. *Estudios sobre historia y ambiente en América II: Norteamérica, Sudamérica y el Pacífico*. Mexico City: Instituto Panamericano de Geografía e Historia, 2002.

Kircher, John. *A Neotropical Companion: An Introduction to the Animals, Plants, and Ecosystems of the New World Tropics*, 2nd ed. Princeton: Princeton University Press, 1998.

McNeill, J. R. *Something New Under the Sun: An Environmental History of the Twentieth-Century World*. New York: W.W. Norton, 2000.

Richards, John F. *The Unending Frontier: An Environmental History of the Early Modern World*. Berkeley: University of California Press, 2003.

Roberts, J. Timmons, and Nikki Demetria Thanos. *Trouble in Paradise: Globalization and Environmental Crises in Latin America*. New York: Routledge, 2003.

Simonian, Lane. *Defending the Land of the Jaguar: A History of Conservation in Mexico*. Austin: University of Texas Press, 1995.

Williams, Michael. *Deforesting the Earth: From Prehistory to Global Crisis.* Chicago: University of Chicago Press, 2003.

CHAPTER 1: AN OLD WORLD BEFORE IT WAS "NEW"

Arnold, Philip P. *Eating Landscape: Aztec and European Occupation of Tlalocan.* Niwot: University Press of Colorado, 1999.

Ayerza, Ricardo, Jr., and Wayne Coates. *Chia: Rediscovering a Forgotten Crop of the Aztecs.* Tucson: University of Arizona Press, 2005.

Balee, William, ed. *Advances in Historical Ecology.* New York: Columbia University Press, 1998.

Butzer, Karl W. "Economic Aspects of Water Management in the Prehispanic New World." *Antiquity* 70:267 (1996): 200–5.

Coe, Sophie D. *America's First Cuisines.* Austin: University of Texas Press, 1994.

Denevan, William M. "The Pristine Myth: The Landscape of the Americas in 1492." *Annals of the Association of American Geographers* 82:3 (1992): 369–85.

Denevan, William M. *Cultivated Landscapes of Native Amazonia and the Andes.* Oxford: Oxford University Press, 2001.

Denevan, William M. "The Native Population of Amazonia in 1492 Reconsidered." *Revista de Indias* 43 (2003): 175–88.

Fisher, Christopher T., Helen P. Pollard, Isabel Israde-Alcántera, Victor H. Garduño-Monroy, and Subir K. Banerjee. "A Reexamination of Human-Induced Environmental Change within the Lake Pátzcuaro Basin, Michoacán, Mexico." *Proceedings of the National Academy of Sciences* 100 (2003): 4957–62.

Krech, Shepard, III. *The Ecological Indian: Myth and History.* New York: W.W. Norton, 1999.

Lentz, David, ed. *Imperfect Balance: Landscape Transformations in the Precolumbian Americas.* New York: Columbia University Press, 2000.

LeVine, Terry Y., ed. *Inka Storage Systems.* Norman: University of Oklahoma Press, 1992.

Mann, Charles C. *1491: New Revelations of the Americas Before Columbus.* New York: Alfred A. Knopf, 2005.

Murra, John V. *The Economic Organization of the Inca State.* Greenwich, CT: JAI Press, 1980.

O'Hara, Sarah L., F. Alayne Street-Perrott, and Timothy P. Burt. "Accelerated Soil Erosion around a Mexican Highland Lake Caused by Prehispanic Agriculture." *Nature* 362 (March 4, 1993): 48–51.

Palerm, Ángel. *Obras hidráulicas prehispánicas en el sistema lacustre del valle de México.* Mexico City: Instituto Nacional de Antropología e Historia, 1973.

Schwartz, Marion. *A History of Dogs in the Early Americas.* New Haven, CT: Yale University Press, 1997.

Whitmore, Thomas M., and B. L. Turner II. *Cultivated Landscapes of Middle America on the Eve of Conquest.* Oxford: Oxford University Press, 2002.

CHAPTER 2: NATURE'S CONQUESTS

Boyer, Richard Everett. *La gran inundación: Vida y sociedad en México, 1629–1638.* Mexico City: Secretaría de Educación Pública, 1975.

Butzer, Karl W., and Elizabeth K. Butzer. "Transfer of the Mediterranean Livestock Economy to New Spain: Adaptation and Ecological Consequences." In *Global Land Use Change: A Perspective from the Columbia Encounter*, ed. B. L. Turner II, 151–93. Madrid: Consejo Superior de Investigaciones Científicas, 1995.

Butzer, Karl W., and Elizabeth K. Butzer. "The 'Natural' Vegetation of the Mexican Bajio: Archival Documentation of a 16th-Century Savanna Environment." *Quaternary International* 43:4 (1997): 161–72.

Crosby, Alfred W. *The Columbian Exchange: Biological and Cultural Consequences of 1492.* Westport, CT: Greenwood Press, 1972.

Crosby, Alfred W. *Ecological Imperialism: The Biological Expansion of Europe, 900–1900.* Cambridge: Cambridge University Press, 1986.

Endfield, Georgina H., and Sarah L. O'Hara. "Degradation, Drought and Dissent: An Environmental History of Colonial Michoacán, West Central Mexico." *Annals of the Association of American Geographers* 89:3 (1999): 402–22.

Gerbi, Antonello. *Nature in the New World: From Christopher Columbus to Gonzalo Fernández de Oviedo*, trans. Jeremy Moyle. Pittsburg: University of Pittsburgh Press, 1986.

Hoberman, Louisa Schell. "Bureaucracy and Disaster: Mexico City and the Flood of 1629." *Journal of Latin American Studies* 6:2 (November 1974): 211–30.

Hoberman, Louisa Schell. "Technological Change in a Traditional Society: The Case of the Desague in Colonial Mexico." *Technology and Culture* 21 (July 1980): 386–407.

Holanda, Sérgio Buarque de. *Visão do paraíso: Os motivos edênicos no descobrimento e na colonização do Brasil*, 4th ed. São Paulo: Editora Nacional, 1985.

Kiple, Kenneth, F. *The Caribbean Slave: A Biological History.* Cambridge: Cambridge University Press, 1984.

Livi-Bacci, Massimo. "Return to Hispaniola: Reassessing a Demographic Catastrophe." *Hispanic American Historical Review* 83 (2003): 3–51.

Melville, Elinor G. K. *A Plague of Sheep: Environmental Consequences of the Conquest in Mexico.* Cambridge: Cambridge University Press, 1994.

Melville, Elinor G. K. "Conquest Landscapes: Ecological Consequences of Pastoralism in the New World." In *Le Nouveau Monde–Mondes Nouveaux;*

L'Experience Americaine, eds. Serge Gruzinski and Nathan Wachtel, 99–113. Paris: Ecole des Hautes Etudes, Siences Sociales, 1996.

Musset, Alain. *De l'eau vive à l'eau morte. Enjeux techniques et culturels dans la Vallée de México (XVIe–XIXe siècles)*. Paris: Éditions Recherche sur les Civilisations, 1991.

Musset, Alain. "De Tláloc a Hipócrates: el agua y la organización del espacio en la cuenca de México, siglos XVI–XVIII." In *Tierra, agua y bosques: historia y medio ambiente en el México central*, ed. Alejandro Tortolero Villaseñor, 127–77. Guadalajara, Mexico: Universidad de Guadalajara, 1996.

Sluyter, Andrew S. "The Ecological Origins and Consequences of Cattle Ranching in Sixteenth-Century New Spain." *Geographical Review* 86:2 (1996): 161–77.

Sluyter, Andrew S. *Colonialism and Landscape: Postcolonial Theory and Applications*. Lanham, MD: Rowman & Littlefield, 2002.

Super, John C. *Food, Conquest, and Colonization in Sixteenth-Century Spanish America*. Albuquerque: University of New Mexico Press, 1988.

CHAPTER 3: THE COLONIAL BALANCE SHEET

Anderson, Robin L. *Colonization as Exploitation in the Amazon Rain Forest, 1758–1911*. Gainesville: University Press of Florida, 1999.

Brown, Kendall W. "Workers' Health and Colonial Mercury Mining at Huancavelica, Peru." *The Americas* 57:4 (April 2001): 467–96.

Brown, Larissa V. "Urban Growth, Economic Expansion, and Deforestation in Late Colonial Rio de Janeiro." In *Changing Tropical Forests: Historical Perspectives on Today's Challenges in Central and South America*, eds. Harold K. Steen and Richard P. Tucker, 165–75. Durham, NC: Forest History Society, 1992.

Cleary, David. "Towards an Environmental History of the Amazon: From Prehistory to the Nineteenth Century." *Latin American Research Review* 36:2 (2001): 64–96.

Cunill, Pedro. "La temprana sementera urbana chilena y los comienzos del deterioro ambiental." In *Siete estudios: Homenaje de la Facultad de Ciencias Humanas a Eugenio Pereira Salas*, ed. Pedro Cunill, 59–80. Santiago: Universidad de Chile, 1975.

Dore, Elizabeth. "Environment and Society: Long-Term Trends in Latin American Mining." *Environment and History* 6 (2000): 1–29.

Endfield, Georgina H., and Sarah. L. O'Hara. "Perception or Deception? Land Degradation in Post-Conquest Michoacán, West Central Mexico." *Land Degradation and Development* 10 (1999): 381–96.

Lipsett-Rivera, Sonya. *To Defend Our Water with the Blood of Our Veins: The Struggle for Resources in Colonial Puebla*. Albuquerque: University of New Mexico Press, 1999.

MacCameron, Robert. "Environmental Change in Colonial New Mexico." *Environmental History Review* 18:2 (1994): 17–40.

MacLeod, Murdo J. "Exploitation of Natural Resources in Colonial Central America: Indian and Spanish Approaches." In *Changing Tropical Forests: Historical Perspectives on Today's Challenges in Central and South America*, eds. Harold K. Steen and Richard P. Tucker, 31–9. Durham, NC: Forest History Society, 1992.

Miller, Shawn William. "Fuelwood in Colonial Brazil: The Economic and Social Consequences of Fuel Depletion for the Bahian Recôncavo, 1549–1820." *Forest & Conservation History* 38 (October 1994): 181–92.

Miller, Shawn William. *Fruitless Trees: Portuguese Conservation and Brazil's Colonial Timber*. Stanford: Stanford University Press, 2000.

Miller, Shawn William. "Stilt-Root Subsistence: Colonial Mangrove Conservation and Brazil's Free Poor." *Hispanic American Historical Review* 83:2 (May 2003): 223–53.

Rostworowski de Diez Canseco, María. *Recursos naturales renovables y pesca: siglos XVI y XVII: Curacas y sucesiones, Costa Norte*, 2nd ed. Lima: Instituto de Estudios Peruanos, 2005.

Schwartz, Stuart B. *Sugar Plantations in the Formation of Brazilian Society: Bahia, 1550–1835*. New York: Cambridge University Press, 1985.

Sweet, David Graham. "A Rich Realm of Nature Destroyed: The Middle Amazon Valley, 1640–1750." Ph.D. diss., University of Wisconsin, 1974.

Watts, David. *Man's Influence on the Vegetation of Barbados, 1627 to 1800*. Hull, England: University of Hull, 1966.

Watts, David. *The West Indies: Patterns of Development, Culture and Environmental Change since 1492*. Cambridge: Cambridge University Press, 1987.

Watts, David. "Ecological Responses to Ecosystem Shock in the Island Caribbean: The Aftermath of Columbus, 1492–1992." In *Ecological Relations in Historical Times: Human Impact and Adaptation*, eds. R. A. Butlin and N. Roberts, 267–79. Cambridge, MA: Blackwell Publishers, 1995.

West, Robert C. *The Mining Community in Northern New Spain: The Parral Mining District*. Berkeley, CA: IberoAmericana, 1949.

CHAPTER 4: TROPICAL DETERMINISM

Brannstrom, Christian. "Polluted Soil, Polluted Souls: The Rockefeller Hookworm Eradication Campaign in São Paulo, Brazil, 1917–1926." *Historical Geography* 25 (1997): 25–45.

Cañizares-Esguerra. Jorge. *How to Write the History of the New World: Histories, Epistemologies, and Identities in the Eighteenth-Century Atlantic World*. Stanford: Stanford University Press, 2001.

Caviedes, César N. *El Niño in History: Storming through the Ages*. Gainesville: University Press of Florida, 2001.

Davis, Mike. *Late Victorian Holocausts: El Niño Famines and the Making of the Third World*. New York: Verso, 2001.

Dean, Warren. *Brazil and the Struggle for Rubber: A Study in Environmental History*. Cambridge: Cambridge University Press, 1987.

Durham, William. *Scarcity and Survival in Central America: Ecological Origins of the Soccer War*. Stanford: Stanford University Press, 1979.

Gallup, John Luke, Alejandro Gaviria, and Eduardo Lora, eds. *Is Geography Destiny? Lessons from Latin America*. Stanford: Stanford University Press, 2003.

García Acosta, Virginia, ed. *Historia y desastres en América Latina*, Vol. 1. Bogotá: La Red/CIESAS, 1996.

Gerbi, Antonello. *The Dispute of the New World: The History of a Polemic, 1750–1900*, revised ed., trans. Jeremy Moyle. Pittsburgh: University of Pittsburgh Press, 1973.

Marquardt, Steve. "Green Havoc: Panama Disease, Environmental Change, and Labor Process in the Central American Banana Industry." *American Historical Review* 106:1 (February 2001): 49–80.

Marquardt, Steve. "Pesticides, Parakeets, and Unions in the Costa Rican Banana Industry, 1938–1962." *Latin American Research Review* 37:2(2002): 3–36.

McNeill, John R. "Ecology, Epidemics and Empires: Environmental Change and the Geopolitics of Tropical America, 1600–1825." *Environment and History* 5 (1999): 175–84.

Pérez, Luis A., Jr. *Winds of Change: Hurricanes and the Transformation of Nineteenth-Century Cuba*. Chapel Hill: University of North Carolina Press, 2001.

Richardson, Bonham C. *Economy and Environment in the Caribbean: Barbados and the Windwards in the Late 1800s*. Gainesville: University Press of Florida, 1997.

Schwartz, Stuart B. "The Hurricane of San Ciriaco: Disaster, Politics, and Society in Puerto Rico, 1899–1901." *Hispanic American Historical Review* 72:3 (August 1992), 303–34.

Schwartz, Stuart B. "Hurricanes and the Shaping of Circum-Caribbean Societies." *Florida Historical Quarterly* 83:4 (2004): 381–409.

Soluri, John. "Accounting for Taste: Bananas, Mass Markets, and Panama Disease." *Environmental History* 7:3 (July 2002): 386–410.

Soluri, John. "Bananas, Biodiversity, and the Paradox of Commodification." In *Territories, Commodities and Knowledges: Latin American Environmental Histories in the Nineteenth and Twentieth Centuries*, ed. Christian Brannstrom, 121–47. London: Institute for the Study of the Americas, 2004.

Stein, Stanley. *Vassouras: A Brazilian Coffee County, 1850–1900*. Cambridge: Harvard University Press, 1957.

Stepan, Nancy Leys. *Picturing Tropical Nature*. Ithaca, NY: Cornell University Press, 2001.

Weinstein, Barbara. *The Amazon Rubber Boom, 1850–1920*. Stanford: Stanford University Press, 1983.

CHAPTER 5: HUMAN DETERMINATION

Cariño Olvera, Martha Micheline. *Historia de las relaciones hombre-naturaleza en Baja California Sur, 1500–1940*. La Paz, Mexico: Universidad Autónoma de Baja California, 1996.

Chalhoub, Sidney. *Cidade febril: cortiços e epidemias na corte imperial*. São Paulo: Companhia das Letras, 1996.

Cushman, Gregory Todd. "The Lords of Guano: Science and the Management of Peru's Marine Environment, 1800–1973." Ph.D. diss., University of Texas, Austin, 2003.

Cushman, Gregory Todd. "'The Most Valuable Birds in the World': International Conservation Science and the Revival of Peru's Guano Industry, 1909–1965." *Environmental History* 10:3 (2005): 477–509.

Folchi Donoso, Maurício. "La insustentibilidad de la industria del cobre en Chile: los hornos y los bosques durante el siglo XIX." *Revista Mapocho* 49 (2001): 149–75

Garavaglia, Juan Carlos. "Human Beings and the Environment in America: On 'Determinism' and 'Possibilism.'" *International Social Science Journal* 44:4 (1992): 569–77.

Guayacochea de Onofri, Rosa. "Urbanismo e salubridad en la ciudad de Mendoza (1880–1916)." *Revista de Historia de América e Argentina* 14 (1987): 171–202.

Hall, Anthony L. *Drought and Irrigation in Northeast Brazil*. Cambridge: Cambridge University Press, 1978.

Konrad, Herman W. "Tropical Forest Policy and Practice during the Mexican Porfiriato, 1876–1910." In *Changing Tropical Forests: Historical Perspectives on Today's Challenges in Central and South America*, eds. Harold K. Steen and Richard P. Tucker, 123–43. Durham, NC: Forest History Society, 1992.

McCook, Stuart. *States of Nature: Science, Agriculture, and Environment in the Spanish Caribbean, 1760–1940*. Austin: University of Texas Press, 2002.

Perló Cohen, Manuel. *El paradigma Porfiriano: Historia del desague del Valle de México*. Mexico City: Universidad Nacional Autónoma de México, 1999.

Romero Lankao, Patricia. *Obra hidráulica de le ciudad de México y su impacto socio-ambiental (1880–1990)*. Mexico City: Instituto Mora, 1999.

Santiago, Myrna I. *The Ecology of Oil: Environment, Labor, and the Mexican Revolution, 1900–1938*. New York: Cambridge University Press, 2006.

Stepan, Nancy Leys. *Beginnings of Brazilian Science: Oswaldo Cruz, Medical Research, and Policy, 1890–1920.* New York: Science History Publications, 1976.

Tortolero Villaseñor, Alejandro. "Transforming the Central Mexican Waterscape: Lake Drainage and its Consequences during the *Porfiriato*." In *Territories, Commodities and Knowledges: Latin American Environmental Histories in the Nineteenth and Twentieth Centuries,* ed. Christian Brannstrom, 121–47. London: Institute for the Study of the Americas, 2004.

Tucker, Richard P. *Insatiable Appetite: The United States and the Ecological Degradation of the Tropical World.* Berkeley: University of California Press, 2000.

CHAPTER 6: ASPHYXIATED HABITATS

Browder, John, and Brian Godry. *Rainforest Cities: Urbanization, Development, and Globalization in the Amazon.* New York: Columbia University Press, 1997.

Ezcurra, Exequiel. *De las chinampas a la megalópolis: El medio ambiente en la Cuenca de México.* Mexico City: Fondo de Cultura Economica, 1990.

Gilbert, Alan. *The Latin American City.* Nottingham, England: Monthly Review Press, 1998.

Joseph, Gilbert M., and Mark D. Szuchman, eds. *I Saw a City Invincible: Urban Portraits of Latin America.* Wilmington, DE: Scholarly Resources, 1996.

Keck, Margaret. "'Water, Water Everywhere, Nor Any Drop to Drink:' Land Use and Water Policy in São Paulo." In *Livable Cities: Urban Struggles for Livelihood and Sustainability,* ed. Peter Evans, 162–97. Berkeley: University of California Press, 2002.

Lewis, Oscar. "Urbanization without Breakdown: A Case Study." *The Scientific Monthly* 75 (1952): 31–41.

McKibben, Bill. *Hope, Human and Wild: True Stories of Living Lightly on the Earth.* New York: Little, Brown and Co., 1995.

Menezes, Cláudio Luiz. *Desenvolvimento urbano e meio ambiente: a experiencia de Curitiba.* Campinas, Brazil: Papirus, 1996.

Pezzoli, Keith. *Human Settlements and Planning for Ecological Sustainability: The Case of Mexico City.* Cambridge: Massachusetts Institute of Technology Press, 1998.

Schwartz, Hugh. *Urban Renewal, Municipal Revitalization: The Case of Curitiba, Brazil.* Alexandria, VA: Hugh Schwartz, 2004.

Simon, Joel. *Endangered Mexico: An Environment on the Edge.* San Francisco: Sierra Club Books, 1997.

Trindade, Etelvina Maria de Castro, et al. *Cidade, homem, natureza: uma história das políticas ambientais de Curitiba.* Curitiba, Brazil: Universidade Livre do Meio Ambiente, Secretaria Municipal do Meio Ambiente, 1997.

Tulchin, Joseph, ed. *Economic Development and Environmental Protection in Latin America.* Boulder, CO: Lynne Rienner Publishers, 1991.

Chapter 7: Developing Environmentalism

Brannstrom, Christian. "Rethinking the 'Atlantic Forest' of Brazil: New Evidence for Land Cover and Land Value in Western São Paulo, 1900–1930." *Journal of Historical Geography* 28 (2002): 420–39.

Carvalho, José Murilo de. "O motivo edênico no imaginário social brasileiro." *Revista Brasileira de Ciências Sociais* 13:38 (October 1998): 63–81.

Castro Herrera, Guillermo. "On Cattle and Ships: Culture, History and Sustainable Development in Panama." *Environment and History* 7 (2001): 201–17.

Coomes, Oliver T. "A Century of Rainforest Use in Western Amazonia: Lessons for Extraction-Based Conservation of Tropical Forest Resources." *Forest & Conservation History* 39:3 (July 1995): 108–20.

Dean, Warren. "Ecological and Economic Relationships in Frontier History: São Paulo, Brazil." In *Essays on Frontiers in World History*, eds. George Wolfskill and Stanley Palmer, 71–100. College Station: Texas A&M University Press, 1983.

Diamond, Jared. *Collapse: How Societies Choose to Fail or Succeed.* New York: Penguin Books, 2005.

Drummond, José Augusto. "The Garden in the Machine: An Environmental History of Brazil's Tijuca Forest." *Environmental History* 1:1 (1996): 83–104.

Drummond, José Augusto. *Devastação e preservação ambiental no Rio de Janeiro.* Niterói, Brazil: Editora da Universidade Federal Fluminense, 1997.

Endfield, Georgina H., and Sarah L. O'Hara. "Conflicts Over Water in 'The Little Drought Age' in Central Mexico." *Environment and History* 3 (1997): 255–72

Faber, Daniel. *Environment Under Fire: Imperialism and the Ecological Crisis in Latin America.* New York: Monthly Review Press, 1993.

Garcia-Johnson, Ronie. *Exporting Environmentalism: U.S. Multinational Chemical Corporations in Brazil and Mexico.* Cambridge: The Massachusetts Institute of Technology Press, 2000.

Goldstein, Karl. "The Green Movement in Brazil." In *Research in Social Movements, Conflicts and Change: The Green Movement Worldwide*, ed. Matthias Finger, 119–93. Greenwich, CT: JAI Press, 1992.

Graham, Wade. "MexEco?: Mexican Attitudes Toward the Environment." *Environmental History Review* 15 (1991): 1–17.

Grove, Richard H. *Green Imperialism: Colonial Expansion, Tropical Island Edens, and the Origins of Environmentalism, 1600–1860.* Cambridge: Cambridge University Press, 1995.

Guha, Ramachandra. *Environmentalism: A Global History.* New York: Longman, 2000.

Guha, Ramachandra, and Joan Martinez-Alier. *Varieties of Environmentalism: Essays North and South.* London: Earthscan, 1997.

Hecht, Susanna, and Alexander Cockburn. *The Fate of the Forest: Developers, Destroyers, and Defenders of the Amazon*. New York: Harper Perennial, 1990.

Howard, Philip. "The History of Ecological Marginalization in Chiapas." *Environmental History* 3:3 (1998): 357–77.

Jacobs, Jamie Elizabeth. "Community Participation, the Environment, and Democracy: Brazil in Comparative Perspective." *Latin American Politics and Society* 44:4 (2002): 59–88.

Keck, Margaret. "Parks, People and Power: The Shifting Terrain of Environmentalism." *NACLA Report on the Americas* 28:5 (March/April 1995), 36–41.

Lutzenberger, José A. *O fim do futuro*. Porto Alegre, Brazil: Editora Movimento, 1976.

Martinez-Alier, Joan. *The Environmentalism of the Poor: A Study of Ecological Conflicts and Valuation*. Cheltenham, England: Edward Elgar, 2002.

McNeill, John R. "Deforestation in the Araucaria Zone of Southern Brazil, 1900–1983." In *World Deforestation in the Twentieth Century*, eds. John F. Richards and Richard P. Tucker, 15–32. Durham, NC: Duke Press Policy Studies, 1988.

Nash, Roderick. "The Exporting and Importing of Nature: Nature-Appreciation as a Commodity, 1850–1980." *Perspectives in American History* 12 (1979): 517–60.

Pádua, José Augusto. "The Birth of Green Politics in Brazil: Exogenous and Endogenous Factors." In *Green Politics Two*, ed. Wolfgang Rüdig. Edinburgh: Edinburgh University Press, 1992.

Pádua, José Augusto. "Cultura esgotadora: Agricultura e destruição ambiental nas últimas décadas do Brasil Império." *Estudos Sociedade e Agricultura* 11 (October 1998): 134–63.

Pádua, José Augusto. *Um sopro de destruição: Pensamento político e crítica ambiental no Brasil escravista (1786–1888)*, 2nd ed. Rio de Janeiro: Jorge Zahar, 2004.

Pattullo, Polly. *Last Resorts: The Cost of Tourism in the Caribbean*. London: Cassell, 1996.

Place, Susan E. "Ecotourism and the Political Ecology of 'Sustainable Development' in Costa Rica." In *Tropical Rainforests: Latin American Nature and Society in Transition*, revised ed., ed. Susan E. Place, 221–31. Wilmington, DE: Scholarly Resources, 2001.

Sedrez, Lise Fernanda. "The Bay of All Beauties: State and Nature in Guanabara Bay, Rio de Janeiro, Brazil, 1875–1975." Ph.D. diss., Stanford University, 2004.

Sonnenfeld, David A. "Mexico's 'Green Revolution,' 1940–1980: Towards an Environmental History." *Environmental Review* 16:4 (1992): 29–52.

Wallace, David Rains. *The Quetzal and Macaw: Costa Rica's National Parks*. San Francisco: Sierra Club Books, 1996.

Wood, Charles, and Marianne Schmink. "The Military and the Environment in the Brazilian Amazon. *Journal of Political and Military Sociology* 21:1 (1993): 81–105.

Wright, Angus. *The Death of Ramon Gonzalez: The Modern Agricultural Dilemma*, revised ed. Austin: University of Texas Press, 2005.

Zerpa Mirabal, Alfonso J. *Explotación y comercio de plumas de garza en Venezuela: fines del siglo XIX–principios del siglo XX*. Caracas: Ediciones del Congreso de la República, 1998.

EPILOGUE: CUBA'S LATEST REVOLUTION

Diaz-Briquets, Sergio, and Jorge Pérez-López, eds. *Conquering Nature: The Environmental Legacy of Socialism in Cuba*. Pittsburg: University of Pittsburg Press, 2000.

Funes, Fernando, Luis García, Martin Bourque, Nilda Pérez, and Peter Rosset, eds. *Sustainable Agriculture and Resistance: Transforming Food Production in Cuba*. Oakland, CA: Food First Books, 2002.

INDEX

CPSIA information can be obtained
at www.ICGtesting.com
Printed in the USA
LVHW040142021222
734253LV00003BA/156